YANKEE Magazine's

Favorite
New England
Recipes

YANKEE Magazine's

Favorite New England Recipes

Compiled by Sara B. B. Stamm
and the Lady Editors of YANKEE Magazine

CLARISSA M. SILITCH   WALTER E. RICHARDSON

Editor   *Designer*

From

YANKEE BOOKS

A division of Yankee Publishing Incorporated
Dublin, New Hampshire

First Edition, 1972
Second Printing, 1973
Third Printing, 1974
Fourth Printing, 1977
Fifth Printing, 1977

Second Edition, 1979
Second Printing, 1981
Third Printing, 1982
Fourth Printing, 1984

Yankee Publishing Incorporated
Dublin, New Hampshire 03444

Library of Congress Catalog Card Number 70-183749
Manufactured in the United States of America
ISBN 0-911658-87-4

Dedication

For John Davies Stamm, my husband, my editor, and my taster.

Contents

Breads; rolls; hot cross buns; popovers; muffins; baking powder biscuits; griddlecakes;
waffles; doughnuts; funnel cakes; Sally Lunn;
cheesy Vermont maple apple Danish; coffee
cakes; cornbreads; eggs; codfish; finnan haddie; kedgeree

Baked beans; brown bread; cassoulet; baked
seafood; egg and cheese dishes; onion pie;
quiches; watercress piecrust; soufflés; macaroni; croquettes and fritters; casseroles and
luncheon dishes; head cheese; sandwiches

The Taste of New England

YANKEE'S newest cookbook is, I hope, a lively sampling of cookery in New England today. The well loved traditional recipes continue in use pretty much as they always have, never neglected or forgotten, and they mix without any noticeable awkwardness, as they have for 350 years, with the contributions of more exotic flavors of newcomers to our shores. The post-war years with rapid interchange of culinary methods, with quick transportation of produce and wide opportunity for travel have brought many innovations. The pages of YANKEE have been full of them. These years have also brought the electric blender, the electric beater, and the electric ice-cream freezer to name only three of the workers that make cooking ten times easier for us than it was for our ancestors. The recipes in this book are planned to use these modern methods or the older homemade ways as you choose. Either method applies.

Thanks are due first to our ingenious contributors for recipes both old and new that breathe the air of New England and the American life. Their recipes are credited to them in the pages that follow. I am grateful to the editors of *The First Parish Cookbook*, Sudbury, Massachusetts, *The Little Compton* (Rhode Island) *Garden Club Cookbook*, *The Somerset Club Cookbook*, Boston, *Chestnuts in the Fire*, Chestnut Hill, Massachusetts, *The Monadnock Garden Club Cookbook*, in Dublin, our own back yard, and *The New Canaan* (Connecticut) *Sewing Circle Cookbook* for permission to publish some of my favorite recipes. My mother, Mrs. John Babbitt, gave me her files and my grandmother's and I hope this book lives up to the excellence of their tables. Mrs. Charlton MacVeagh was one of our most generous contributors.

In general, while these recipes may be followed exactly with excellent results, the interested cook can feel free to make substitutions as taste or expediency suggest. The time of year and the preferences of her family will often offer suggestions that will make a recipe her own. Herbs, spices, and wines are elements which are particularly subject to personal whim. Fresh herbs, fresh ground pepper, a good quality of wine, when called for, contribute subtly to the superiority of a dish. Fresh butter and cream are incomparable, but oleomargarine with its sweet meadow flavor and its low cholesterol is often to be used when the pleasanter word "butter" appears. Dried herbs are much more concentrated than fresh ones and should be added by pinches, stirred to release their flavor, then tasted.

Variety in combining flavors and textures and a little thought for showmanship play a great part in keeping meals that are essentially simple from being humdrum. The paper frills around the ham bone, the flourishes of parsley or cherries, the Thanksgiving turkey's necklace of cranberries should not be forgotten. After all, eating is one of the recurrent and dependable pleasures of life and eating well together forges a deep bond. In the course of assembling this book, I have leafed through the files of YANKEE for more than a quarter of a century. Friends, relations, editors and their relations, too, have dug back into family secrets to find the fibre of New England cooking for our book. Really, the present day cook, New England or of New England ancestry, can hardly contemplate this particular regional aspect of caring for and loving one's family without realizing that, for the distaff side, cookery is a tenacious heritage.

Sara B. B. Stamm
October 25, 1971
Walpole, N. H.

We open with a few sample menus for everyday and special occasions.

MENUS

Three weekend breakfasts for mornings when no one is counting time or calories.

SUMMER

orange juice with fresh mint
chicken hash   mushroom puffs
blueberry popovers with sweet butter
raspberries and cream, brown or white sugar
coffee

WINTER

orange juice
broiled veal kidneys, Canadian bacon, and tomatoes
fried cucumbers
sour cream corn bread   cherry jam
stewed prunes in Madeira
coffee

A BOSTON SUNDAY BREAKFAST

orange juice
codfish cakes   eggs goldenrod   crisp bacon
apple muffins   bitter orange marmalade
strawberries in season, served whole with powdered sugar
coffee

Two special seasonal buffet menus that make luncheon entertaining flexible.

SUMMER LUNCHEON BUFFET

Spread your table in a shady corner of the garden.

cold cherry soup with yoghurt

chicken pâté in jelly   hominy croquettes   white wine

spinach salad, *Princess Louise*

French bread with herb butter

cheese tray

deep-dish pear pie   whipped cream

coffee

WINTER LUNCHEON BUFFET

hot almond soup with sour cream

halibut mousse with lobster sauce   white wine

green beans in casserole

broiled mushrooms

corn sticks

pineapple sherbet   brownies   walnut wafers   coffee

CHURCH SUPPER MENU

This is one of the bountiful menus served by the Reverend George Niles at the First Church, Unitarian, in Walpole, New Hampshire. It is typical Church Supper fare. Church suppers are served country-style—plenty of everything, crowding the board. Not recommended for weight watchers!

baked ham (clove-studded)

the bean pot

baked macaroni and cheddar cheese

pineapple-cabbage cole slaw

fresh sliced tomatoes with tarragon

watermelon rind pickles

India relish

hot corn bread

Boston cream pies

coffee (by the gallon)

tea

MOVABLE FEASTS

There are all sorts of occasions when a previously prepared picnic lunch is called for, when going to football games or sailing to an off-shore island, planning a day at sea or simply facing a long motor trip where tedium can be turned into a special event by opening a hamper to reveal a delectable lunch.

cold avocado soup
cold sautéed chicken   chilled white wine
watercress sandwiches   pâté sandwiches
cherry tomatoes and endive sections   olives
whole strawberries with powdered sugar or grapes
butterscotch squares   coffee

---

sorrel soup (hot or cold)
rare roast beef sandwiches with horseradish sauce   red wine
stuffed eggs   ripe olives   gherkins   potato ribbons
carrot strips and hearts of celery
melon slices   filled cookies   coffee

---

large shrimp cooked on skewers with olive oil and garlic
butterfly leg of lamb cooked in a bed of herbs
buttered baked potatoes   red wine
French bread, hot
finger salad, small scraped carrots, scallions, radishes,
basil beans, ripe olives
broiled bananas   Indians

THE DINNER THAT COOKS ITSELF

Here is a dinner menu (and it is really a banquet) that can be made ready the day before it is cooked, leaving the hostess free to spend the whole day away from home, then return and whisk out a feast.

hearts of celery and olives
crabmeat mayonnaise   lemon halves   melba toast
roast beef   horseradish sauce   Yorkshire pudding   Burgundy
endive salad with watercress dressing
forgotten torte
coffee mints

Everything should be on hand the day before the dinner. In the evening set the table. Have the celery and endive clean and in the refrigerator with the crabmeat and olives. Make the mayonnaise, the horseradish sauce, the watercress dressing and the batter for the Yorkshire pudding, and put them on ice. Leave the roast out of the icebox if you plan to start the cooking early in the morning using the method described in *Roast Beef II*. Prepare the torte and leave it in the oven.

In the morning cook the roast for an hour. During the hour in the evening while it cooks again, the other elements of the dinner can be assembled. While the roast "rests" for half an hour, the hostess can rest too.

DINNER FOR EARLY SPRING

fresh asparagus with hollandaise sauce
baked chicken with peaches   spinach and sour cream
Moselle wine
vanilla soufflé with whipped cream and fresh strawberry sauce
coffee

DINNER THAT CAN WAIT

For those times when you cannot be at all sure when everyone will be ready to eat due to the delays of modern life or the uncertainty of travel, here is a dinner that will keep serenely, indefinitely, to comfort the most tired guest and leave the hostess free from care.

oyster bisque   melba toast
steak and kidney pie   currant jelly   red wine
prune ice box cake with whipped cream
coffee   chocolate mints

The bisque, the pie, and the icebox cake may be prepared ahead of time, the day before if you wish. Put the pie (room temperature) into a 350° oven 30 minutes before you sit down to eat the soup which has been heated for 5 minutes. Make the melba toast in the oven with the pie.

YANKEE Magazine's

Favorite
New England
Recipes

Chapter 1.
Yankee Breads & Breakfasts

Traditionally the Yankee breakfast has been a fine, warm affair, a minor feast that can hold its own with any other meal. Yankees rose early (most of them still do), and the chores that had to be done while breakfast was prepared produced a happy appetite for fish cakes, baked beans, and pie. The only restriction to dishes that should please a hungry man was that they had to be something kept over from the day before or possible to cook in a reasonably short time.

When I was young in Vermont, there was a fine-looking man who lived across the street from us. His wife told us that in his whole life he had never missed having a piece of pie for breakfast each morning. We looked upon this fortunate creature with an awe that was not unmixed with envy, for the fine old New England breakfast had disappeared already from our table. Oatmeal, ham, creamed codfish, cornbread . . . yes; pie . . . no.

Nowadays we have reached a compromise in our family. Everyday breakfasts are good—sustaining but simple. On Saturday and Sunday everything goes. And all of it disappears, too. Family and guests enjoy these weekend occasions. Orange juice and coffee are served to early risers as they appear, and by the time everyone is on hand the large breakfast is ready. This large, late breakfast offers a good opportunity for entertaining, besides. Some people call it brunch, but it seems to me that this poor mongrel of a word is not very appetizing by comparison with the crisp healthy sound of the older word and the fine pictures it conjures up of English and New England repasts.

BREAD HINTS

In old New England it was usual to make dough for bread each evening and let it rise overnight. Kneading, a second rising, and baking took place in the morning and the housewife got up early enough to have the bread ready when the men and children had done the chores and came in to breakfast. Our generation can turn out bread as fine as any produced in the kitchens of long ago. Flour, expertly milled, and yeast that functions more predictably and more quickly have removed the hazards from breadmaking.

There are many advantages to making bread and rolls at home. They are infinitely better tasting than the best that you can buy. Commercial breads, although often excellent, have to be adapted to a wide taste, and must be baked with preservatives to make them keep well. Homemade bread is a great economy, too. And, of course, bread may be varied in dozens of ways by an interesting cook. Most important, bread baking in the oven makes your house smell so good that everyone is happier there. It is not hard to make. Even if you have never tried, a couple of loaves will soon make you an expert.

General rules apply to most breads made with yeast, although recipes differ slightly. The type of flour, the amount of shortening, the amount of time for rising can all vary the formulas a little. But a good loaf is one of medium size with a rounded top and a medium brown crust free from cracks; the grain is fine and the crumb feels moist and elastic to the touch. Before use in bread dough, milk should be boiled or scalded and then cooled, or your bread may be sour. One teaspoon to one tablespoon of sugar and one teaspoon of salt per loaf is a good general rule when working with yeast. Shortening increases tenderness and improves the keeping quality of bread. Yeast reacts best at a temperature of 80° to 85° (80° within the bread). Be sure to grease the bowl in which you set the dough to rise and cover with a damp towel. If you have no place with this approximate temperature, the pan of dough may be placed in a large basin of warm (90-95°) water, and the water maintained at that temperature during the rising period. An oven heated low and then turned off works well, too.

To mix and bake bread in 5 hours, use one package of yeast to 2 cups of liquid. The first rising will take 2-3 hours, the second 1-2 hours, and the baking about 1 hour. A little experience will tell you exactly when each process is right. To test whether the dough has risen properly, make an impression in the dough with your finger; if the impression remains, the rising is complete. The bread is baked when the crust is well-browned, shrinks from the sides of the pan, and sounds hollow when tapped. Brush it with butter and turn it out immediately to cool on a rack. When cool, store wrapped in wax paper or cellophane to retain its moisture. Well-wrapped bread freezes well.

HOMEMADE BREAD

The recipe of YANKEE's food editor for many years, Grace "Mom" Weldon, this bread is just plain good and makes fine toast.

1 package dry yeast	1 teaspoon salt
1 cup warm (not hot) milk	1 tablespoon sugar
3 tablespoons butter	3 cups sifted flour

In a large, warm bowl dissolve the yeast in the milk. Add the butter, salt and sugar, then sift in the flour until no more can be worked in with a spoon or fingers. Cover lightly and let rise for about 2 hours in a warm place until the dough is three times its original bulk. Turn out on a floured board and knead lightly. Shape and place the dough in a well greased bread pan. Cover and let rise again until twice its original size (about an hour). Bake the bread in an oven preheated to 365° for 40 minutes. When done, remove the bread to a cooling rack and rub the top lightly with butter.

1 loaf

OLD FASHIONED VANILLA-FLAVORED WHITE BREAD

Excellent, served thinly sliced with butter and strawberry jam, for tea.

2 packages dry yeast	1/2 cup (melted) butter
2 and 2/3 cups lukewarm milk	1 teaspoon (or more) vanilla
5 cups white flour	2 eggs
3/4 teaspoon salt	1/2 cup sugar

Sprinkle dry yeast over milk, stir in, and add gradually one cup of the flour. Mixture should be smooth. Spread damp towel over bowl and set to rise in a warm (not hot) place. Wait 2-3 hours for mixture to double in bulk, then add salt, melted butter, and vanilla. In a separate bowl, beat eggs with sugar until light yellow, and pour into first mixture. Add remaining flour until dough is kneadable (stiff enough so as not to stick to your hands), then turn out on floured board and knead until velvety-smooth. Put into greased (butter) bowl covered with damp towel and let rise a second time. When the dough has again doubled, punch it down and turn out again on floured board. Grease loaf pans (2) and lightly shape dough into oblongs to fit. Let the dough rise in the pans for an hour. Each pan should be half full. Bake in 400° oven for 15 minutes, then turn heat down to 375° for 40-60 minutes. Bread is done when bottoms give a hollow sound when tapped and toothpick inserted comes out dry. Turn loaves out onto drying (cake) racks, and brush with melted butter. Or brush with beaten egg and sprinkle poppy seed over loaves.

2 loaves

OATMEAL BREAD

Mary L. Douglas
Swansea, Mass.

1 full cup old-fashioned oatmeal
1/2 cup molasses
1 and 1/4 teaspoons salt
1 yeast cake

1 tablespoon sugar
2 cups boiling water
2 full tablespoons butter
3-4 cups sifted flour

Dissolve the yeast cake in a little tap water, and sprinkle the sugar on top until it rises. In a large bowl mix together the oatmeal and molasses and salt. Boil the water, dissolve the butter in it and add to the oatmeal. Sift in the flour until no more can be added, when partly cool add the yeast and mix well. Let rise in a warm place free from drafts for almost 2 hours or until doubled in bulk. Knead on a floured board and put in 2 greased pans to rise a second time. When doubled, bake in a 350° oven for about 40 minutes. Remove to a cooling rack and brush with butter. This recipe may be used to make rolls, too. Shape them accordingly.

2 loaves

CRACKED WHEAT BREAD

Marion W. Andros
Walpole, N.H.

1 cup whole-grain cracked wheat
 (from a Country Store)
4 cups boiling water
2 teaspoons salt
1/2 cup molasses

4 tablespoons butter
1 package dry yeast
8 cups unbleached flour
 (approximately)

Pour the boiling water over the cracked wheat and let stand 3 hours or more (overnight if you wish). Heat to lukewarm and add the salt, molasses, and butter. Sift the yeast with 2 cups of the flour and stir into the cracked wheat mixture. Sift in the remaining flour to make a fairly firm, non-sticky dough. Turn out on a floured board and knead until smooth and elastic. Put dough into a greased bowl and cover. Let rise in a warm place until doubled in bulk (about 2 hours). Knead again lightly and divide the dough in fourths. Shape into loaves and place in greased loaf pans. Cover with a damp towel and let rise again until doubled in bulk (about 1 and 1/4 hours). Bake in oven preheated to 400° for 10 minutes, reduce the heat to 350° and bake 50 minutes longer. Turn out and cool on a rack. Brush the tops with butter. Loaves may be frozen. Makes 4 small loaves, about 1 and 1/4 pounds each.

4 loaves

WHEAT GERM WHITE BREAD

A very fine-textured, high-rising bread.

1 package dry yeast (1 yeast cake)
1 and 1/4 cups lukewarm water
1 tablespoon sugar
1 egg, beaten
1 cup scalded milk
6 tablespoons butter, melted

1 and 1/2 teaspoons salt
1/2 cup honey
1/4 teaspoon baking soda
7 cups white flour
1 cup wheat germ (toasted)

Sprinkle yeast over 1/2 cup of the lukewarm water, stir, and add sugar. Let mixture stand in warm place for 45 minutes. Then beat in the egg, melted butter, rest of water, scalded milk (milk is scalded when, on being heated, bubbles form around edge of pan), salt, honey, and soda. Add flour and wheat germ gradually until batter is too stiff to beat. Then turn dough out onto floured board and knead in rest of flour. Knead till smooth, then place in greased bowl and cover with damp towel. Let stand in a warm place (70-80°) until dough has doubled in bulk. Punch down dough, knead, and replace in greased, covered bowl, and wait until it doubles in size again. Punch down again, and separate into three loaf-size portions, sealing edges carefully. Place each loaf into greased loaf pan. Again, let loaves rise until they double their size. Put loaves in cold oven. Set at 400° for 15 minutes. Then change oven heat to 375° and bake 35-45 minutes more. Brush loaves with melted butter when done.

3 loaves

POTATO BREAD

3 cups mashed potatoes
1/3 cup potato water
a scant tablespoon salt
1 tablespoon shortening

1 tablespoon sugar
2 packages yeast
5 cups white flour
1 cup barley flour

Dissolve the yeast in the lukewarm potato water, add the salt, shortening, sugar, then the mashed potatoes and mix well. Stir in the flours until no more can be added and set in a warm place covered with a cloth to rise, about 3 hours. Knead well, divide the dough in three parts and put in loaf pans to rise again in a warm place until again doubled in bulk. Bake for an hour in a 375° oven.

3 loaves

FRENCH BREAD

Twentieth Century Americans have adopted French bread for their own. Made without milk or shortening, it is best eaten, as the French do, shortly after it is baked.

1 package yeast
2 cups lukewarm water
4 cups sifted flour

1 tablespoon sugar
2 teaspoons salt

Dissolve the yeast in 1 cup of the water. Sift the flour, sugar and salt, stir in the yeast. Add just enough of the second cup of water to hold the dough together. Mix until soft and sticky. Cover with a clean cloth, set in a warm spot and let rise until double (2-4 hours). When the dough is high and spongy, punch it down and beat for several minutes with floured hands. Divide the bread in two parts and place each part in long loaves (roll out the dough and roll into a tight cylinder, pinching the edges firmly together) on a greased cookie sheet or in greased round glass baking casseroles. Cover again and let rise until double in size. Start oven at 400°. Brush the bread with melted butter and bake for 1 hour.

2 loaves

HERB BREAD

Slice French bread 3/4 inch thick—to but not through the bottom crust. Brush with 1/4 cup of butter creamed with 4 tablespoons of herbs (parsley with chives or thyme or dill, or tarragon with chives). Press the bread firmly together and heat for 10 minutes in a 400° oven.

GARLIC BREAD

Rub the crusty loaf with a clove of garlic and proceed as above.

CHEESE BREAD

Mix grated cheese with butter and spread between the slices.

ANCHOVY BREAD

Add a few mashed anchovies to the butter and spread between the slices.

DILL BREAD

Mrs. M. Carey
New Castle, Penna.

Made with unusual ingredients, this is a moist, flavorful loaf especially recommended for ham sandwiches.

1 package dry yeast
1/4 cup warm water
1 cup lukewarm creamed cottage cheese
2 tablespoons sugar
1 tablespoon soft butter

1 tablespoon finely chopped onion
2 teaspoons dill seed
1 teaspoon salt
1/4 teaspoon soda
1 egg
2 and 1/4 to 2 and 1/2 cups flour

Dissolve the yeast in the warm water. In a large bowl, combine the cottage cheese, sugar, butter, onion, dill seed, salt, soda, and the egg. Add to the yeast mixture, and gradually add enough flour to make a stiff dough, beating well after each addition. Place dough in a greased bowl to rise, and cover it with a light towel. When the dough has doubled in bulk, punch down, turn into a well-buttered round 2-quart casserole or a conventional bread pan and let rise again until light. Bake the bread in a moderate oven (375°) for 40-50 minutes. Brush the surface with butter.

Poppy seed, caraway, or sesame seed may be substituted for the dill seed or used with it.

1 loaf

MRS. GEORGE WASHINGTON'S POTATO ROLLS

2 large potatoes
1 teaspoon salt
2 tablespoons sugar
3 tablespoons butter
1 and 1/2 cups potato water

3/4 cup scalded milk
1 package yeast
7 cups sifted flour
(approximately)

Peel and cook the potatoes for about 30 minutes or until tender, drain them and save the water. Mash the hot potatoes, adding the salt, sugar and butter and beat well; add the potato water and hot milk and cool until lukewarm. Add the yeast and stir in 4 cups of the flour, beating well; then add enough of the remaining flour to make a dough stiff enough to knead. Knead on a floured board until smooth and elastic; brush the top with more melted butter and place in a large greased bowl; cover and let rise slowly for 5 hours in a warm place until the dough has doubled in bulk. Place on a floured board and pat out to a thickness of about 1/2 inch, but do not knead again. Pinch off small pieces and shape into small rolls. Place them in greased pans and let rise until very light and more than doubled in bulk. Bake in a hot (400°) oven for 20 minutes or until done.

48 small rolls

TWO-HOUR ROLLS

1 cup scalded milk	1 yeast cake
2 tablespoons butter	1 egg yolk, beaten slightly
2 tablespoons sugar	3 cups sifted bread flour
1 teaspoon salt	1 egg white, beaten stiff

Combine milk, butter, sugar, and salt in a mixing bowl and let cool until lukewarm. Then add yeast, egg yolk, and 1 and 1/2 cups flour. Stir until smooth. Fold in the egg white and the rest of the flour. Let rise in a warm place for 2 hours, then form into rolls. Let rise again for 30 minutes in well greased muffin tins, lightly covered. Put 3 small balls of dough into each cup for clover leaf rolls. Or cut them with a round cutter, elongate each round, fold over a piece of butter and you have Parker House Rolls.

PUMPKIN BISCUITS

1/2 cup puréed pumpkin	1/2 cup scalded milk
1/4 cup sugar	1/4 yeast cake dissolved in
1/2 teaspoon salt	1/4 cup lukewarm water
1/4 teaspoon mace	2 and 1/2 cups flour
4 tablespoons butter	

Add the pumpkin, sugar, salt, mace, and butter to the milk. Cool to lukewarm and add the dissolved yeast cake, then the flour; cover and put in a warm place to rise overnight. Shape into biscuits, place side by side in a greased pan, let rise again, and bake in a 375° oven. This recipe may also be made using squash.

HOT CROSS BUNS

Served during Lent, and particularly on Good Friday.

1 cup milk, scalded	3 cups flour
1/2 cup sugar	1/2 teaspoon cinnamon
3 tablespoons melted butter	1/2 cup currants
1/2 teaspoon salt	1/4 cup shredded citron
1 yeast cake, or dry yeast	pinch of ground cloves
1/4 cup warm water	1 egg, well beaten
1 egg, well beaten	confectioners' sugar and milk

Combine the milk, sugar, butter, and salt. When lukewarm, add the yeast cake dissolved in water. Add the egg and mix well. Sift together the flour, cinnamon, and cloves, add the currants and citron, and mix thoroughly. Cover and let rise in a warm place (75-85°) until double in bulk. Shape into round buns and place close together in a well buttered pan. Let rise again. Brush the top of each bun with beaten egg. Make a cross on each bun with a sharp knife. Bake in a hot oven (400°) for 20 minutes. Remove from oven and brush over lightly with crosses made of confectioners' sugar moistened with milk.

POPOVERS

It is not hard to make high, puffy popovers, in fact given one lesson a child can do it. Their appearance is impressive and always seems to bring a gasp of joy. Serve them with plenty of butter and jam for breakfast, or split them and fill them with creamed chicken for a pleasant breakfast, luncheon, or supper dish.

2 eggs	1 cup flour
1 cup milk	dash of salt

Stir the ingredients together but do not beat. Batter should be a bit lumpy. Coat 6 earthenware or Pyrex cups very generously with melted butter. Divide the batter among them and place in an oven at 425°. The oven may be preheated or not as convenient. Bake for about 45 minutes. If you wish to slow down the popovers, the last half of the cooking (after they have popped) may be done at a lower temperature.

6 popovers

BLUEBERRY POPOVERS

Add 1/2 cup of berries, lightly sugared, to the batter. Absolutely wonderful.

CHEESE POPOVERS

Place a 3/4-inch cube of Swiss cheese in each baking cup.

MUFFINS

2 cups flour	1 well beaten egg
3 teaspoons baking powder	1 cup milk
1/2 teaspoon salt	3 tablespoons melted butter
3 tablespoons sugar	

Sift the dry ingredients together. Mix together the egg, milk, and butter. Stir the egg mixture into the flour mixture, *quickly*. This is the secret of tender muffins. Turn immediately into greased muffin tins, filling them two thirds full. Bake in a hot (425°) oven for 20-30 minutes, depending upon the size of the muffins.

12 medium-size muffins

VARIATIONS ON MUFFINS

BLUEBERRY MUFFINS

Add 1 cup blueberries mixed with 2 tablespoons sugar to the muffin dough. These are wonderful for breakfast, lunch, or supper in August—hot, juicy, and delicious.

CHERRY MUFFINS

Unusual and good. Add 3/4 cup chopped cherries mixed with 2 tablespoons sugar to the muffins. Reduce the milk by 2 tablespoons if the cherries are very juicy.

CRANBERRY MUFFINS

Add 3/4 cup chopped cranberries mixed with 3 tablespoons sugar to the sifted dry ingredients.

NUT MUFFINS

Add 1/2 cup coarsely chopped nuts to the sifted dry ingredients.

BRAN MUFFINS

Using the recipe for Muffins, substitute 1 cup of bran for 1 cup of the flour, increase the baking powder to 3 and 1/2 teaspoons, and reduce the milk to 2/3 cup. Add the bran to the dry ingredients. If you wish, brown sugar may be used instead of granulated sugar, and 1/2 cup raisins may be added to the muffins.

SOUR CREAM MUFFINS

Using the recipe for Muffins, reduce the baking powder to 1 teaspoon and add 1/2 teaspoon baking soda. Use 1 and 1/4 cups sour cream in place of the milk and shortening. These muffins are good with 1/2 cup of chopped dates added.

12 muffins

BAKING POWDER BISCUITS

Mrs. Armande Madore
St. Johnsbury, Vt.

2 cups flour
1 teaspoon salt
4 teaspoons baking powder

4 tablespoons Crisco
3/4 cup milk

Sift together the flour, salt, and baking powder and cut in the shortening. Gradually add the milk to make a firm, soft dough. Turn onto a lightly floured board, and knead just enough to shape into a smooth ball. Pat to 1/2 inch thickness and cut with a floured biscuit cutter. Place on an ungreased baking sheet or pan—one half inch apart for crusty biscuits and close together for tall soft biscuits. Bake in a hot oven (450°) for 12-15 minutes. Baking powder biscuits are quick to make and useful on many menus. They taste especially good served with a cone of fresh honey.

14 2-inch biscuits

VARIATIONS ON
BAKING POWDER BISCUITS

All of these are good for buffet or cocktail parties. Nut and Orange biscuits are nice for tea.

CHEESE BISCUITS

Roll the dough 1/4 inch thick. Cut biscuits. Place a small square of cheese—Cheddar, Roquefort, or any that you like—on half of the biscuits and top, sandwich fashion with the other half. Press edges together.

SAUSAGE BISCUITS

Form sausage meat into tiny flat cakes and sandwich between biscuit rounds as for cheese biscuits.

BACON BISCUITS

Crumble crisp bacon into the biscuit dough before shaping.

NUT BISCUITS

Add 1/2 cup of chopped black walnuts to the biscuit dough.

ORANGE TEA BISCUITS

Press a small lump of sugar dipped in orange juice into each biscuit, then sprinkle the biscuits with grated orange rind.

RAGAMUFFINS

A favorite Vermont recipe contributed by Dorothy Crandall, who ate them as a child in Essex Junction, Vermont, and because they are sort of ragged looking called them Ragamuffins. Delicious with cold milk or with coffee.

1 recipe baking powder biscuit
   dough (see p. 12)
1 cup soft butter

1 cup soft maple sugar
1/2 cup butternuts or walnuts,
   chopped (optional)

Roll the dough out very lightly on a board until it is about 1/2 inch thick. Spread it with soft butter, maple sugar, and nuts. Roll it up like a jelly roll, slice, and bake in a flat pan in a 425° oven until light brown. Or if you like more crust, bake in muffin tins.

SCONE HOT CROSS BUNS

3 cups sifted flour
4 and 1/2 teaspoons baking
   powder
1 teaspoon salt
1/4 cup sugar
1 and 1/2 teaspoons cinnamon

1/4 teaspoon allspice
6 tablespoons shortening
3/4 cup currants
1 egg, beaten
2/3 cup milk

Sift together the flour, baking powder, salt, sugar, and spices. Cut in the shortening and add the currants. Add the milk to the beaten egg, then add to the flour mixture until all is moistened. Turn the dough out on a lightly floured board and knead gently for 30 seconds. Roll the dough out about 3/4 inch thick and cut with a biscuit cutter. Place the scone rounds in a lightly greased pan or on a baking sheet. Brush them with milk and bake in a 425° oven for 15 minutes. After baking, mark a cross on the top of each bun with confectioners' sugar icing.

GRIDDLECAKES AND WAFFLES

Long the breakfast standby of New England, griddlecakes and waffles give real warmth and substance to keep you through a cold winter day. They are usually served with butter and hot maple syrup or molasses, or with maple sugar. Sausages or bacon and fried apple slices should accompany them.

The batter used for these breakfast cakes is very similar to the batter used for popovers. Griddlecakes can be baked on a heavy iron or aluminum griddle or pan, or on a soapstone griddle which is very lightly rubbed with grease. Waffles used to be made in a cast iron waffle iron. Now an electric one is generally used. After a preliminary rubbing down of the waffle iron with unsalted fat, it should not be necessary to grease it again. The batter has enough fat in it to prevent sticking. The iron or griddle is hot enough for baking when a drop of water "dances" rapidly on its surface. Waffles should be crisp and light, griddlecakes or pancakes tender and golden brown. Thin pancakes may be filled with creamed cottage cheese and herbs and served as a luncheon or supper dish. Waffles may be topped with creamed chicken for lunch, or with crushed fruit and sweetened whipped cream for dessert.

GRIDDLECAKES

1 cup sifted flour	1 egg
1 teaspoon baking powder	3/4 cup milk
1/2 teaspoon salt	1 tablespoon melted butter

Sift the dry ingredients together. Combine the egg and milk and all except butter; beat until smooth and add the butter. Bake on a lightly greased hot griddle, turning once.

APPLE PANCAKES

Add 1/2 cup of finely chopped apple to the batter.

BLUEBERRY PANCAKES

Add 1/2 cup of fresh blueberries to the batter. Frozen ones may be used in winter, but drain them carefully first.

JELLY PANCAKES

Butter hot griddlecakes, spread them with a tart jelly or jam and roll tightly. Sprinkle with sugar and serve.

MAPLE FIRSTS

(Excerpts from an article by W. T. Arms, YANKEE, March '58)

In the 1760s, Britain's periodical Dodsley's Register *recorded that "a method of making sugar and molasses from the sap of a certain tree called the Maple, common in the New England colonies, has just been discovered and put into practice at several portions of New England, but especially at Bernardston, twenty miles from Athol." The earliest reference to New England sugar making goes as far back as 1609 when Marc Lescarbot, historian in the Lake Champlain area wrote: "The Indians get juice from the trees and from it distil a sweet and agreeable liquid."*

Indian catch buckets were actually made from large pieces of birch bark, folded and then stitched with basswood fibres. The seams were made sap-tight with pine resin. Sap was then poured into large, hollowed-out tree trunks in which the liquid was boiled and made into syrup or sugar by adding an endless succession of red hot stones.

Before 1765 the Yankees had been slow to imitate the Indians in sugar making, but toward the close of the French and Indian Wars the Reverend Samuel Hopkins of Springfield suggested that "It would be prudent for colonial farmers to spare their maple trees and utilize them in supplying themselves with their own sugar and molasses."

GEORGE WASHINGTON'S BREAKFAST

This recipe is contributed by Stuyvie Wainwright, aged 5, of New York. It is completely authentic, and we imagine that it was accompanied by delicious smoked ham. Cherry jam would have tasted good with the hoe cakes, but knowing of the early encounter of the Father of Our Country with this lovely fruit tree, one must assume that there was no cherry jam upon his breakfast table.

HOE CAKES

corn meal   water
salt

Mix ingredients to make a thin batter and cook on a hot griddle until brown on each side. Serve with butter and honey.

RYE PANCAKES

Here's a recipe that dates back to the early 1700's, when great fields of rye waved in the wind all along the Taunton River Valley in Massachusetts. The molasses or sugar required for these pancakes was brought up the river in small sloops or brigs before the days of the Old Colony Railroad. A cherished family tradition handed down from generation to generation, this recipe was contributed to YANKEE by Miss Helen H. Lane.

1 and 1/2 pints rye meal   1 teaspoon cream of tartar
1/2 pint flour   1 egg
1 gill sugar or molasses (1/2 cup) 1 pint milk or water
1 teaspoon salt   1/2 tea cup New England rum

Combine ingredients and fry pancakes in deep fat. Fill individual butter plates with sugar. Drop enough vinegar on the sugar to make it spreadable as butter. As you eat the pancakes, dab them with the mixture.

TUESDAY PANCAKES

With the approach of Lent our forebears had one last feast before the fasting began, traditionally serving pancakes on Shrove Tuesday.

6 eggs
1 and 1/2 cups sifted flour
1/4 teaspoon salt

1 tablespoon sugar
2 cups milk

Beat the eggs until light, add the other ingredients and beat approximately 5 minutes until the batter is smooth. Coat the bottom and sides of an 8-inch frying pan with melted butter. When hot, pour in about 5 tablespoons of batter, turning the pan so that it will form a large, thin, flat, pancake. Cook until the batter bubbles, then turn and cook the other side. Put the pancake on a hot plate, sprinkle it heavily with powdered sugar and cinnamon, spread cooked apples or whipped cream on it and roll the cake like a jelly roll. Serve with maple syrup.

STUMP JUMPERS' BUCKWHEAT CAKE

Mrs. George A. Dunham
Danville, Vt.

1/2 cup sugar
1/2 cup flour
2 teaspoons baking powder
3/4 teaspoon salt
1 rounded cup buckwheat flour
    (or packaged buckwheat pancake
    mix)
3 tablespoons shortening

1 egg
1 cup sweet milk or 1 cup
    buttermilk or thick sour
    milk (if buttermilk or sour
    milk is used, omit baking
    powder and add 1 teaspoon
    soda)

Sift the dry ingredients into a large bowl. Add the milk gradually, then the shortening, melted, and the egg. Mix well. If you use an electric mixer, beat at medium speed for at least 3 minutes. If a thick cake is desired, pour the batter into a well greased round 9-inch cake pan. Any medium-sized square pan is equally good. Bake at 425° for 35 minutes or until well browned. Delicious served hot with plenty of butter and a steaming cup of coffee.

WAFFLES

2 cups sifted flour
3 teaspoons baking powder
1/2 teaspoon salt

3 eggs, separated
1 and 1/4 cups milk
4 tablespoons melted butter

Mix and sift dry ingredients. Beat egg yolks well and combine with milk; add to dry mixture and beat until smooth; add melted butter, then fold in stiffly beaten egg whites. To prevent overflow, turn into hot waffle iron enough batter to partly fill each compartment. Close iron and bake until steam is no longer visible.

6 waffles

DOUGHNUTS

Served with cold cider, milk, or quantities of hot coffee, doughnuts are another staple of the New England diet. They may be made in a number of shapes and in countless different ways. Rings, rounds, or twists, not to mention doughnut holes; plain, sugared, chocolate, spiced—every family has its own favorite variation.

The temperature of the fat is of prime importance in achieving a perfect doughnut. If it is not hot enough, the doughnuts will be greasy. If it is too hot, the doughnuts will not be cooked through. The fat should be at 360-370°. The easiest way to determine temperature, of course, is with a thermometer, but our grandmothers knew that the fat was just right for frying doughnuts when a cube of bread would brown in it in 60 seconds.

Do not fry too many doughnuts at a time, or the fat will be cooled. As soon as the doughnuts rise to the top of the kettle, turn them once to brown the other side. Drain them on absorbent paper, place in a crock while warm, and leave the top ajar until they have cooled completely.

AUNTIE'S DOUGHNUTS

From Mrs. Gertrude E. Olsen of Mansfield, Massachusetts, comes this recipe. "My mother was always known as 'Auntie', or 'The Doughnut Lady' to the people of our community. Everyone loved her, and everyone loved her doughnuts. Each Saturday, she replenished our doughnut crock, and each Saturday the paper-boy, the mailman, the milkman, and the grocer lingered to chat a bit and enjoy some hot doughnuts straight from the kettle on the old wood-burning range. We children could hardly wait for the first doughnut holes, which she would fry on the pretext of testing the fat, but really to see our delight in savoring their goodness to the accompaniment of ice-cold milk. Here is the recipe as she wrote it out for me when I was married."

1 quart flour	1 cup sugar
1 teaspoon soda	butter the size of a walnut
1 teaspoon cream of tartar	2 eggs
1 heaping teaspoon salt	2 cups (approx.) sour milk
1 heaping teaspoon ground nutmeg	

Cream the sugar and the butter. Add the eggs, not beaten. Stir together and add sour milk. Sift together the dry ingredients and add the liquid mixture. Stir up well. If too thin to roll, add flour to handle. Roll, and fry in deep fat. Dip the doughnuts quickly in hot water immediately after cooking to remove the fat. Dip some in sugar, some in cinnamon and sugar, leave some plain. Place in the crock while warm, and leave top ajar until the doughnuts cool. (If you have no sour milk, add another teaspoon cream of tartar to sweet milk, but the doughnuts won't be as good.)

SPICED DOUGHNUTS

To be served with apple cider.

2 eggs, beaten
1 cup sugar
1 cup milk
5 tablespoons shortening, melted
4 cups flour

4 teaspoons baking powder
1/4 teaspoon cinnamon
1/4 teaspoon nutmeg
1/4 teaspoon ground cloves
1/4 teaspoon salt

Add the sugar, milk, and shortening to the beaten eggs. Sift the flour before measuring, then resift it with the baking powder, spices, and salt. Combine the egg mixture with the flour mixture and stir until blended. Roll the dough one quarter inch thick and cut into desired shapes with a floured cutter. Fry at 360° to 370° for about 3 minutes, first on one side, then the other. Sprinkle with sugar.

30 doughnuts

DOUGHNUTS IN RHYME

1 cup of sugar, 1 cup of milk;
Two eggs, beaten fine as silk:
Salt and nutmeg (lemon will do)
Of baking powder teaspoons two,
Stir enough of flour in,
To roll on pie board, not too thin;
Cut in diamonds, twists or rings,
Drop with care the doughy things
Into the fat that swiftly swells
Evenly the spongy cells.
Watch with care the time for turning,
Fry them brown, just short of burning;
Roll in sugar, serve when cool,
This is the never failing rule.

Submitted by Mrs. M. E. Cotter
Wilbraham, Mass.

POTATO DOUGHNUTS

Very light.

2 cups mashed potato (not hot)
1 cup sweet milk
2 cups sugar
4 eggs
4 tablespoons melted butter

6 cups flour
6 teaspoons baking powder
1 teaspoon nutmeg
1/4 teaspoon cinnamon
1/2 teaspoon salt

Roll the dough out as soft as possible and fry, a few at a time in fat heated to 360°. Drain on paper towels.

FUNNEL CAKES

Mrs. Lois Kenyon
Wyckoff, N.J.

A Pennsylvania Dutch favorite contributed by a YANKEE reader.

1 egg, well beaten
2/3 cup milk
1 and 1/4 cups flour
2 tablespoons sugar
1 teaspoon baking powder

1/4 teaspoon salt
a funnel having a 3/8 to 1/2-inch hole
deep fat at 375°

Beat the milk with the egg. Blend the dry ingredients and gradually add the milk mixture, beating constantly until the batter is smooth. Place your finger over the opening of the funnel and fill it with batter. Holding the funnel as close to the surface of the fat as possible, remove your finger and drop the batter into the fat swirling it in circles from the center out to form a spiral cake about 3 inches in diameter. Immediately replace your finger on the funnel hole and form other cakes, as many as will float uncrowded. Fry until the cakes are puffy and golden brown, turning once. Remove with a slotted spoon to paper toweling to drain. Sift confectioners' sugar lightly over the cakes or serve them with molasses or maple syrup. It is intriguing to watch the cook make funnel cakes for breakfast or lunch. The batter forms rings around rings and the cakes may be made up to 6 inches across if you wish.

2 dozen cakes

SALLY LUNN

2 cups flour
3 teaspoons baking powder
1/2 teaspoon salt

2 eggs, separated
1/2 cup milk
1/2 cup melted butter

Mix and sift the dry ingredients. Add the milk to the beaten egg yolks and add to the dry ingredients stirring until just mixed. Stir in the melted butter, then fold in the stiffly beaten egg whites. Bake in a well greased 9-inch square pan in a moderate oven (350°) for about 30 minutes.

9 squares

CHEESY VERMONT MAPLE APPLE DANISH

Mrs. Barbara Howard
Burlington, Vt.

This dreamy confection was invented by Mrs. Howard to show off three of Vermont's most famous products. The pastry is as easy as letting the butter soften to room temperature before starting, and following all instructions for chilling between rolling. Note that the dough should be chilled *overnight*, and plan accordingly.

PASTRY DOUGH

3/4 cup milk
1/3 cup soft maple sugar, firmly packed
2 teaspoons salt
1/3 cup butter or margarine
2 packages dry yeast

1/4 cup warm water (*not hot*)
1/2 teaspoon almond extract
3 eggs, beaten
4 and 1/2 cups sifted all-purpose flour
1 cup soft butter or margarine

FILLING

4-6 slightly tart apples (such as firm McIntosh, Cortland, or Spy)
sharp Vermont Cheddar cheese, shredded or grated

cinnamon
soft maple sugar
2-4 tablespoons butter or margarine

ICING

2 cups sifted confectioners' sugar
milk

1/2 to 1 teaspoon maple flavoring

Dough: Scald the milk; stir in the maple sugar, salt, and 1/3 cup butter or margarine. Let cool until lukewarm. Meanwhile, dissolve yeast in the warm water. Let stand at least 5 minutes. Combine yeast and lukewarm milk mixture. Mix in the almond extract and the beaten eggs, then add the flour, gradually. Blend all the ingredients thoroughly, but do not overmix. Place the dough in a greased 9" x 13" pan and refrigerate for 1-2 hours.

Turn the dough out onto a floured board. Roll into a rectangle, 12" x 16". Spread 1/3 cup of the remaining butter or margarine over two-thirds of the dough. Fold the unspread portion of the dough over half the covered portion. Fold the third section over the first two. Roll dough out again to the original size. Repeat this process twice, until the entire cup of soft butter is used up. Put the dough in the pan, cover, and chill overnight.

Roll half of the dough into a rectangle at least 9" x 16" x 1/4" for cockscombs or swirls. Roll dough to approximately 12" x 16" for baby bunting or "envelope" shapes. Shape as desired and fill with cheesy maple-apple filling. Cover and let rise until very light and puffy (at least doubled in bulk). Bake at 375° for about 12 minutes, or until delicately browned. While warm, frost lightly with maple icing.

Filling: Melt enough butter or margarine in a large, heavy skillet to form a thin layer over the bottom. Pare, core, and thinly slice 2-3 apples for each half of the dough. Sauté the apple slices in the melted butter over low heat, until *just* tender. Remove from heat. Place apples in the center of each piece of dough, approximately one tablespoonful for most shapes. Sprinkle on a dash of cinnamon, then generously top with maple sugar and shredded sharp cheddar cheese. The more cheese the better—but be careful not to use so much that the sugar or cheese will ooze out during baking.

Icing: Mix icing ingredients, adding enough milk for a semi-liquid icing. Frost.

24 pastries

APRICOT STREUSEL COFFEE CAKE

Mrs. Barney A. Parslow
Elnora, N.Y.

1 and 1/2 cups flour
3/4 cup sugar
3 teaspoons baking powder
1/2 teaspoon salt
1/4 cup shortening,
  or 4 tablespoons butter

1 egg
1/2 cup milk
1 teaspoon vanilla
1/2 cup stewed apricots or
  apricot jam

TOPPING

1/4 cup brown sugar
1 tablespoon flour
1 teaspoon cinnamon

1 tablespoon melted butter
1/4 cup chopped pecans

Sift the dry ingredients together in a bowl, then cut in the shortening with a pastry blender or 2 knives until the mixture looks like meal. Stir in the egg, milk, and vanilla. Spread half of this mixture in a greased and floured 6" x 10" baking pan. Spread stewed apricots or apricot jam over this layer. Cover with the rest of the batter. Sprinkle the topping over all. Bake at 375° for 25-30 minutes.

SOUR CREAM COFFEE CAKE

1/2 cup butter
1 cup sugar
2 eggs beaten
1 cup sour cream

2 cups flour (sift before measuring)
1 teaspoon baking powder
1 teaspoon baking soda
1 teaspoon vanilla

FILLING AND TOPPING

1/2 cup brown sugar
1/2 cup chopped nuts

1 teaspoon cinnamon
raisins

Cream the butter and sugar together and add the eggs, sour cream, and the flour sifted with the baking powder and soda and the vanilla. Put half of the batter in a well buttered tube pan. Sprinkle half of the filling mixture and about 1/2 cup of raisins over the batter. Pour in the remainder of the batter and sprinkle it with the rest of the topping. Bake in a 350° oven for 35 minutes, or until done.

PECAN COCONUT CAKE

Mrs. Fritz Nelson
Worcester, Mass.

This cake is excellent with coffee, a nice treat for Sunday morning breakfast.

1/3 cup butter
1 cup brown sugar, firmly packed
2 eggs, unbeaten
1 and 1/2 teaspoons vanilla
1/3 cup milk

1/3 cup sweetened shredded coconut
1 and 1/2 cups sifted all-purpose flour
1 and 1/2 teaspoons baking powder
1/2 teaspoon salt

TOPPING

1/2 cup all-purpose flour
1/2 cup brown sugar
1/4 cup hard butter

1/2 cup pecan nuts
1/3 cup sweetened shredded coconut

Mix together the butter, sugar, eggs, vanilla, and coconut until well blended. Sift together flour, baking powder, and salt, add this to the first mixture alternately with the milk, and beat until smooth. Pour into a greased 8-inch square pan. Mix topping ingredients all together and spread over the batter. Bake at 375° for 30 minutes.

OLD-FASHIONED CORNBREAD

1 cup cornmeal
1 cup sifted flour
1/4 cup sugar
3 teaspoons baking powder
1 teaspoon salt

1 egg, well beaten
1 cup milk
1/4 cup melted shortening,
  butter, or chicken fat

Mix dry ingredients and wet ingredients separately. Stir lightly and pour into a well greased 9-inch square pan. Bake in a 425° oven for 20-25 minutes. If you are roasting meat at the same time, the cornbread may be baked for a longer time at a lower temperature.

SOUR CREAM CORNBREAD

A cornbread with a lighter texture.

3/4 cup yellow cornmeal
1 cup unsifted flour
1/4 cup sugar
2 teaspoons baking powder
1/2 teaspoon soda

3/4 teaspoon salt
1 cup sour cream
1/2 cup milk
1 egg unbeaten
2 tablespoons melted shortening

Preheat oven to 375°. Place all of the ingredients in a mixing bowl and mix with a wire whisk. Pour the batter into a greased 9-inch square pan and bake for 25 minutes. Or if you wish, bake the batter in muffin tins for about 20 minutes.

APPLE CORNBREAD

Add 1 apple, peeled, cored, and finely diced to either of the above cornbreads.

MAPLE CORNBREAD

1 and 1/3 cups flour
2/3 cup cornmeal
3 teaspoons baking powder
1/2 teaspoon salt

1/3 cup maple syrup
1/2 cup melted shortening
2 eggs, slightly beaten

Sift the dry ingredients together and add the syrup, shortening, and eggs. Stir until well mixed, but do not beat. Turn into greased pans and bake 25 minutes in a hot (425°) oven.

CONNECTICUT DABS

Ellen Ormsbee Warder
Newfane, Vt.

1 cup white corn meal
3/4 cup boiling water
1 dessert spoon butter
salt

1 egg, beaten very light
3 tablespoons cream (sour cream
   is fine, too)

Mix the ingredients together in the order given. Drop the mixture by spoonfuls onto a well buttered hot pan and bake for 15 minutes in a 450° oven.

RHODE ISLAND TOADS

New Bedford tradition says these toads are to be eaten with creamed codfish.

1 cup corn meal
1 cup flour
2 teaspoons baking powder
1 egg

salt
milk
sugar, if desired

Mix the meal, flour, baking powder, and salt. Add the egg, unbeaten, and enough milk so that walnut-sized portions can be dripped into deep fat (360°) for frying to golden brown.

HIGHLAND EGGS

Mrs. Janet Kinloss Cheney
Morro Bay, Calif.

These eggs are very light and tender due to a "secret ingredient" which cannot be detected—a little vinegar.

4 eggs
1 teaspoon vinegar
salt and pepper to taste

1/2 cup milk
butter the size of a walnut

Break the eggs in a bowl and mix in the vinegar, salt, and freshly ground pepper. Melt the butter in a pan, add the milk, then the eggs, and cook very gently stirring with a wooden spoon. The eggs are good with the addition of a little grated orange rind, chopped parsley, or chopped chives.

Serves 2

INDIVIDUAL OMELET (see p. 34)

BEDSPREAD FOR TWO (see p. 35)

EGGS GOLDENROD (see p. 36)

SCOTCH EGGS

Mrs. Nicholas Cameron
Harrisville, N.H.

7 eggs
1/2 cup flour
salt and freshly ground pepper

1/2 pound sausage meat
vegetable oil for deep fat frying
breadcrumbs

Hard boil 6 eggs. Drain and place in cold water to cool. Mix the flour, salt, and pepper on a piece of wax paper, and roll the shelled eggs in the mixture. Divide the sausage meat into six equal parts and shape around each egg until each is evenly covered. Beat the remaining egg and brush it over the sausage meat. Roll each egg in breadcrumbs. Heat the oil to 390° and fry the eggs until they are golden brown in the deep fat—about 3 minutes. Drain the eggs on paper toweling. Cut crosswise and serve with toast.

CODFISH BALLS

The real Bostonian Sunday Breakfast, of course, is codfish balls (or cakes, or creamed codfish), baked beans, and brown bread.

2 and 1/2 cups salt cod	1 egg
2 and 1/2 cups potatoes	pepper
2 tablespoons butter	

Soak the fish in water for half an hour, then drain and flake it. Boil it with the peeled and cubed potatoes until the potatoes are tender. Drain. Put back on the fire momentarily to dry completely. Mash the mixture, add butter and pepper and beat until fluffy. Add the egg and continue beating. Drop by tablespoons into deep hot fat (375°) and fry until golden brown. Codfish *cakes* may be made by dropping the mixture onto a hot, lightly greased griddle and browning on both sides. They are good served with fried tomatoes.

Serves 6

CODFISH CAKES
Mrs. William Endicott, Sr.
Danvers, Mass.

These are fluffier, fancier fare than the preceding recipe.

2 cups salt codfish	1 egg white, beaten
2 cups potatoes, mashed	cream

Soak the codfish overnight. Pick apart in fine pieces. Cut potatoes into small pieces and boil together with the codfish. When the potatoes are done, mash them together and add the beaten white of one egg and enough cream to make the mixture light and fluffy. If the potatoes are dry, more cream should be added. Drop the mixture from the end of a spoon into deep hot fat until light brown. These fish cakes should be uneven and fluffy. Sliced hardboiled eggs mixed in a curried cream sauce make a good combination with these cakes.

EGGS BOSTONIA

codfish cakes (p. 28)	3/4 teaspoons salt
1 cup cream sauce (p. 245)	1 tablespoon white vinegar
pepper	paprika
8 eggs	parsley

Form the fishball mixture into eight flattened patties about 1/2 inch thick. Make the cream sauce and season highly with pepper. Just before serving fry the fishcakes, four at a time, in deep fat at 385° for 3 or 4 minutes until golden brown. Drain on paper toweling and place in a deep, heated platter. Poach the eggs in one large or two small skillets containing an inch of water to which the salt and vinegar have been added. Small rings to contain the eggs are very helpful. When the whites are firm remove the eggs with a skimmer to the fishcakes. Cover with cream sauce and sprinkle with paprika. Garnish with parsley.

Serves 4

PROVINCETOWN
CREAMED CODFISH

Albert E. Snow
Orleans, Mass.

1/2 pound salt codfish
2 tablespoons butter
2 tablespoons flour
1/4 teaspoon pepper

1 cup milk
dash of Tabasco sauce
1 egg, beaten

Cut the codfish into one quarter inch slices across the grain. Soak it in lukewarm water overnight to draw out the salt and soften the fish. Drain the fish in the morning and simmer it in fresh water for 10 minutes. Melt the butter in a saucepan, add the flour and pepper and blend well. Gradually add the milk. Cook until thickened and add a dash of Tabasco sauce. Pour a small amount of the cream sauce into the beaten egg, stirring constantly, then mix the fish, egg, and sauce together and serve on hot buttered toast.

PARKER HOUSE CODFISH TONGUES

Dip fresh codfish tongues in milk, roll in flour, and fry in butter until golden brown. Pour over them freshly browned butter, to which has been added lemon juice and fresh chopped parsley.

FINNAN HADDIE DELMONICO

2 cups finnan haddie
4 hardcooked eggs, sliced
1 and 1/2 cups cream sauce (p. 245)

cayenne
pepper
chopped parsley

Soak the finnan haddie for 30 minutes. Drain and flake the fish removing any bones. Simmer for 25 minutes in fresh water. Combine the fish with the cream sauce and sliced hardcooked eggs. Season with cayenne and pepper and serve on hot buttered toast sprinkled with chopped parsley.

Serves 6

CONNECTICUT KEDGEREE

2 cups cooked rice
2 cups cooked flaked fish
4 hardcooked eggs, chopped

2 tablespoons minced parsley
1/2 cup top milk
salt and pepper

To hot rice add remaining ingredients and reheat in a double boiler. Serve immediately.

Serves 6

QUAHOG FRITTERS (see p. 43)

CREAMED DRIED BEEF (see p. 45)

BOSTON BAKED BEANS (see p. 31)

Chapter 2.
Various Dishes

What are *various dishes*? Well, that's what I call dishes good for lunch or supper, for a buffet party, a first course, or sometimes just a snack. They include egg and cheese dishes, our famous New England baked beans, casseroles, and other old favorites that "taste even better the next day."

NEW ENGLAND'S FIRST MOLASSES

Sunrise one morning during the late 1600s revealed a weathered sloop riding at anchor in Boston Harbor. Shorefront observers saw that it rode low in the water, evidently carrying a heavy cargo. They had no way of knowing that this cargo was the first of its kind ever to reach New England and was to initiate changes in New England's eating and drinking habits, as well as play its part in bringing a country yet undreamed of to civil war.

Down in the sloop's creaking hold, hogsheads of molasses crowded each other, lumbered aboard weeks before in the West Indies. Soon the sweet syrup would be on every Yankee table,

poured over breakfast dishes and desserts, mixed into hasty pudding, and used as the sweetening ingredient in countless New England recipes. Shortly, men would be distilling it into rum, most of which would go to Africa to be traded for slaves, these to be traded in the South for sugar molasses, and money—to the completion of the triangle and the enrichment of the Yankee trader.

Not too long after the landing of that first cargo of molasses, Boston housewives and their cooks were experimenting with the new ingredient in cookies, cakes, and candies—not to mention Baked Beans!

BOSTON BAKED BEANS

This dish, New England's favorite Saturday night supper, is apt to be eaten again with codfish balls for breakfast on Sunday morning, and I doubt if a church supper has even been held here that didn't offer big pots of beans along with baked ham, chicken pie, and cole slaw.

1 quart pea beans	1 teaspoon salt
1/2 pound piece salt pork	1 teaspoon soda
1/3 cup sugar	1/2 teaspoon dry mustard
1/3 cup molasses	boiling water

Wash and pick over the beans and soak them overnight in cold water. In the morning drain them and cover with fresh water. Simmer until the skins break. Put the beans in a bean pot, score the pork and press on top of the beans where it will brown, filling the pot three-quarters full. Add the sugar, molasses, salt, soda, and mustard. Cover with boiling water. Cover the pot and bake without stirring for 8 hours in a slow oven, 250°. Keep beans almost covered with water. Remove the pot's cover for the last half hour of baking.

Serves 8

BAKED BEANS II

Here's another baked beans recipe for those who like their food more spicy. This recipe comes from the Lighted Christmas Tree Inn in Marlow, New Hampshire.

1 quart pea beans	1 teaspoon salt
2 large onions, chopped	3/4 cup black molasses
3/4 pound salt pork, diced	1 teaspoon dry mustard
ham bone	1/2 teaspoon ginger
1 or 2 cloves garlic, chopped	2 tablespoons vinegar

Soak the beans overnight. Next morning, parboil them in fresh water until they are soft, along with the onions, salt pork, garlic, and ham bone. Salt to taste. Put them in the bean pot with real black molasses (some like brown sugar as well), mustard, ginger, and vinegar to add piquancy. Leave in the oven with anything else baking (except cake), covered at first and uncovered for the last hour of cooking. The longer the beans bake, the better they are. They are best the second day's baking. (250° for 6-8 hours should do it. Add water if necessary.)

Serves 8

BOSTON BROWN BREAD (STEAMED)

1 cup rye flour
1 cup yellow corn meal
1 cup graham flour
1 teaspoon salt

1 teaspoon soda
3/4 cup molasses
2 cups sour milk
1 cup raisins

Mix and sift the dry ingredients. Dissolve the soda in a small quantity of water and stir into the molasses. Combine with the sour milk, then mix into the dry ingredients. Flour the raisins and add to the batter. Mix thoroughly and pour into two greased molds filling two-thirds to the top. (Old baking powder cans used to be the standard molds.) The cover should be tight-fitting, and should be buttered before being placed on the mold. It should then be tied down with a string so that the bread will not force off the cover as it rises. Place the molds on a rack in a kettle containing boiling water which comes halfway up around the molds. Cover and steam for 3 hours, adding more boiling water if needed. Use a string to slice brown bread.

BAKED BROWN BREAD

Mrs. Mariam Bresett
Belchertown, Mass.

This recipe is similar to the preceding one but can be whipped up at an hour's notice.

2 cups buttermilk
3/4 cup molasses
1 cup graham flour
1 cup white flour
1 cup yellow corn meal

1 cup raisins
1/4 cup melted shortening
1 teaspoon soda
1 teaspoon salt

Combine the ingredients and bake for one hour in a greased loaf pan in a 350° oven.

CASSOULET

A New England adaptation of an old French dish that comes down to us through Canadian settlers, this is a highly flavored version of baked beans that well deserves the praise it always gets. The recipe will fill a 4-quart casserole and serve at least 12-14 as a side dish with ham or lamb. If it is to be the main dish, count on 6-8 servings. Cassoulet is even better when prepared a day or two in advance and reheated.

2 pounds dried white beans	6 cloves garlic, crushed
(yellow eye or soldier beans)	2 onions, cut up
2 tablespoons salt	1/2 pound salt pork or
1 bay leaf	bacon scraps
1 sprig thyme, or 1/2	
teaspoon dried thyme	

Soak the beans in water overnight. They will double in bulk. In the morning, rinse them and place in water to cover. Add the rest of the above ingredients, bring to a boil, and simmer very gently for about 1½ hours, or until just tender. Discard the bay leaf and the sprig of thyme. Remove the pork or bacon and cut it into cubes.

1/2 pound chicken livers	2 tomatoes, sliced
1/4 pound garlic sausage	1/2 can tomato paste

Cut the chicken livers in pieces and brown them with the cubes of salt pork. Cube the garlic sausage. Arrange a layer of the beans in a large earthenware pot; spread part of the chicken livers, sausage, and cubed salt pork over them. Continue in layers until all the ingredients are used. Pour all the juices in which the beans were cooked over the dish and add (now or later) some drippings from a ham or lamb if you are cooking either. Taste for seasoning.

1 cup breadcrumbs	1/2 cup chopped parsley

Top the cassoulet with a mixture of breadcrumbs and parsley and place in a very slow (250°) oven for 4 hours or longer. The finished dish should be liquid and succulent.

BAKED SEAFOOD

1 large green pepper	1/2 teaspoon salt
1 small onion	pepper
1 cup chopped celery	1 teaspoon Worcestershire sauce
1 cup crab meat	buttered breadcrumbs
1 cup shrimp	chopped parsley
1 cup mayonnaise	3-4 tablespoons white wine

Chop the pepper, onion, and celery rather fine. Combine the crab and shrimp, cut in pieces, with the vegetables and mayonnaise. Add the seasonings and mix well. Place in a buttered baking dish and cover with buttered crumbs and parsley. Bake 30 minutes in a 350° oven. Just before serving, add the white wine.

Serves 6

INDIVIDUAL OMELET

2 eggs	salt and pepper
2 teaspoons water	1 tablespoon butter

Use an 8-inch omelet pan with sloping sides; one that is kept exclusively for making omelets will give you the best results. Have fresh eggs at room temperature, beat them lightly with the water, salt, and pepper until just blended. Heat the butter in the omelet pan over rather high heat, tilting the pan to coat the entire surface. When the butter sputters, pour in the egg mixture and scramble quickly once to cook most of the egg. Cook over lowered heat, shaking the pan to keep the omelet loosened from the pan and rolling the pan to let the uncooked egg slip to the bottom. When just a filmy coating of the liquid egg rests on top, fold the outer edges toward the center. Slide the omelet to the edge of the pan and turn onto a warm plate.

OMELET VARIATIONS

An omelet can be made in less than 2 minutes and can be filled with all sorts of good things to make a wonderful light meal. Put the warmed filling in just before folding the omelet. A few sliced mushrooms cooked in butter, a little crumbled bacon, some sour cream, cottage cheese, grated Swiss or Parmesan cheese, together or alone. Chopped herbs, parsley, chives, and watercress, or whatever ones are available may be mixed with the egg before making the omelet. Small amounts of leftover vegetables, meat, or fish may be folded into the omelet.

Suggested fillings for lunch-time omelets are: cooked asparagus tips; purée of spinach with sour cream; diced chicken, chicken livers, or ham in cream; crabmeat, lobster, or fish, creamed.

An omelet filled with jam or jelly and dusted with powdered sugar makes a breakfast or supper dish which children love. Adults do, too. Omit the pepper and use only a bit of salt. Sour or whipped cream may be folded into these sweet omelets.

Garnish a filled omelet with a hint of its contents—a sprig of watercress, a lobster claw, three slices of mushroom, as the case may be.

LOBSTER OMELET

Narcissa Chamberlain
Marblehead, Mass.

1/2 cup cooked, sliced lobster meat
1 tablespoon butter
1/4 cup dry white wine
1/2 cup thick cream sauce (p. 245)
6 eggs, made into one large
   or three small omelets (p. 34)

Heat the lobster meat in the butter with the wine and simmer until partly reduced. Blend in the cream sauce. Fold the lobster meat and part of the sauce into the center of the omelet or omelets. Pour the rest of the sauce over the top and serve.

Serves 3-4

OMELETTE A LA VIACROZE

Another omelet recipe of Narcissa Chamberlain's.

6 eggs, beaten
1 onion chopped and cooked soft
   in butter and 1 tablespoon
   parsley

3 mushrooms cooked until slightly soft in butter, 1/4 cup diced ham, and 2 tablespoons meat extract butter

Make a flat omelet with half your eggs and slide it onto a hot plate. Cover with the onion and mushroom and ham mixture. Top with another round omelet made with the remaining eggs. Quite a sandwich.

Serves 3

BEDSPREAD FOR TWO

A very ample bedspread.

6 eggs
12 medium oysters
anchovy paste
butter

toast
salt and freshly ground white pepper

Stir the eggs in a soup plate, and in a second soup plate cut up the oysters moderately fine. Rub the bottom of a chafing dish with anchovy paste. Put in a good sized piece of butter (3 tablespoons) and proceed to cook eggs gently to a creamy scramble. Just as they are turning, throw in the oysters and stir until well blended and cooked through. Season to taste and serve on toast lightly spread with anchovy paste and garnished with watercress or parsley.

Serves 2

EGGS BOSTONIA (see p. 28)

EGGS GOLDENROD

This pretty and soothing dish fills in for many occasions and is particularly popular with small children.

12 hardcooked eggs
2 cups cream sauce (p.245)

toast
parsley

Slice 10 of the eggs on a platter, cover with the cream sauce, and sieve the remaining eggs over them. Be sure the ingredients and the platter are good and warm. Surround with hot buttered toast points and garnish with parsley.

Serves 6

EGGS A LA HITCHCOCK

Mary B. Kidder
Devon, Penna.

A subtly flavored chafing-dish specialty.

1 pint cream, light or heavy
1 tablespoon Worcestershire
  sauce
1/2 tablespoon tomato catsup
1/2 tablespoon walnut catsup

1 saltspoon Tabasco sauce
salt and pepper to taste
6 large eggs
rounds of buttered toast
parsley or watercress

Heat the cream in a chafing dish, and when it is hot add the seasonings. Drop the eggs into the hot sauce. When they are set serve them on the rounds of buttered toast. Pour the remaining sauce over the eggs and garnish the plates with parsley or watercress.

Serves 6

COUNTRY STYLE ONION PIE

3 pounds onions
1 pint coffee cream
3 eggs, beaten

salt and pepper
pastry for one pie (p. 277)

Peel and slice the onions. Fry in butter until golden brown. Beat the eggs and cream together, season, and add to onions. Line a deep pie plate with pastry. Pour in the onions and cover with pastry. Bake in a 350° oven for 1 hour. The crust should be golden brown. For a change, crumbled crisp bacon or slivers of cheese may be put into the pie.

SPINACH QUICHE

Evart Andros
Walpole, N.H.

Excellent.

flaky pastry (p. 277)
2 pounds fresh spinach
2 tablespoons chopped scallions
2 tablespoons butter
3 eggs
1 and 1/2 cups heavy cream

1/2 teaspoon salt
1/2 teaspoon white pepper
1/2 teaspoon nutmeg
1/4 cup grated Gruyère cheese
1 tablespoon butter

Line a 9-inch pie pan or quiche dish with the pastry and chill it. Wash the spinach thoroughly and discard all thick stems. Plunge the spinach into boiling water for about 1 minute, drain it well and pat it dry with paper towels. Chop the spinach fine, add the chopped scallions, and cook the greens in the 2 tablespoons butter for several minutes, or until *all* liquid has evaporated. In a bowl combine the eggs, lightly beaten, with the cream and salt, pepper, and nutmeg. Add the spinach and pour into the pastry shell. Sprinkle the top with the grated cheese and dot it with 1 tablespoon of butter cut in bits. Bake the quiche in a moderate oven (375°) for 25-30 minutes until set. Serve hot.

Serves 6

MUSHROOM QUICHE

Use the same recipe, substituting 1 pound of mushrooms, sliced, for the 2 pounds of spinach. Use a watercress piecrust.

WATERCRESS PIECRUST

Adds "zing" to a meat or vegetable pie.

1 cup sifted flour
1 and 1/2 teaspoons baking powder
1/2 teaspoon salt
pinch of powdered thyme

2 tablespoons lard
1/3 cup finely chopped watercress
      leaves, well dried
1/2 cup cold milk

Sift the flour again with the baking powder, salt, and thyme. With two knives or a pastry blender, cut the lard and watercress leaves alternately into the flour. Add the milk gradually, and roll out on a floured board.

1 crust

CHEESE WOODCHUCK

This comfortable supper dish is a Maine "receipt" from a family whose ancestors were among the first settlers.

1 small onion, minced	1/2 pound diced cheese
2 tablespoons butter	1/2 teaspoon savory*
1/2 teaspoon salt	2 eggs, well beaten
2/3 cup milk	6 slices toast
1 and 1/2 to 2 cups corn, scraped from the cob	

Sauté butter and onion together, add seasonings, milk and corn, and cook slowly, stirring constantly, for about 10 minutes. Stir in the cheese and savory, and cook till cheese is melted. Then add the eggs and cook very gently, stirring constantly, 2-3 minutes longer. Serve on the toast slices, with pickle or relish as an accompaniment.

Serves 6

*Use Worcestershire Sauce

VERMONT CHEDDAR PUDDING

*Emily Holt
New York, N.Y.*

This pudding is something between a cheese soufflé and a Welsh Rabbit, but is much easier to concoct than either and guaranteed to please everybody. By simple arithmetic it can easily be adapted for two, four, or even 20.

8 slices white bread	1/2 teaspoon dry mustard
butter	salt, white pepper, and paprika
1/2 pound sharp Vermont Cheddar cheese	6 eggs
2 tablespoons grated Parmesan cheese	milk and cream
	1 teaspoon Worcestershire sauce

Lightly toast and butter the bread. Cut it into squares or triangles and place a layer in a buttered casserole. Cover with a layer of thinly sliced cheese, dust with Parmesan and seasonings and repeat these layers; the top should be cheese, dusted with mustard and paprika. Beat the eggs well and add enough half milk and half cream, or rich milk, to make 3 cups. Add Worcestershire sauce. Pour over the casserole and allow to stand for at least one hour, occasionally depressing with a wooden spoon so that the liquid covers all of the ingredients. If necessary add more whole milk. Preheat the oven to 400° for at least 10 minutes, cover the casserole with a cover or aluminum foil and place in the oven for 12 minutes. Remove the cover and bake for 25-30 minutes longer, until the casserole is puffed and browned. Serve at once with iced tea, coffee, or cold beer, with a green salad. This can be made in a roasting pan if the number of your guests so indicates.

Serves 6

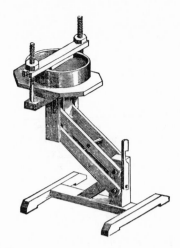

WELSH RABBIT

A good Cheddar cheese is the crucial ingredient for this dish. The better the cheese, the tastier the rabbit.

6 cups grated Cheddar cheese (about 1 and 1/2 pounds)	1 teaspoon dry mustard
1 tablespoon butter	Worcestershire sauce to taste
4 egg yolks	salt
1 cup beer	Tabasco sauce
	6 slices hot buttered toast

Melt the butter in the top of a double boiler over simmering water. Stir in the cheese and cook until melted and smooth. Stir the egg yolks into the beer with a whisk and add this mixture very slowly to the cheese, stirring. Add the seasonings and continue to cook and stir until the mixture is thick. Taste and add more seasoning if needed. Serve at once on hot buttered toast or crisp heated crackers.

Serves 6

This zestful dish is a good one to remember for an impromptu snack, for if you keep a good piece of cheese on hand the ingredients are never lacking. There are a number of pleasant ways to vary the dish. For a more substantial meal, garnish the rabbit with crisp bacon or fried ham.

TOMATO RABBIT

Place broiled tomatoes or drained canned tomatoes which have been heated on the toast before pouring the rabbit sauce over it.

OYSTER RABBIT

Add a half pint of oysters with their liquor to the cheese rabbit.

SCOTCH WOODCOCK

Place a poached egg on the toast before pouring the sauce over it.

TOMATO FONDUE

1 and 1/2 cups canned tomatoes
1 and 1/2 cups soft breadcrumbs
1 teaspoon salt
1/4 teaspoon paprika

2 cups Cheddar cheese, diced
4 egg yolks, slightly beaten
4 egg whites, beaten stiff

Add tomatoes to crumbs, season with salt and paprika and place over low heat. Add the cheese and melt it, stirring occasionally. Remove from heat, add the egg yolks, fold in the egg whites. Pour into a greased baking dish and bake at 350° for 40-45 minutes.

Serves 6

CHEESE SOUFFLE

A beautiful and useful dish for any day of the week, cheese soufflé can be counted on to fill an emergency easily and with style. For variety, try making a soufflé with Swiss cheese, with a combination of cottage cheese and Roquefort, or put a surprise ingredient (crabmeat, sliced tomatoes, or hearts of artichoke) in the bottom of the dish. The recipe given is for a 6-cup soufflé mold and serves three amply. If it is to be the main dish for four or five people, make 1 and 1/2 times the recipe (6 egg yolks, 7 or 8 whites) and use an 8-cup mold. For 6 servings it is best to double the recipe and use two 6-cup molds. Egg whites beat up better if they are at room temperature.

2 and 1/2 tablespoons butter
3 tablespoons flour
1 cup milk
1/2 teaspoon salt

a good pinch of mustard,
    cayenne, or both
1 cup diced cheddar cheese
4 egg yolks
5 egg whites

Set a rack in the middle of the oven and preheat the oven to 400°. Butter a straight-sided soufflé dish well, and shake a little grated cheese around it.

Melt the butter, remove from the heat and stir in the flour and a bit of the milk. Return to low heat and gradually add the rest of the milk, the seasonings and the cheese and stir well. You will have a thick sauce.

Separate the eggs, stirring the yolks one by one into the sauce and dropping the whites (adding an extra one) into a clean, dry mixing bowl. Beat the whites until they stand in stiff peaks.

Stir a large spoonful (or the white that clings to the beater) into the sauce, then very quickly and lightly fold in the rest of the egg white. Spoon the mixture into the prepared soufflé dish and place on the rack in the center of the oven. Immediately reduce the oven heat to 375°. In 25-30 minutes, the soufflé will be well puffed but still creamy in the center. Allow it to cook for 5 minutes longer and take it to the table where you have already assembled the other elements of the meal and the guests.

Serves 3

QUICK CHEESE SOUFFLE

1 can Cheddar cheese soup   4 eggs, separated
pinch of dry mustard

Preheat the oven to 400° and place a rack in the center of the oven. Stir the cheese soup over low heat, adding the mustard, and stirring in the egg yolks one by one. Beat the whites and fold them in as in the preceding recipe. Spoon into a buttered soufflé dish, set in the oven, reduce the heat to 375°, and bake for 30 minutes.

Serves 3

HAM, CHEESE, AND
MUSHROOM SOUFFLE

4 tablespoons butter   1 and 1/2 cups sliced, sautéed
3 tablespoons flour   mushrooms
2 cups milk   1 cup chopped cooked ham
3/4 cup grated cheese   4 eggs, separated
1/2 cup minced celery   3/4 teaspoon curry powder
1/2 cup minced pimiento   1 and 3/4 teaspoons grated onion
                              salt and pepper to taste

Melt the butter in a skillet, stir in the flour and add the milk gradually, stirring constantly until the sauce is smooth and thick. Add the cheese and stir until melted. Add the celery, pimiento, mushrooms, ham and well beaten egg yolks, curry powder, and onions. Season to taste. Cool to lukewarm and fold in the egg whites, beaten until stiff. Turn into a well greased casserole and bake in a 350° oven for 35-40 minutes until firm and well browned.

Serves 6

BAKED MACARONI AND CHEESE

A reliable old favorite good served with beef, lamb, or ham, hot or cold or as a buffet dish. If the recipe is doubled, allow a little longer time for baking.

1 8-ounce package macaroni
2 cups cream sauce (p. 245)
2 cups grated Cheddar cheese

1/2 cup buttered breadcrumbs
paprika

Cook the macaroni, broken in 2-inch pieces in 2 quarts boiling water with 1 teaspoon salt for 9-12 minutes or until soft. Rinse thoroughly in cold water and arrange layers of macaroni with cheese and cream sauce in a buttered baking dish, ending with a layer of cheese. Sprinkle the buttered breadcrumbs on top, dot with paprika and just before serving brown for 20-25 minutes in a 375° oven.

Serves 6-8

MACARONI RING

A most versatile dish, the ring may be served with grilled ham and filled with a vegetable, peas, creamed mushrooms, or creamed carrots. Or fill the ring with creamed chicken or fish and surround with a vegetable.

1 cup macaroni
2 teaspoons onion juice
1 and 1/2 tablespoons chopped parsley
2 tablespoons chopped green
   pepper
1 teaspoon salt

1/2 cup grated cheese
1 cup light cream
1 cup soft breadcrumbs
1/4 cup melted butter
3 eggs, well beaten

Break the macaroni in pieces and cook it in boiling salted water until nearly tender (about 7 minutes). Mix the drained macaroni with the other ingredients. Pour into a well buttered 2-quart ring mold (the mixture will rise during the cooking because of the eggs). Bake in a 350° oven for 45 minutes, or until firm.

Serves 6

CHESTNUT CROQUETTES

Mrs. Helen B. Haaland
Woodbury, Conn.

2 cups hot mashed chestnuts
4 tablespoons butter
2 eggs
salt and pepper

2 tablespoons minced onion
1 egg
breadcrumbs

Mix the chestnuts, butter, 2 eggs, slightly beaten, and seasonings. Shape into croquettes, roll in crumbs, then in beaten egg, and again in crumbs. Fry in deep hot fat (375-390°) until the crumbs are brown—2-5 minutes.

Serves 6

HOMINY CROQUETTES

Boil 1 cup hominy grits in 6 cups salted water for 1 hour. Mix 1 and 1/2 cups hot hominy with 2 beaten eggs and 2 tablespoons butter. Season to taste. Shape into balls and fry in deep hot fat until lightly browned. Serve with lots of grated cheese.

HAM FRITTERS

1 and 1/2 cups ground cooked ham
2 cups sifted flour
2 cups boiling water

4 eggs
3/4 tablespoon curry powder
cooking fat for deep frying

Stir the flour into rapidly boiling water and continue to cook, stirring vigorously, until the batter leaves the sides of the pan. Lower the heat and beat in the eggs, one at a time. Remove from the heat and stir in the curry powder and the ham. Bring the fat up to 390° on a thermometer and drop the batter by teaspoons into it. Cook until golden brown all over, then drain on absorbent paper. Serve with Cumberland sauce (p. 248) or brown mushroom sauce (p. 246).

QUAHOG FRITTERS

Albert E. Snow
Orleans, Mass.

1 pint quahogs, chopped fine (squeeze out and discard the blacks)
1 small onion, chopped fine
1 tablespoon olive oil or melted shortening

1 thin clove garlic, mashed
1 egg, slightly beaten
1/2 teaspoon baking powder
salt and pepper
flour

Mix ingredients well, using enough flour to make a batter with the consistency of whipped cream; thin when necessary with the quahog liquor. Fry by tablespoonfuls in piping hot fat in a frying pan. Do not use deep fat. Fry slowly after once starting. Serve hot. Delicious with tomato catsup. Takes the place of meat on your dinner menu.

CHICKEN ROLL

2 cups flour
4 teaspoons baking powder
1/2 teaspoon salt
4 tablespoons shortening

3/4 cup milk
2 cups diced, creamed chicken
(see cream sauce, p. 245)

Make biscuit dough and roll it out to 1/4 inch thickness. Spread with chicken and roll as a jelly roll. Bake in a hot oven for about 25 minutes. Serve with chicken gravy and currant or cranberry jelly.

Serves 4-6

CHICKEN LIVERS WITH MUSHROOMS

1 pound chicken livers
3 tablespoons flour
salt and pepper
cooking oil

4 tablespoons butter
1 large onion, coarsely chopped
1/2 cup sliced mushrooms
sherry

Toss the chicken livers in the flour seasoned with salt and pepper and fry them, a few at a time, in the oil until nicely browned. Cook the onion in the butter in another pan until soft. Add the mushrooms and cook for a few minutes longer, stirring. Add the livers and sherry and simmer all together for about 5 minutes. Serve on hot buttered toast.

Serves 4

CHICKEN TIMBALES

A long-time New England favorite, chicken timbales are attractive and digestible. Usually served with rice, they may be accompanied by a mushroom sauce (p. 246). This old family recipe from Tremont, Maine, was contributed by Mrs. Elaine Guthrie Lorillard.

10 crackers, finely crumbled
(Saltines or soda crackers)
2 tablespoons butter
1 and 3/4 cups milk
2 eggs, slightly beaten

2 cups cooked chicken, diced fine
2 teaspoons onion juice
1/2 teaspoon paprika
1 teaspoon salt
1/2 teaspoon pepper

Mix cracker crumbs, butter, and milk in a pan, stirring and heating until the mixture is of a creamy consistency. Pour it over the eggs and add the chicken, onion, and other seasonings. Butter individual molds, fill, and place in a pan of hot water. Bake for 30 minutes at 325°, or until a silver fork comes out clean when tested.

TASTY CORN-SAUSAGE CASSEROLE

Mrs. R. L. DeRoy
Centredale, R.I.

1 pound sausage meat
1 No. 2 can cream style corn
2 eggs

1/4 teaspoon salt
1 and 1/2 cups soft breadcrumbs

Brown the sausage until crumbly. While it cooks combine the corn, eggs, and salt. Place half of this mixture in a greased casserole, cover with the sausage lifted from the skillet with a perforated spoon. Top with the rest of the corn mixture. Stir the bread crumbs together with the fat remaining in the skillet and spread over the casserole. Bake until set and browned at 400° for 20-25 minutes.

Serves 4

CREAMED DRIED BEEF

1/2 pound dried beef
2 tablespoons butter
2 tablespoons flour

1 cup light cream
pepper

Separate the pieces of meat and soak them in hot water for 10 minutes to remove some of the salt. Meantime melt the butter, add the flour and, gradually while stirring, the cream to make a cream sauce. Season with the pepper and add the drained dried beef. This may be served on hot buttered toast or poured over stuffed baked potatoes.

FRIED SALT PORK

1 pound fat salt pork

Cut the salt pork in 12 thin slices, or have the butcher do this for you, and fry turning, until well browned. Crisp salt pork is often served as an accompaniment to creamed dried beef over baked potatoes. It may also be served with a cream gravy made by adding a cup of thick cream to one tablespoon of salt pork fat left in the pan. As soon as the cream is hot, pour it over the salt pork slices.

Serves 4

NEW ENGLAND CHICK
AND OYSTER PIE

Mrs. M. W. Sullivan
Boston, Mass.

A dish native to Boston that has much merit. It is a bit unusual, very, very good, and it can be prepared at any time during the day, then set aside for supper.

3 cups cooked chicken, cut in
   large chunks
2 cups oysters
butter
1 teaspoon salt

white pepper
2 cups medium cream sauce
   (p. 245)
pie crust (p. 37 or p. 277)

Combine the chicken and oysters in a buttered casserole. Dot with 2 tablespoons of butter, add the salt and pepper, and pour the cream sauce over all. Cover the dish with a pie crust, slit to allow steam to escape. Bake in a hot oven (400°) for 35 minutes.

Short Cuts: A can of cream of chicken soup mixed with a half can of milk and oyster liquor makes a quick cream sauce. Try leftover mashed potatoes, whipped with egg, as a topping for the pie (instead of pie crust)—bake at 350°.

Serves 8

FRUGAL PIE

This pie, adapted from an old cookbook, makes a thrifty yet nutritious meal.

1 pound left-over meat, cut in
   small pieces (or ground chuck)
1 pound cold potatoes, peeled
2 small onions
1 sprig flavoring herb (thyme or
   a bay leaf)

1 teaspoon flour
2 tablespoons drippings
1 tablespoon milk
1 cup left-over gravy
salt and pepper

Skin, scald, and slice the onions, then brown them slightly with half of the drippings in a pan. Pour off the drippings. Break the flour with a little cold water (make a paste), and add it to the onions, along with the rest of the gravy, the herb sprig, salt, and pepper. Simmer for about 15 minutes, until the onion is tender, stirring to prevent the flour from sticking to the pan. Remove the sprig and let the sauce cool. Pour it into a pie dish, and put the meat into it. Mash the potatoes, and add to them the milk and the other half of the drippings. Lay the potatoes smoothly on top of the meat; score them across with a knife. Put the pie into the oven to brown (425°). When browned, it is ready. Lacking an oven, place the pie on the hob or hot plate for a few minutes to warm it through (do not allow it to boil), then brown it in front of the fire. The top of the pie may be glazed by brushing it over with a little milk.

Serves 4

TOURTIERE

Mrs. Rose A. Fournier
Worcester, Mass.

A Canadian recipe for pork pie.

1 pound ground pork
1 onion, chopped
3 medium potatoes, boiled and
    cut up fine
1/2 teaspoon cinnamon

1/2 teaspoon cloves
salt and pepper to taste
left-over gravy
pie crust (p.277)

Fry the onions in a little butter, add the meat, and stir until done. Add the seasonings, then the potatoes and the gravy. Bake between two crusts in a hot (425°) oven until brown. Good warmed over, too.

STEAK AND KIDNEY PIE

3 pounds lean beefsteak (top of the
    round is good), cut into 1-inch
    cubes
2 pair veal kidneys, cut to
    similar size (or 3 pair lamb
    kidneys)
3/4 cup flour
1 and 1/2 teaspoons salt
black pepper

butter or bacon fat
12 small onions
6 carrots scrubbed and cut into
    large pieces
1/2 pound mushrooms
2 crushed cloves garlic
1 cup beef stock
a glass of good red wine
herbs

Dredge the pieces of meat in seasoned flour and brown them well in fat in a large frying pan over a hot flame. At the same time cook the onions and carrots in enough salted water to cover. As the pieces of meat are done, put them into a 3-quart deep pie dish alternately with the onions and carrots. Slice the mushrooms into the frying pan with more butter, cook briefly, and add to the casserole. To the juices in the pan add the remaining flour and garlic. Gradually pour in the water in which the vegetables were cooked, plus the beef stock and red wine, stirring to make a smooth sauce.

Season the sauce with herbs as available, fresh or dried parsley or chervil, marjoram or thyme, chives or green onions. Taste the sauce. If you wish, add more salt or herbs, or a dash of Kitchen Bouquet to taste. Pour it over the meat and vegetables. Make a pie crust (p.277). Fold it, slash it in several places to let steam escape, put it over the pie and flute the edges. Glaze the crust if you wish by brushing egg yolk over the surface and ornament it with pastry cut-outs. Put the pie in a 350° oven 50 or 60 minutes before you are ready to eat it.

Serves 6-8

HAM MOUSSE

Martin Shallenberger
Herrod's Creek, Ky.

This dish, fine enough for any luncheon or buffet party, uses up the last bits of a baked ham.

1/2 pint heavy cream
1 cup water
1 and 1/2 packages gelatin

2-3 cups ham leftovers—meat, jelly, and cloves

Whip the cream and set aside. Mix the water, gradually, with the gelatin. Mix half of it with half of the whipped cream and coat the inside of a nice mold with this. Put the mold in the refrigerator to chill. Now in a food grinder or a blender purée the ham leftovers. Mix with the remaining cream and gelatin. If a blender is used, the mixture will fluff up considerably. Add a drop of red food coloring if it seems desirable. Add to the mold in which the gelatin coating will now have set. Chill again to set the ham mousse. Serve with Cumberland sauce (p. 248), baking powder biscuits, and a green salad.

Serves 6

HAM-YAM RAMEKINS

Mrs. Robert Boyce
Worthington, Ohio

2 cups mashed yams
1/2 cup diced green pepper
2 tablespoons butter
1 can condensed mushroom soup
2/3 cup milk
1 tablespoon grated onion
black pepper

1 tablespoon sharp prepared mustard
3 tablespoons flour
1/4 cup cold water
3 cups cooked ham, cubed
pineapple and marshmallow pieces

Pare, slice, and boil 2 medium-sized yams until tender. Drain and mash them and beat in a little warm milk until fluffy. (Canned, drained yams can be used instead.) Cook the green pepper in butter for about 3 minutes. Combine the soup and milk in a saucepan and add the onion, pepper, and mustard. Blend together the flour and water, add to the soup mixture, and stir over low heat until thickened. Add the green pepper and ham, and divide the mixture into six buttered ramekins. Top each with mashed yams and garnish with pieces of pineapple and marshmallow. Bake in a 350° oven for 20-25 minutes.

Serves 6

TETE A FROMAGE

This old recipe for head cheese makes an excellent spread for sandwiches or crackers.

4 pounds fresh pork (allow for
   bones and leave fat in meat)
4 large onions, chopped
salt and pepper
water to barely cover

1 tablespoon mace
1/2 teaspoon ground cloves
   (no more)
parsley, chopped
salt and pepper to taste

Boil pork, onions, salt and pepper slowly for 3-4 hours until the meat falls from the bones. Add mace, cloves, parsley, and more salt and pepper if needed. The meat will cook more quickly if cut into small pieces. Be sure to cook the bones with the meat because they are the source of the jelly that solidifies the mixture. Remove the bones, skim the pot and store the head cheese in molds in the refrigerator.

SHRIMP AND ARTICHOKE CASSEROLE

Mrs. Ivan Albright
Woodstock, Vt.

This dish was a favorite of Adlai Stevenson when he was our representative to the United Nations. Serve it with rice or buttered noodles, a mixed greens salad, and garlic bread.

6 tablespoons butter
4 tablespoons flour
3/4 cup milk
3/4 cup heavy cream
salt and pepper to taste
1 No. 2 can artichoke hearts,
   drained, or 1 package frozen
   artichoke hearts, cooked

1 and 1/2 pounds shrimp (fresh,
   frozen, or canned)
1/4 pound sliced mushrooms
1/4 cup sherry
1 tablespoon Worcestershire
   sauce
1/4 cup grated Parmesan cheese
paprika

Preheat the oven to 375°. Melt the butter and sauté the mushrooms for 2 minutes; stir in the flour and blend. Gradually add the milk and cream, stirring constantly with a whisk. When thick, add salt and pepper. Arrange the artichokes in a buttered baking dish and place the shrimp over them. After adding the sherry and Worcestershire to the mushroom sauce, pour it over all. Sprinkle with cheese and paprika and bake for 20-30 minutes.

Serves 6

HUNGARIAN STEAK CASSEROLE

Mrs. W. R. Torrey, Jr.
Huntington, Conn.

A husband's delight—Hungarian style.

2 pounds round steak, cut in
   1/2-inch cubes
3 tablespoons shortening
1 large onion, diced
1 clove garlic, crushed
2 tablespoons flour
1 3-ounce can mushrooms and
   broth

1/2 cup chopped celery
1 cup sour cream
1 8-ounce can tomato sauce
1 teaspoon salt
pepper
1 tablespoon Worcestershire
   sauce

Brown the steak cubes in hot shortening, add the onion and garlic, and cook until golden. Stir in the flour and the remaining ingredients, mix thoroughly, and turn into a buttered casserole. Bake uncovered for 1 and 1/2 hours at 350°.

Serves 6

CREAMED TURKEY ON SWISS FONDUE

An interesting and original way to use left-over turkey.

3 tablespoons butter
5 tablespoons flour
1 cup turkey stock
1 cup cream
1 teaspoon salt
1/4 teaspoon paprika
2 cups cooked diced turkey

1 and 1/2 cups chopped
   mushrooms
1/2 cup ripe olives, sliced
2 tablespoons chopped pimiento
1 teaspoon lemon juice
2 egg yolks, beaten
2 tablespoons milk

Make a cream sauce from the first six ingredients, stirring over a low flame until thick and smooth. Add the turkey, mushrooms, olives, pimiento, and lemon juice to the sauce and cook gently for 5 minutes. Then beat the egg yolks with the milk and add to the mixture. Stir and cook over low heat for 2 minutes. Make the Fondue.

FONDUE

2 cups scalded milk
2 cups soft breadcrumbs
3/4 pound sharp cheese, cut in bits
2 tablespoons butter

1 teaspoon salt
6 egg yolks, beaten
6 egg whites, beaten to form
   peaks

Mix together the milk, breadcrumbs, cheese, butter, and salt. Stir in the beaten egg yolks. Then fold the egg whites into the mixture. Pour the fondue into a buttered square baking dish and bake in a 350° oven for 20 minutes. Cut the hot fondue into squares and cover with the turkey sauce.

Serves 8-10

RAGOUT OF TURKEY

1 tablespoon flour	pinch of nutmeg
2 tablespoons butter	dash of Worcestershire sauce
1 and 1/2 cups gravy or stock	3 cups diced cooked turkey
1/4 teaspoon salt	1/4 cup sherry

Brown the flour in the butter, stirring constantly; stir in the gravy or stock and cook until thickened. Season with salt, nutmeg, and Worcestershire sauce. Add the turkey and cook for 10 minutes or until heated through. Serve on rice or buttered toast.

Serves 4-6

YODELING GOOD SWISS CASSEROLE

Sam Bullock
Somerset, N.J.

A fine veal casserole to accompany a raw spinach salad.

1 and 1/2 pounds veal cutlets, 1/4 inch thick	2 cups wide noodles, cooked
	1/2 pound Swiss cheese, sliced
1 and 1/2 teaspoons paprika	1/4 cup butter
3 tablespoons flour	1/2 cup light cream
1 teaspoon salt	2 teaspoons chopped chives
1 and 1/2 cups beef gravy	

Cut the veal into serving pieces. Place a slice of cheese on half of them and top with a second piece of veal. Press the edges together. Combine the flour, paprika, and salt and coat the veal with them. Brown well in butter and remove the veal from the skillet. In the same skillet stir together the gravy and cream and simmer for 5 minutes. Arrange alternate layers of noodles, sauce, and veal in a buttered 2-quart casserole, sprinkle with chives, cover, and bake for 1 and 1/2 hours at 375°.

Serves 6

DABNEY SANDWICH

No one seems to remember which of the many Dabneys in Boston's Somerset Club was the inventor of this practical and pleasant sandwich. It is ideal, for instance, to take with one on the New Haven Railroad's *Yankee Clipper*, thereby neatly avoiding the crowd in the diner.

1 and 1/2 cups cooked chicken	salt and pepper
1/2 cup minced onion	butter
lettuce	mayonnaise

Combine ingredients (except the lettuce) and spread the mixture between slices of buttered dark or graham bread. Add a crisp leaf of lettuce.

4 sandwiches

ONION SANDWICH

This is just such a zestful sandwich as delighted that Yankee President, Calvin Coolidge. It is particularly good made with rye bread.

1 large sweet onion	mayonnaise
3 hard cooked eggs	1/2 teaspoon dry mustard
2 small pickles	salt and pepper

Chop the onion, eggs, and pickles fine and add enough mayonnaise to have a good spreading consistency, and mustard, salt, and pepper to taste. Spread lavishly. Serve with tomato wedges and ripe olives.

spread for 6 sandwiches

Cal and Mrs. Coolidge leave the Ashuelot House after an onion sandwich snack.

Chapter 3.
Afternoon Tea

The ritual of afternoon tea is an old New England tradition, whether one takes one's tea from pottery cups while sitting around the kitchen table or sips China tea in heirloom lustre filled from a silver service on a fair white cloth. Even in "the office," the ritual is not unknown. In any form, it provides a welcome and refreshing break in the day—a time to relax, to chat, and to pamper a sweet tooth.

Of course, one need not take time out from afternoon tea to enjoy the sweet breads, cakes and bars that follow—they taste just as good at supper or lunch or after school!

TEA BREADS

DATE AND APRICOT NUT BREAD

1/2 cup dried apricots	1 teaspoon salt
1/2 cup white raisins	1/4 teaspoon soda
1/2 cup dates	1 cup brown sugar, firmly packed
3/4 cup coarsely chopped nuts	1 egg, well beaten
3 cups sifted all-purpose flour	1 and 1/2 cups milk
3 teaspoons baking powder	2 tablespoons melted butter

Cut the apricots in strips with scissors and place in a bowl with the raisins. Cover with boiling water and let stand for 15 minutes. Drain well. Sift together the flour, baking powder, salt, and soda into a mixing bowl. Add the sugar, fruits, and nuts. Mix well. Stir in the egg mixed with the milk and butter. The batter will be rather thin. Pour it into a well-greased loaf pan. Let stand for 20 minutes. Bake in a 350° oven for 1 hour, then cool on a rack.

GINGERBREAD

This recipe was passed down through six generations to Dorothy Hale Wires of Rockport, Massachusetts. She writes that during the War of 1812 "the little settlement of Sandy Bay, now Rockport, was in constant fear of attack from marauding British privateers then prowling Cape Ann waters. In the early days of the War many families planned escape through the woods to the larger settlement in Gloucester, some five miles away, which provided better protection. My great aunt Lucy Hale Knutsford, known to all as 'Aunt Lute', used to tell me many stories which in turn had been told her by her mother, Betsy Tarr Hale, who having been born in 1800, thus was 12 years old at the time of the War. During the anxious days when fears of raids were uppermost in the minds of Sandy Bay residents, Betsy's mother used to keep ever in readiness clothing and food so that her family could quickly leave their home to follow woodland paths to the Gloucester settlement. Every morning she baked a fresh gingerbread for food along the way, should it be necessary to go. Aunt Lute always cherished this recipe and our family has enjoyed it for six generations. This is it just as given me by Aunt Lute."

Take 1/2 cup sugar, 1/2 cup molasses, 1/2 cup melted shortening, 1 egg, 1/2 teaspoon cinnamon, 1/2 teaspoon ginger. To this add alternately 1 cup flour to which has been added 1 teaspoon soda and 1/2 teaspoon salt, and 1 cup boiling water. More flour should be added, if necessary, to make a fairly stiff batter. Then lastly add 1/2 teaspoon vinegar. Bake in moderate oven until a straw comes out clean, or until it doesn't sizzle on holding the pan to the ear (325° for about 35 minutes).

VICTORIAN GINGERBREAD

1 cup sugar
1 cup melted butter
1 cup sour cream
1 cup dark molasses
2 cups flour

2 eggs
1 teaspoon baking soda
2 teaspoons ginger
1/2 teaspoon allspice
pinch of cinnamon and of mace

Beat the eggs well and add to them the sour cream, molasses and sugar. Stir in the flour sifted with the soda and spices. Add the melted butter and beat well. Fill a cake pan 3/4 full and bake the gingerbread in a moderate (325°) oven for about 35 minutes, or until done. Serve hot as a bread for tea with butter, or hot with whipped cream as a dessert which is particularly popular with children, or serve cold as a cake.

LEMON BREAD

6 tablespoons butter
2 eggs
1 cup white sugar
1 and 1/4 cups pastry flour
1 teaspoon baking powder
grated rind of 1 lemon
1/2 cup milk

1/2 teaspoon salt
1/2 cup chopped maraschino
   cherries
1/2 cup chopped walnuts
sugar
lemon juice

Cream together the butter and sugar and beat in the eggs. Add the baking powder and salt to the flour and mix alternately with the milk; then add the grated lemon rind, the cherries, and walnuts. Bake in a loaf pan for 1 hour in a 350° oven. Mix together 1/2 cup white sugar and the juice of 1 lemon and pour over the baked loaf in the pan. Let stand for 10 minutes.

ORANGE NUT BREAD

Almonds, pecans, or walnuts may be used, and pistachio nuts make a particularly pretty slice. Serve spread with sweet butter or cream cheese.

3/4 cup sugar
2 tablespoons solid shortening
1 egg
3/4 cup milk
3/4 cup orange juice
4 tablespoons grated orange rind

3 cups flour
3 and 1/2 tablespoons baking
   powder
1 teaspoon salt
1 teaspoon nutmeg
3/4 cup chopped nuts

Heat the oven to 350°. Grease a 9 x 5 x 3″ loaf pan. Mix the sugar, shortening, and egg together thoroughly. Stir in the milk, orange juice and rind. Sift together and stir in the flour, baking powder, salt and nutmeg. Blend in the nuts. Pour into the greased pan and let stand for 20 minutes. Bake for 60-70 minutes.

WINCHESTER NUT BREAD

Wonderful on a winter day.

3/4 cup water
1/2 cup light brown sugar
1/2 cup molasses
3/4 cup milk
1 cup bread flour
1 and 1/2 teaspoons salt

2 and 1/2 teaspoons baking
   powder
1 teaspoon soda
2 cups whole-wheat flour
3/4 cup nuts—walnuts or pecans

Dissolve the sugar in the water and add the molasses and milk. Sift the flour, salt, baking powder, and soda together and add the whole-wheat flour unsifted. Mix all together, add the nuts, and bake in a greased pan in a slow oven (275°) for 2 hours.

PUMPKIN WALNUT BREAD

4 and ½ cups flour
2 tablespoons baking powder
1 teaspoon cinnamon
½ teaspoon mace
½ teaspoon salt
1 and ½ cups light brown sugar

½ cup melted butter
1 and ½ cups pumpkin puree
   (fresh or canned)
3 eggs, lightly beaten
1 cup milk
2 cups chopped walnuts

Sift together the dry ingredients. Combine the butter and the sugar and add to them the eggs and pumpkin. Add the dry ingredients alternately with the milk to the pumpkin mixture. mixing well after each addition. Stir in the nuts. Pour into well greased loaf pans and bake in a 350°F. oven for about 1 hour.

FRESH PUMPKIN PUREE

Wipe a pumpkin with a damp cloth, cut it in half and remove the seeds and fiber with a spoon. Put the halves shell side up on a baking sheet and bake them in a 300° oven for about an hour or until very tender. Scrape the pumpkin from the shell and put through a sieve or purée in the blender.

COOKIES

For easy cookie making use two good-sized cookie sheets and four sheets of heavy aluminum foil. Grease the foil lightly before starting (it will not be necessary to grease it again), and rotate two sheets of foil upon each cookie sheet. This method makes for quick removal of the cookies and easy clean-up.

APPLESAUCE COOKIES

1/2 cup butter
1 cup sugar
1 egg
1/2 cup thick applesauce
1 and 3/4 cups sifted flour
1/4 teaspoon salt

1 teaspoon baking powder
1/2 teaspoon soda
1/2 cup raisins
1 tablespoon grated orange rind

Cream the butter, add the sugar gradually, creaming and beating until light and fluffy. Add the egg and beat. Stir in the applesauce. Sift together the flour, salt, baking powder, soda, and add the orange peel and raisins. Mix all together and drop by teaspoonfuls, 2 inches apart, on a lightly greased cookie sheet. Bake in a 350° oven for 15 minutes.

BEACON HILL COOKIES

These crunchy chocolate meringues make delicious snacks with milk or tea.

1/8 teaspoon salt
2 egg whites
1/2 cup sugar
1/2 teaspoon vinegar
1/2 teaspoon vanilla

1/2 cup sweetened shredded coconut
1/4 cup chopped walnuts
6 ounces semi-sweet chocolate chips, melted

Add the salt to the egg whites and beat until foamy throughout. Add the sugar very gradually, beating well after each addition. Continue beating until stiff peaks form. Add the vinegar and vanilla and beat well. Fold in the coconut, nuts, and the melted chips. Drop by teaspoonfuls on a greased baking sheet and bake in a moderate (350°) oven for 10 minutes.

30-36 cookies

BEDFORD COOKIES

Wickedly rich and almost irresistible to those who like sweets.

1/2 pound butter
1 tablespoon powdered sugar
1 teaspoon vanilla

2 cups sifted flour
1 cup chopped nuts (walnuts, hazelnuts, or pecans are good)

Cream the butter and gradually add the sugar, vanilla, and flour. Mix in the nuts and form into balls the size of a walnut. Press flat with a fork and bake the cookies for 10 to 15 minutes in a 350° oven. Remove from oven, and while still hot shake the cookies in a bag of powdered sugar.

BROWN SUGAR COOKIES

Mrs. Edna W. Marshall
Chicopee, Mass.

This recipe comes from Mrs. Marshall's great grandmother, Harriet Bradstreet, a descendant of Massachusetts Governor Simon Bradstreet.

> *"When we were growing up, one of our greatest pleasures was gathering nuts from the trees around our farm—mostly shagbarks and butternuts. After we had filled our canvas bags and returned home, we spread them out on the floor of the storage attic over the woodshed to dry.*
>
> *"A day would come when we were housebound because of rain or snow, and Mother would say: 'If you children will crack some nuts and take out enough nut meats, I'll bake you some cookies just like my mother used to bake for me when I was a little girl. Get the woodbox well filled, and you may help me make them when all is ready.'*
>
> *"Our favorite great uncle told us that one hot summer day, my grandmother-to-be, then a young girl, carried a plate of these cookies and a pitcher of cold lemonade out to the hayfield where he and a young man who became my grandfather were working. He liked to say that my grandfather fell in love either with the cookies or with the pink-cheeked, blue-eyed girl who served them."*

1 cup shortening	1/2 teaspoon salt
1 cup firmly packed brown sugar	2 teaspoons baking powder
1 egg, beaten	1/2 teaspoon nutmeg
1/2 cup seedless raisins	1/2 cup sour cream
2 cups sifted flour	1/2 cup nut meats
1/2 teaspoon baking soda	

Cream the shortening and the sugar, add the egg and the raisins. Mix and sift the remaining dry ingredients and add alternately with the sour cream to the raisin mixture. Then add the nuts. Drop by teaspoonfuls onto greased cookie sheets and bake for 12 to 15 minutes in a 400° oven. Cookies always come out plump and golden regardless of the type of stove used.

BUTTER COOKIES

1 cup butter
1 cup sugar
2 eggs, well beaten
1 teaspoon vanilla

1/4 teaspoon almond extract
2 cups flour
1/4 teaspoon salt

Cream the butter until light and gradually add the sugar. Beat in the eggs and flavorings and add the flour and salt a little at a time to make a stiff dough. Chill, then roll 1/8 inch thick and cut out. (This dough is good for fancy shaped cookie cutters.) Decorate the cookies if you wish with pieces of candied fruit or nuts. Bake in a 350° oven until lightly browned, about 10 minutes.

BUTTERSCOTCH COOKIES

Mrs. Harry Mathews
Brookline, Mass.

2 cups light brown sugar
2 eggs
1 cup butter
2 cups flour

1 teaspoon cream of tartar
1 teaspoon salt
1 cup chopped dates
1 cup chopped walnuts

Cream the butter and sugar, and sift flour together with the cream of tartar and salt. Combine all these ingredients and drop by teaspoons on greased cookie sheets. Bake in a moderate oven (350°) for 3 or 4 minutes. Don't let the cookies get too brown.

CARAWAY (also FILLED, or JUMBLE) COOKIES

Mrs. Leon Dawes Thayer
Cummington, Mass.

A basic cookie recipe. Rolled thin with caraway generously added (or chopped nuts or fine coconut), it makes a crisp delicacy with an old-fashioned flavor. Not so thinly rolled, with chopped raisins or dates, it makes a moister cookie. Cut round with a doughnut shaped round on top it makes old-fashioned "jumbles" to be topped with tart jelly. The same dough may be used for filled cookies with mincemeat or other raisin filling.

1 cup sugar
1/2 cup shortening
3/4 cup sour milk
1 teaspoon soda
2 cups all-purpose flour

1/2 teaspoon vanilla (use lemon extract for jumbles)
caraway seeds, raisins, nuts, etc. to taste

Mix ingredients and roll on a floured board. Bake on cookie sheets in a 300° or 350° oven until lightly browned, 10 to 15 minutes, depending upon the thickness of the cookies.

CHOCOLATE MINT COOKIES

1 cup butter
2 cups sugar
3 eggs, well beaten
1 cup sifted flour

1/4 teaspoon soda dissolved in 3 tablespoons hot water
1/2 teaspoon vanilla extract
thin chocolate-covered mints
pecan halves

Cream the butter and sugar together until fluffy. Blend in the beaten eggs and then the flour, little by little. Add the soda and vanilla extract and blend well. Chill the dough in a covered bowl until firm. Add more sifted flour, but not one speck more than is necessary to reach a consistency that can be rolled out. On a floured surface, roll about 1/8 inch thick and cut in rounds about 3 inches across. In the center of half the rounds place a thin chocolate mint. Place another round on top and press the edges together with a fork. Press a pecan half on each cookie. Bake on buttered cookie sheets in a hot (425°) oven until lightly browned—about 12 minutes.

CORNFLAKE MACAROONS

1 egg white beaten stiff
1/2 cup sugar
1/2 cup shredded sweetened coconut

1 cup cornflakes
1/4 teaspoon almond extract
1/2 teaspoon vanilla extract

Mix ingredients in the order given and drop from the tip of a spoon onto a buttered cookie sheet. Bake for 20 minutes in a 350° oven.

FILLED COOKIES

Jane Goyer of West Boylston, Massachusetts, contributed this recipe handed down from her grandmother, Malina Goodney. She calls them "Old-Fashioned Honeymoon Cookies;" her grandmother called them "Big Surprises." Under whatever name, they have long been popular with New England's children—a moist, rich treat with a glass of cold milk.

FILLING

1/2 pound round plump fresh raisins

1 cup nut meats (Grandma used black walnuts)

1 large juicy apple (Baldwins are best)

1 tablespoon dark brown sugar (pack firmly)

1 tablespoon fresh lemon juice

1 teaspoon cinnamon

1/2 teaspoon nutmeg

DOUGH

1/4 cup soft butter

1/2 cup sugar

1 large fresh egg, beaten

2 cups all-purpose flour

2 teaspoons baking powder

speck of salt

ICING

1/2 cup fine confectioners' sugar

1 tablespoon cream

Prepare the filling first. Put the raisins, nuts, and cored apple through a food chopper, add the sugar, lemon juice, and spices and mix well. Then make the dough. Beat the butter, sugar, egg, until creamy. Add the flour sifted with the baking powder and salt. Combine the two mixtures and beat well. Divide the dough in half. Roll thin on a floured board, using a little more flour if necessary to prevent sticking. Cut in rounds, with a glass tumbler whose rim has first been floured. On each round place a teaspoon of the filling. Roll out the rest of the dough and cut into rounds. Place them over the filling, pressing down firmly around the edges. Seal the edges with a fork and prick the top of each cookie. Bake at 350° for about 15 minutes, or until pale brown. Allow to cool, then brush over with thin creamy icing.

GINGERSNAPS

3/4 cup (1 and 1/2 sticks) butter

1 cup sugar

1 egg

1/4 cup molasses

1 tablespoon ground ginger

1 teaspoon cinnamon

1/2 teaspoon salt

2 teaspoons soda

2 and 1/2 cups flour

Cream the butter and gradually add the sugar. Beat until light. Beat in the egg and the molasses, then little by little the sifted dry ingredients. Form into small balls, roll in more granulated sugar and place on ungreased cookie sheets about 2 inches apart. Bake at 350° for 10 to 12 minutes.

GOLDEN BREADCRUMB COOKIES

Children love these.

1 egg beaten lightly
1 cup sugar
1/2 cup shortening
1 teaspoon vanilla
1 teaspoon salt
1 and 1/2 cups toasted
 breadcrumbs

1/4 cup milk
1/4 cup water
1 cup maraschino cherries,
 chopped fine
1 and 1/2 cups sifted flour

Mix the egg, sugar, shortening, and vanilla together. Then add the salt, breadcrumbs, milk, water, cherries and flour, little by little. Mix well, and drop by teaspoons onto greased cookie sheets. Bake at 375° for 12-15 minutes.

HEALTH COOKIES

Mrs. Jean Burke
Rockingham, Vt.

Crisp, and good as they are healthy.

1 cup brown sugar
1/4 cup white sugar
1/4 cup honey
1 cup shortening
2 eggs, unbeaten
1 teaspoon vanilla
1/2 cup white flour

1 teaspoon baking soda
1 teaspoon salt
1/2 cup wheat germ
1 and 1/4 cups whole-wheat
 flour
2 cups oatmeal

Cream the sugars, honey, and shortening together thoroughly, then add the eggs and vanilla and mix together until fluffy. Sift the flour, baking soda and salt together. Mix the wheat germ and the whole-wheat flour into the dry mixture. Add to the creamed mixture, blending all ingredients. Then stir the oatmeal into the dough with a table knife. Drop by teaspoons onto an ungreased cookie sheet and bake at 350° for 8-10 minutes.

LACY OATMEAL COOKIES

A classic old favorite.

2 and 1/4 cups old-fashioned
 oatmeal
2 and 1/4 cups light brown
 sugar
3 tablespoons flour

1/2 teaspoon salt
1/2 pound butter, melted
1 egg, beaten
1/2 teaspoon vanilla

Combine the oatmeal, sugar, flour, and salt and stir. Add the egg, melted butter, and vanilla. Drop, spacing well apart, by teaspoonfuls on well greased and floured cookie sheets. Bake for 12 minutes in a 325° oven. Use a spatula or a pancake turner to remove from sheet.

LUMBERJACK COOKIES

Lumbering is a unique occupation and projects a day-to-day life unlike any other. In the upper reaches of the rivers, when spring freshets deepen the water enough to float the logs, men of a particularly courageous breed shepherd the raw wood down the rivers, sometimes for hundreds of miles, to the sawmills. They spend many days on the logs and on a raft with a shanty on it that brings up the rear. In the shanty is a man at whom the others characteristically jeer but deeply value—the cook.

One morning early in this century, such a log drive was moving along the Muskegon past a riverside farm, when a dignified little woman marched to the water's edge and waved to them. She wished to parley with the lumberjack cook. Just why is explained by Mrs. Paul V. Bretz of St. Paul, Minnesota. "The great lumbering industry of Michigan was beginning to wane, but there was still some lumbering along the Muskegon. When the logs were being floated down the river to the mills, there was always a cook shanty on a raft following the log drive. It was a great treat for children to have a meal with the lumberjacks on this river raft. They could look forward to fried salt pork, boiled potatoes, boiled beans, hot breads, cookies, and strong black coffee. Good hearty fare.

"These were molasses cookies and so good that my husband prevailed upon his mother to go to the river and learn the recipe from the cook. We always called them 'Lumberjack Cookies,' and here is the recipe:"

1 cup sugar
1 cup molasses
1 cup shortening
1 cup sour milk

1 teaspoon salt
ginger, vanilla, and mace (or nutmeg) to taste
flour enough to make a soft dough

Drop by tablespoons on a lightly greased cookie sheet and bake in a moderate oven (350°) until done, about 10 minutes.

SISTER MINNIE'S MOLASSES COOKIES

A recipe from the old Shaker Colony in Alfred, Maine, now but a memory. It closed in 1925.

2 and 1/4 cups flour
2 level teaspoons soda
1 teaspoon ginger
1 teaspoon cinnamon
1/4 teaspoon salt
1/2 cup shortening

1/2 cup sugar
1 egg
1/2 cup molasses
1/2 cup warm water (not hot)
raisins as desired

Cream the shortening and sugar until light and fluffy. Add the unbeaten egg and molasses and beat well. Sift the flour, soda, salt, and spices together. Add a little at a time to the creamed mixture, cutting in a few raisins at the same time. Add the water. Drop by small teaspoons on an ungreased baking sheet. Sprinkle with sugar and put a raisin on each cookie. Bake in a 375° oven for 15-20 minutes or until browned.

40 large cookies

PETTICOAT TAILS

A pretty name for a pretty cookie.

1 cup soft butter
1 cup confectioners' sugar
2 and 1/2 cups sifted flour

1/4 teaspoon salt
1 teaspoon vanilla
1 cup chopped almonds

Cream together the butter and sugar. Add the salt to the flour and sift. Add flavoring and half of the nuts. Shape into a roll about 2 inches in diameter, wrap in waxed paper, and chill. Slice very thin, cover cookies with remaining almonds and bake at 400° for 8 to 10 minutes.

48 cookies

TRUE SCOTCH SHORTBREAD

A cookie with excellent keeping properties.

3 cups flour	1/2 pound butter, medium soft
1/2 pound rice flour	6 tablespoons sugar

Sift the flours together and add, gradually, with the sugar to the butter. Knead to a soft dough. Shape into medium-thick, round cakes the size of a saucer, place on rimmed, greased cookie sheets, prick with a fork and flute the edges. (For modern consumption the shortbread may be more useful cut in cookie size squares or diamonds or in fancy shapes.) Bake in a 400° oven for 30 minutes.

OLD-FASHIONED SUGAR COOKIES

1/2 cup butter	2 tablespoons milk
1/2 teaspoon salt	2 cups sifted flour
grated rind of 1 lemon	1 teaspoon baking powder
1 cup sugar	1/2 teaspoon soda
2 eggs, well beaten	1/2 teaspoon nutmeg

Cream the butter, add the salt and lemon rind, and gradually the sugar. Beat in the eggs and the milk, and little by little add the dry ingredients sifted together. Drop by spoonfuls on cookie sheets. Sprinkle each cookie with sugar and bake in a 375° oven for about 12 minutes.

WALNUT WAFERS

1 tablespoon butter	1/2 cup flour, sifted
1 cup brown sugar	1 teaspoon baking powder
2 eggs, well beaten	1 cup chopped nutmeats
1 teaspoon vanilla	

Cream together the butter and the sugar, then add the eggs, vanilla, and the flour sifted with the baking powder. Stir in the nuts and drop at good intervals on greased cookie sheets. Bake in a moderate (350°) oven for 12 minutes.

FUDGY BROWNIES

4 squares unsweetened chocolate
1/2 cup butter
2 cups sugar
4 eggs, beaten

1 cup sifted flour
1 teaspoon vanilla
1 cup coarsely chopped walnuts

Melt the chocolate and butter together over hot water. Cool slightly. Gradually add the sugar to the eggs, beating thoroughly after each addition. Stir in the flour, then add the vanilla and nuts. Spread in a greased 9-inch square pan and bake in a slow oven (325°) about 40 minutes. Cool in the pan. Cut into squares.

24 brownies

CHOCOLATE PEPPERMINT BROWNIES

Bake brownies as above, then arrange 10-20 chocolate peppermint patties over the hot brownies; return to the oven for about 3 minutes to soften. Then spread to cover the entire top of the brownies. Cool and cut.

BUTTERSCOTCH SQUARES

1 cup butter
2 cups brown sugar
2 eggs beaten
1 and 1/2 cups all-purpose flour

2 teaspoons baking powder
2 cups coarsely chopped pecans
1 teaspoon vanilla
dash of salt

Heat the butter and sugar until dissolved. Cool. Add the eggs, blend, and sift in the combined flour and baking powder. Mix well. Add the remaining ingredients. Spread and bake on a greased cookie sheet in a 350° oven for about 15 minutes. Cut in squares.

DATE BARS

Mrs. John Babbitt
Walpole, N.H.

This is the recipe of my mother, and I still think them the most delicious small cakes for tea, for picnic boxes, or to pass with fruits or ices.

1 cup sugar
3 eggs, separated
1 cup nuts
1 package dates
1/4 cup sour cream

1 teaspoon vanilla
1 cup flour
1 teaspoon baking powder
salt

Mix the egg yolks and sugar; add the other ingredients, the beaten egg whites last. Bake in a shallow pan for 30 minutes in a 350° oven. Cut while warm into bars and roll in powdered sugar.

INDIANS

2 squares chocolate, melted
1/2 cup butter
3 eggs, beaten
1 cup sugar
1/3 cup bread flour

1/2 teaspoon baking powder
1/2 teaspoon salt
1 cup chopped walnuts
1 teaspoon vanilla
1/2 cup chopped dates (optional)

Add the butter to the chocolate and melt. Add the sugar slowly to the eggs, then add the flour mixed with the baking powder and salt, the nut meats, vanilla, and the chocolate mixture. Spread in a greased 8-inch square pan. Bake 25-30 minutes in a moderate (350°) oven. Cut while warm.

MARBLE SQUARES

1 cup butter or margarine
1 and 1/2 teaspoons vanilla
2 cups sugar
4 eggs

2 cups sifted flour
1/2 teaspoon salt
1 cup chopped walnuts
2 squares chocolate

Melt the chocolate and set aside to cool. Cream together butter, vanilla, and sugar until light and fluffy. Add the eggs one at a time, beating well after each. Add flour and salt and mix until blended. Stir in the nuts and divide the batter in half and add the cooled chocolate to one half. Drop the batters alternately by teaspoonfuls into a greased pan 13 x 9 x 2″. Run a knife through the batter several times to marbelize. Bake in a moderate oven (350°) about 45 minutes. Cool and frost with Chocolate frosting (p. 77). Cut into squares.

THE ANYTIME CAKE

Mrs. Jean Burke
Rockingham, Vt.

A useful cake for breakfast, tea, or "anytime."

1 cup sugar
1 cup shortening
3 eggs
1 and 1/2 teaspoons vanilla
2 and 1/2 cups sifted flour

1/2 teaspoon baking powder
1 teaspoon baking soda
1/4 teaspoon salt
1 cup sour cream

NUT MIXTURE

1/4 cup nut meats, ground or
chopped very fine

1 teaspoon cinnamon
1/4 cup sugar

Mix the ingredients of the Nut Mixture together and set aside. Cream the sugar and shortening until fluffy, then add the eggs and beat again until fluffy. Add vanilla. Sift the dry ingredients together. Add the flour mixture alternating with the sour cream to the sugar, shortening, and egg mixture. Grease and flour a large tube or angel food pan. Spoon 1/3 of the batter into the pan, and sprinkle 1/3 of the nut mixture over the batter. Repeat with another layer of batter and nuts; follow this with the remaining batter. With a table knife, stir the contents of the pan in a circular motion to distribute the nut mixture. Sprinkle the remaining nut mixture over the top. Bake at 350° 45-50 minutes. No other frosting is necessary or desirable.

BLUE HEAVEN CAKE

J. Almus Russell
Bloomsburg, Penna.

The name of this cake derives from its pleasant, bluish color.

1/2 cup poppy seeds
3/4 cup milk
3/4 cup shortening
1 and 1/2 cups sugar
2 and 1/2 cups flour
3 teaspoons baking powder

1/4 teaspoon salt
1/4 cup golden raisins (optional)
3/4 cup milk
1 teaspoon vanilla
4 egg whites

Soak poppy seeds in 3/4 cup of milk over night. Cream the butter and sugar. Sift the dry ingredients together. Combine 3/4 cup of plain milk with the first 3/4 cup of milk and the poppy seeds which have been soaked in it. Add alternately the dry ingredients and the milk mixture to the creamed butter and sugar. Add the vanilla. Fold the beaten egg whites into the mixture. Bake in a greased 13 x 9 x 2" pan at 375° for 25 minutes.

PRIZE COCONUT CAKE

1 and 3/4 cups sifted cake flour
2 and 1/4 teaspoons baking powder
3/4 teaspoon salt
1/2 cup butter
1 cup plus 2 tablespoons sugar

2 eggs
2/3 cup milk
1 teaspoon vanilla
2/3 cup sweetened shredded
   coconut

Measure sifted flour, baking powder, and salt and sift together. Cream the butter and gradually add the sugar and cream until light and fluffy. Add the eggs one at a time, beating well after each addition. Alternately add the flour mixture and the milk, beating after each addition until smooth. Stir in the vanilla and the coconut. Pour the batter into two 8-inch layer pans lined on the bottom with paper. Bake in a moderate oven (350°) for 30 to 35 minutes. Cool for 10 minutes in the pans, then remove and finish cooling on cake racks. Frost with Seven-Minute Coconut frosting (p. 78).

CHEESE-FILLED CHOCOLATE CAKE

3/4 cup shortening
3 tablespoons cocoa
1 and 1/2 cups sugar
3 eggs
1 and 1/2 teaspoons vanilla

1 and 1/2 cups flour, sifted
1/2 teaspoon baking powder
1 cup cottage cheese
pinch of salt

Mix the cocoa with creamed shortening. Beat the eggs until thick and add the sugar gradually, then add the chocolate mixture. Add the vanilla and cottage cheese and beat for 1 minute. Sift the dry ingredients and blend into this mixture. Bake in a buttered 8-inch square pan in a 350° oven for 40 minutes. Cool and frost with Fluffy Chocolate frosting (p. 77), or serve warm with lightly whipped cream.

CHERRY DEVIL'S FOOD CAKE

Mrs. Curtis R. Borden
Lake Worth, Fla

This light, moist cake is great for church suppers or when friends drop in for tea.

2/3 cup shortening
2 eggs, separated
1 and 3/4 teaspoons soda
3 cups sifted flour
2 cups sugar
4 squares melted chocolate

1 teaspoon salt
2 4-ounce bottles maraschino
    cherries, drained
cherry juice plus buttermilk to
    make 2 cups

Put the cherries to drain way ahead of when you plan to mix the cake (cut them in quarters for faster draining). Cream together the shortening and sugar; add the egg yolks and mix thoroughly. Stir in the melted chocolate. Sift together twice the flour, soda, and salt. Add to the creamed mixture alternately with the cherry juice-buttermilk. Fold in the stiffly beaten egg whites and then the cup of cherries. Bake at 350° for 50 minutes. Use a 10 x 14" cake pan or two 9-inch round pans. Frost with white frosting.

FASNACLOICH JELLY CAKE

This unique delicacy was for years a closely guarded secret, the recipe being given out only to family members. The cake actually improves with age, being better a few days after it is baked; the flavor is enhanced, and the sliver-thin layers take on a slightly chewy texture. Although it can be made in the regulation two or three layers, it is much the best when made in six very thin layers—spread evenly in the pans to a thickness of about a quarter inch.

1 cup sugar
1/4 cup melted butter
1 egg
1 cup (approximately—see directions) thick sour milk (add 2 teaspoons vinegar to sweet milk)
1 teaspoon baking powder

1/2 teaspoon soda sifted with
    2 cups flour, 1 teaspoon
    (some prefer 2) nutmeg,
    pinch of salt
1 jar currant jelly
· powdered sugar

Cream the butter and sugar. Break the egg into a cup measure and fill the cup with sour milk. Add to the butter and sugar. Add the other ingredients and beat well. Pour the batter very thinly in greased cake pans, just covering the bottom (use a spatula to make sure the batter lies evenly over the bottom). The recipe will make 3-6 layers, depending on thickness. Bake in a moderate oven (350°) until the edges are brown and drawn away from the side of pan. While the cake is baking, whip the currant jelly with a fork until liquid. When the cake is cool, spread the top of each layer with jelly. Dust top with powdered sugar.

OLD ENGLISH FRUITCAKE

Mrs. Wm.Newberry
Sheboygan, Wis.

Sometime in November, prepare this sumptuous Christmas cake. Easy and interesting to assemble, it will perfume your house with a foretaste of Christmas. This 5-pound cake is big enough to see a large, hospitable family through the Christmas season. Some may even be left for the new year. Far, far better than any cake it is possible to buy, the total cost of its ingredients is surprisingly modest.

4-5 pounds fruit and nuts:
- 1 pound dark raisins
- 1 pound white raisins
- 1/2 pound currants
- 1/2 pound candied cherries
- 1/2 pound candied pineapple
- 1/4 pound candied citron
- 2 ounces candied orange peel
- 2 ounces candied lemon peel
- 1/4 pound blanched whole almonds
- 1/4 pound whole pecans

- 1/2 cup Madeira
- 1/2 cup dark rum
- 2 cups flour
- 1 teaspoon baking soda
- 1/2 teaspoon each: cinnamon, cloves, mace, and allspice
- 1/2 cup butter
- 1 cup brown sugar, firmly packed
- 1 cup white sugar
- 5 eggs, lightly beaten
- 1 teaspoon almond extract

Put the raisins and currants in a large bowl, add the Madeira and the rum and let stand, covered, overnight. Then add the candied fruits and mix well. Sift the spices and soda with 1 and 1/2 cups of the flour, combine the remaining flour with the nuts. Add all to the fruits, mixing lightly.

In another large bowl, beat the butter until light and cream in the sugars until light and fluffy. Beat in the eggs and almond extract. Add the fruit and nut mixture to the batter and stir well. Turn the batter into a well greased tube or springmold pan. A 10-inch pan will do for this 5 and 1/2 pound cake, or two smaller cakes may be made. Bake the large cake in an oven preheated to 275° for 3 and 1/2 to 4 hours, or until a cake tester inserted near the center of the cake comes out dry. The smaller cakes will take half the time.

Let the cake stand in the pan on a wire rack for half an hour, run a knife around the pan, if a springmold, loosen it and remove the cake gently to a piece of heavy aluminum foil large enough to enclose it completely. Fold the closing double to seal the cake completely. Once or twice before Christmas, open the foil and pour a little additional rum or wine on the cake.

When ready to use, decorate the top of the cake with a wreath of pecans and maraschino cherries and thin slices of candied fruit.

WELLESLEY FUDGE CAKE

An old favorite, rich and good.

4 squares unsweetened chocolate	1 teaspoon salt
1/2 cup hot water	1/2 cup vegetable shortening*
1 and 3/4 cups sugar	3 eggs
2 cups sifted cake flour	3/4 cup milk*
1 teaspoon soda	1 teaspoon vanilla

*To use butter or margarine, decrease milk to 2/3 cup

Melt the chocolate in the water in the top of a double boiler, stirring occasionally. Add 1/2 cup sugar; heat and stir for 2 minutes. Cool the mixture to lukewarm. Measure sifted flour, soda, and salt and sift together. Cream shortening and gradually add the remaining 1 and 1/4 cups of sugar and cream together until light and fluffy. Add the eggs, one at a time, beating thoroughly after each addition. Then alternately add the flour mixture and the milk, beating after each addition until smooth. Blend in the vanilla and the chocolate mixture. Pour the batter into two 9-inch layer pans lined on bottoms with paper and bake in a moderate oven (350°) for 30-35 minutes or until the cake springs back when lightly pressed. Frost with Fluffy Chocolate frosting (p. 77), Seven-Minute frosting, Marshmallow, Coconut, or Peppermint frosting (p. 78).

GRANDMOTHER SUMMERS' 1-2-3-4 CAKE

This recipe makes a very large cake. For convenience the ingredients may be cut in half.

1 cup butter	1 cup milk
2 cups sugar	4 teaspoons baking powder
3 cups cake flour	grated nutmeg
4 eggs, separated	

Cream the butter and sugar until light, add the well beaten yolks, then alternately the milk and the dry ingredients which have been sifted together. Fold in the stiffly beaten egg whites. Bake in an oven preheated to 375° in a buttered cake pan, or layer pans, for 25-35 minutes.

If you wish the cake may be cut into triangle shaped pieces and frosted on all sides except the bottom with Canadian frosting (p. 77), the pieces then rolled in almonds which have been blanched and browned lightly in the oven and rolled fine.

SILVER NUT CAKE

3/4 cup shortening
1 and 1/2 cups sugar
2 and 3/4 cups flour
3 teaspoons baking powder
1/2 teaspoon salt

1 cup milk
1 cup chopped English walnuts
1/2 teaspoon vanilla
1 teaspoon almond extract
4 egg whites

Cream together the shortening and the sugar. Sift the flour with the baking powder and salt and add to the creamed mixture alternately with the milk. Add the flavorings and the nuts, and then carefully fold the egg whites, beaten stiff, into the batter. Put in a cake pan which has been buttered and floured and bake 1 hour at 350°. This cake is nice frosted with Mocha or Maple Cream frosting (p. 78 and p. 77).

ROXBURY SPICE CAKES

Mrs. G. Leighton Bridge
Walpole, N.H.

2 eggs, separated
1/2 cup sugar
1/4 cup butter
1/2 cup molasses
1 teaspoon soda
1/2 cup seeded raisins

1/2 cup sour milk or cream
1 and 1/2 cups flour
1 teaspoon cinnamon
1/2 teaspoon cloves
1/4 teaspoon nutmeg
1/2 cup walnuts

Beat the egg whites until stiff. Cream together the butter and sugar and add the beaten egg yolks. Dissolve the soda in the sour milk and add alternately with the sifted dry ingredients to the above mixture. Fold in the egg whites, then the raisins and nuts. Bake in muffin tins for about 30 minutes in a 350° oven. Frost with Seven-Minute frosting (p. 78).

SPICE CAKE

Mrs. John Babbitt
Walpole, N.H.

No commercial mix can match this delicious old spice cake.

1 cup sugar
1/2 cup lard (scant)
1 egg, beaten
1 cup raisins
1 and 1/2 cups bread flour
1 teaspoon baking powder
1 teaspoon soda

1/2 teaspoon salt
1 rounded teaspoon cinnamon
1/2 teaspoon cloves
1 teaspoon nutmeg
1 cup sour cream or sour milk
1 teaspoon vanilla

Cream together the lard and the sugar and add the beaten egg. Cover the raisins with cold water and simmer until the water is gone. Cool. Meantime, add the flour which has been sifted with the baking powder, soda, salt, and spices alternately with the sour cream or sour milk to the sugar mixture. Add the raisins and vanilla and turn into a greased 8-inch square pan and bake in a moderate oven (350°) for about 35 minutes. Frost with Seven-Minute frosting (p. 78).

MOTHER'S SPONGE CAKE

4 eggs, separated
1 and 1/2 cups sugar
1/2 cup cold water (or orange juice, or water flavored with 1 tablespoon lemon juice)

1 and 1/2 cups flour sifted with 1 and 1/2 teaspoons baking powder and a pinch of salt
1 teaspoon vanilla (if you do not use fruit juice)

Beat the egg whites until they stand in soft peaks, beating in 1/4 cup of the sugar a little at a time. Without washing the beater, beat the yolks in another bowl with the water or fruit juice and the rest of the sugar until they are a creamy lemon color. Add the remaining ingredients to the second mixture, then fold in the egg whites. Bake in a tube pan in an oven preheated to 350° for 50-60 minutes, or until the cake springs back when pressed lightly with a finger. Invert on a wire cake rack until cool. Loosen with a spatula and unmold.

WHITE PLUM CAKE

A recipe adapted from *The Ladies' Friend,* June 1864, for YANKEE by Hyla Snider, this cake was often used as a wedding cake or for special occasions. It is nice to have on hand, as it is firm and keeps well.

2 cups butter (1 pound)
8 egg yolks, beaten
2 cups sugar
4 cups all-purpose flour
2 teaspoons baking powder
dash of salt
1 cup slivered almonds
4 ounces thinly sliced citron

4 ounces chopped candied lemon peel
1 cup sultana raisins
1/8 teaspoon mace
2 tablespoons milk
1/4 cup brandy
8 egg whites, beaten stiff

Cream the butter; add the egg yolks and beat thoroughly. Add the remaining ingredients, reserving the egg whites until last. Bake in a greased tube pan lined with greased paper at 325° for 1 hour or until done.

LEMON CURD TARTS

Mrs. Kenneth Hulbert, Jr.
Morristown, N.J.

Depending upon size, this rule will fill 12 or 18 little tarts. Mrs. Hulbert says: "My English aunt frequently served Lemon Curd Tarts with a cup of tea—nothing can describe the flavor of these tangy treats."

3 eggs
1/2 cup butter

1 cup sugar
1/2 cup lemon juice

Beat the eggs until light. Melt the butter in the top of a double boiler, then add to it the sugar and the eggs. Mix well and cook over hot water, stirring constantly for 5 minutes. Add the lemon juice and cook 3 minutes longer until thick and smooth. Chill and fill tiny tarts for tea time.

FROSTINGS

CANADIAN FROSTING

1/2 cup butter
2 cups confectioners' sugar

1 tablespoon cream
1/2 tablespoon vanilla

Beat the butter and sugar to a cream and gradually add the cream and vanilla.

CHOCOLATE FROSTING

4 tablespoons butter
2 cups confectioners' sugar
2 squares melted chocolate

1/2 teaspoon vanilla
dash of salt
2 or 3 tablespoons cream

Cream the butter until soft; gradually stir in 1 cup of sugar, then the melted chocolate and the other ingredients and the rest of the sugar. This is enough to frost one cake or 24 cup cakes.

FLUFFY CHOCOLATE FROSTING   *Mrs. L. C. Stuart*
Westfield, N.J.

4 tablespoons butter
1 and 1/2 cups confectioners' sugar
1 teaspoon vanilla

3 squares chocolate, melted
1/4 teaspoon salt
2 egg whites, beaten stiff

Cream together the butter and 3/4 cup of the sugar until light, add the salt, vanilla, and chocolate and mix well. Fold the remaining sugar, 2 tablespoons at a time into the egg whites. Add the chocolate mixture, folding gently but thoroughly only enough to blend. This is a very fluffy frosting that spreads like whipped cream.

MAPLE CREAM FROSTING

1 pound soft maple sugar

1 cup cream

Boil the sugar and cream together, without stirring, until a soft ball can be formed when the mixture is tried in cold water. Cool until of spreading consistency, beat well, and spread on the cake.

MOCHA FROSTING

4 tablespoons butter	1 tablespoon breakfast cocoa
1 egg yolk	1 tablespoon instant coffee
1 and 1/2 cups confectioners' sugar	

Cream butter, add sugar gradually and the egg yolk and flavorings. Beat well.

SEVEN-MINUTE FROSTING

2 egg whites	1/3 cup water
1 and 1/2 cups sugar	2 teaspoons light corn syrup
few grains of salt	1 teaspoon vanilla

Beat together the egg whites, sugar, salt, water, and corn syrup in the top of a double boiler; place over boiling water and continue beating with a rotary beater—electric if you have one—for 4-7 minutes or until the frosting thickens and holds its shape when dropped from the beater. Remove from the stove, add the vanilla, and continue beating until thick enough to spread. Approximate yield—frosting for the tops and sides of two 9-inch layers, or for 24 cupcakes.

FLUFFY MARSHMALLOW FROSTING

Beat 1 cup diced marshmallows into the frosting before spreading on the cake.

COCONUT FROSTING

Put layers together and cover the cake with Seven-Minute frosting. Sprinkle it at once with 1 and 1/2 cups shredded coconut.

PEPPERMINT FROSTING

Instead of the vanilla add a few drops of oil of peppermint to the frosting.

ORANGE FROSTING

Substitute 1 teaspoon orange extract for 1 teaspoon vanilla.

LEMON FROSTING

Substitute 1 teaspoon lemon extract for 1 teaspoon vanilla.

Chapter 4.
Hors d'Oeuvres

A few suggestions for small appetizers, some of which may be used as a first course or for a buffet party, others as tidbits for friends who drop in.

ANCHOVY CANAPES

Mrs. Adele Mac Veagh
Dublin, N.H.

two 2-ounce cans flat anchovy fillets
2 medium garlic cloves, chopped fine
1 teaspoon tomato paste
1 to 1 and 1/2 tablespoons olive oil
2 teaspoons lemon juice or red wine vinegar
freshly ground black pepper
8-10 slices French bread
1 teaspoon finely chopped parsley

Drain the anchovies and place in a heavy bowl with garlic and tomato paste. Mash the mixture to a smooth purée. Dribble in the oil, a few drops at a time, stirring until the mixture becomes thick and smooth. Stir in the lemon juice (or vinegar) and pepper. Preheat the oven to 500°. Brown the bread lightly on one side. While the bread is still warm, spread the untoasted side with the anchovy mixture. Arrange the bread on a baking sheet and bake for 10 minutes. Sprinkle with parsley and serve at once.

ANCHOVY PUFFS

1 3-ounce package cream cheese
1/2 cup butter
1 cup flour
anchovy paste

Blend the cheese and butter, add the flour and chill. Roll very thin and cut with a 2-inch cookie cutter. Spread rather generously with anchovy paste, fold over and crimp the edges. Bake in a hot (400°) oven for 8-10 minutes. Serve at once.

48 puffs

ANGELS ON HORSEBACK

1 pint oysters
bacon strips cut in half
Worcestershire sauce
salt and pepper

Wrap the oysters in bacon strips and secure with toothpicks. Season and bake them in a 375° oven (turning once) until the bacon is crisp.

Two interesting ways to serve avocados as a first course.

AVOCADOS WITH HOT SAUCE

Mrs. John Goold
Ogunquit, Me.

1 very ripe, very cold avocado,
  halved and stoned
watercress
2 tablespoons catsup
2 tablespoons butter

2 tablespoons white rum
1 tablespoon brown sugar
2 teaspoons lime juice
few dashes of Tabasco sauce
fresh ground white pepper

Combine the ingredients for the sauce and bring the sauce to the table bubbling hot, preferably in a metal ramekin. Pour into the cavities of the cold avocado halves and accompany with hot buttered Triscuits. Garnish with watercress. The contrast of the hot with the cold, the piquant with the bland, and the soft with the crisp is very appetizing.

Serves 2

AVOCADOS WITH RED CAVIAR AND SOUR CREAM SAUCE

1 very ripe, very cold avocado,
  halved and stoned
4 ounces red caviar

1/2 cup sour cream
1 egg yolk
1 teaspoon onion juice

Combine the last three ingredients to make the sauce. Spoon the caviar into the avocado halves, and over it the sauce. Serve ice cold with hot buttered Triscuits and lemon wedges.

AVOCADO MIX

1 avocado
1 tablespoon grated onion
1 tablespoon lemon or lime juice

4 slices crisp bacon, crumbled
salt and pepper to taste

Mash the avocado, and put through a sieve or purée in the blender. Add the other ingredients, and serve with crackers as a dip.

BACON ROLL-UPS

Bacon roll-ups always disappear quickly and are easy, as you can get them ready ahead of time. One good combination is a piece of pineapple and half of a water chestnut rolled in a half strip of bacon. Secure it with a toothpick and bake in a hot (400°) oven for ten minutes or so or until the bacon is crisp. Marinate with a little pineapple juice and serve.

The Woodstock Inn in Woodstock, Vermont, serves kumquats wrapped in bacon, and they are delicious. Even better with an almond slipped inside the kumquat.

BASIL BEANS

These are crisp and wonderful to add to a salad or to nibble with cocktails. Keep a batch on hand all during the summer when beans are ripening. They will last in the refrigerator for a week or so.

Fill a crock, large or small, with a brine made with 12 measures of water to one of salt. Add a small dash of vinegar and a small piece of garlic. Put a good amount of basil into the brine, then prepare the beans. Pick them while still young, remove the stem and string (if any) and parboil them for just two or three minutes, until a bit tender and bright in color. Submerge them in the brine. Cool, then chill.

DILL BEANS

Dill beans are made the same way—just use dill instead of basil.

CURRIED CANTALOUPE DIP

Mrs. H. T. Webster
New Canaan, Conn.

fresh melon balls
1/2 pint sour cream
2 tablespoons mayonnaise
1/2 teaspoon curry
1/2 teaspoon catsup
1 teaspoon lemon juice
a dash of salt

Combine the sour cream with the mayonnaise and seasonings and blend well. Garnish with mint leaves and serve as a dip for melon balls.

THE CHEESE TRAY

A cheese tray fills many useful roles. Accompanied by a variety of crackers or by French bread, it is an attractive addition to a buffet table, at a cocktail party, or it may accompany the salad if you want to make that a final course. Served with fresh fruit it takes the place of dessert.

Try to find a large flat wicker basket or a large platter of natural wood. Arrange four or five cheeses on it. In summer the cheeses look well placed on fresh grape leaves. Or you may want to use paper doilies, particularly if you serve a runny cheese. Cheddar cheese, Swiss, Blue cheese, Edam and one or two of the French cheeses make a good choice. A cheese crock (see p.83) may be served with these others. It's an easy way to make your meal more interesting.

CHEESE PEAR FOR THE CHEESE TRAY

Form an 8-ounce cream or Neufchâtel cheese into the shape of a pear rolling it between the hands inside a small plastic bag. Remove the cheese from the bag and roll it lightly on a breadboard, rubbed if you wish with garlic or onion, in some fine breadcrumbs with nuts and nut crumbs. Shake paprika on one side of the pear to give it a sun-kissed look and plant a few bay leaves atop to complete the picture.

CAMEMBERT CHEESE BALLS

1/2 package Camembert cheese	scant cup milk
1 package cream cheese	salt and cayenne pepper
2 tablespoons butter, creamed	1 egg, beaten
3 tablespoons flour	breadcrumbs

Purée the cheese, and add the butter, flour, milk, and seasoning. Stir over low heat until thick and pour on a plate to cool. Form into small balls, roll in flour, and brush with beaten egg. Roll in the breadcrumbs and either chill for later use, or fry immediately in deep fat and serve.

CHABLIS CHEESE

This needs at least a week to ripen. Use an earthenware container or crock.

8 ounces cream cheese
4 ounces Liederkranz cheese
celery salt

4 tablespoons Chablis wine
garlic clove

Mash the cream cheese and beat in the Liederkranz. Season with celery salt. Beat in the wine. Rub the inside of the earthenware crock with a clove of garlic. Spoon the mixture into the crock, cover tightly, and let stand for a week or longer.

HOT CHEESE APPETIZERS

2 cups grated Cheddar cheese
1 package cream cheese
2 tablespoons soft butter

1/2 teaspoon baking powder
1 beaten egg

Beat the mixture until creamy and pile on small rounds of bread or on crackers. Place under the broiler until slightly brown and puffy. Sprinkle with chopped parsley and mustard seed.

CHEESE BITES

Peter McHenry
Lawrenceville, N.J.

Mozzarella or Swiss cheese
1 egg lightly beaten
flour

seasoned breadcrumbs
deep fat

Cut the cheese in 3/4 inch cubes, roll them in flour and dip them in the egg, then in seasoned breadcrumbs. Dip them again in the egg, again in the breadcrumbs, and fry them in hot fat. Serve on toothpicks.

CHEESE CROCK

Mrs. John McCracken
New Canaan, Conn.

1 pound sharp Cheddar cheese
1 package cream cheese
1 tablespoon olive oil

pinch of dry mustard
liqueur or spirits
1 crushed garlic clove

Grate the cheddar and blend it with the cream cheese and oil. Add the mustard, garlic and a few jiggers of whatever liquor you choose. Put in a small crock, and after it is well blended keep the crock in the ice box ready for crackers and an unexpected guest. Never use it all up. Keep adding to it.

CRABMEAT MAYONNAISE

A light but formal first course that is convenient for the hostess as it can be made ready ahead of time.

1 pound fresh or frozen crabmeat
hearts of 1 bunch celery
lemon juice, to taste
salt, to taste

homemade mayonnaise
capers
young lettuce leaves

Pick over the crabmeat to be sure it is free of pieces of membrane or shell. Mix with the minced hearts of celery, and toss gently in the mayonnaise, adding salt and lemon juice to taste. Arrange the crabmeat on lettuce leaves on individual plates and top with another spoonful of mayonnaise and one of capers.

Serves 6

HAM ROLLS

ham, sliced thin
1 teaspoon dry mustard

1 tablespoon sour cream
1 strip of bacon for each ham slice

Mix the mustard and sour cream. Spread the mixture on the ham slices. Roll each slice, wrap in a strip of bacon, and fasten with a toothpick. Bake the ham rolls at 400° until the bacon is crisp.

HOT HORS D'OEUVRE

1/2 pound tiny frankfurters
  (small meat balls or chicken
  livers)
4 tablespoons chili sauce

2 tablespoons brown sugar
1 teaspoon dry mustard
a dash of sherry

Combine and bake (in a dish that can be used for serving) for about 20 minutes in a 350° oven. Spear with toothpicks and pass with paper napkins.

CURRIED OLIVE CANAPE

a 4 and 1/2-ounce can ripe
  olives, chopped
1/4 cup grated onion
3/4 cup grated Cheddar cheese

1/4 cup mayonnaise
1/4 teaspoon curry powder
8 slices bread
parsley

Combine the first five ingredients. Remove the crusts from the bread and toast lightly. Cut in quarters and spread with the mixture. Broil until bubbly and sprinkle with parsley.

32 pieces

PECAN OR WALNUT ILLUSIONS

whole nuts, freshly toasted
3 tablespoons ground nuts
1 small package cream cheese

3 minced ripe olives
1 tablespoon chopped chives

Soften the cheese with a fork until it is smooth. Add the chopped olives and chives. Shape into small balls, roll in the chopped nuts, and flatten into small patties. Press half a nut on top of each. Chill in the ice box before serving.

HOT PECAN SPREAD

Victor Davies
Chester, N.J.

an 8-ounce package cream
   cheese, softened
2 tablespoons sherry
a 2 and 1/2-ounce jar sliced
   dried beef
1/4 cup finely chopped green
   pepper

2 tablespoons dried onion flakes
1/2 teaspoon garlic salt
freshly ground pepper
1/2 cup sour cream
1/2 cup coarsely chopped pecans
2 tablespoons butter
1/2 teaspoon salt

Combine the softened cream cheese and sherry and mix until well blended. Stir in the dried beef (cut up if necessary), the green pepper, onion flakes, and seasonings, and mix well. Fold in the sour cream. Spoon into a small, ovenproof baking dish. Heat and crisp the pecans in melted butter and salt and sprinkle them over the cream cheese mixture. Bake at 350° for 20 minutes. Serve hot with crackers.

ROQUEFORT BISCUITS

2 cups sifted flour
1 teaspoon salt
3 teaspoons baking powder

1/4 cup Roquefort cheese
1/4 cup butter
2/3 cup milk

Sift together the flour, salt, and baking powder. Cut in the crumbled Roquefort and the butter with a pastry blender or two knives until the mixture is of the consistency of coarse corn meal. Add the milk slowly and lightly. Turn on to a floured board, knead a little and roll to 1/2-inch thickness. Cut in small rounds with a floured cutter and bake on a greased baking sheet in a 425° oven for 12 minutes or until done. Split and put a piece of butter and a sliver of country ham in each biscuit and serve quickly.

THIN SANDWICHES

Thin, firmly made sandwiches have a versatility that is hard to beat. They can go to picnics, tea parties, or cocktail parties, cut in size and shape to suit the occasion. Use white or whole-wheat bread that is melba thin. If you can, buy it that way. If not there is a wonderful gadget that will divide a normal slice of bread perfectly. And some people are able to slice thin, thin bread from an unsliced loaf with a sharp knife.

CUCUMBER SANDWICHES

Spread the bread for the sandwiches with softened cream cheese or a combination of cream and cottage cheese. Sprinkle with salt and pepper and a little onion juice, slice cucumbers thinly on the bread, top with another slice, press firmly together, and refrigerate until needed. At that time remove the crusts from the sandwiches and cut into desired shapes.

MUSHROOM SANDWICHES

Spread the bread for the sandwiches with softened sweet butter. Sprinkle with salt and pepper, a little onion juice and chopped parsley, slice mushrooms thinly on the bread and top with another slice, press firmly together, and refrigerate until needed. At that time remove the crusts from the sandwiches and cut into desired shapes.

PATE DE FOIE GRAS SANDWICHES

Spread the bread for the sandwiches with softened sweet butter. Spread with pâté de foie gras, or if you use a lesser liver pâté, use more butter and less pâté proportionately. Proceed as above. Garnish with watercress.

SARDINE SPREAD

Use as a spread, a dip, or to stuff celery sticks.

8 ounces cream cheese	1 large onion, minced fine
3 tablespoons lime or lemon juice	salt to taste
1 tin sardines, mashed	2 hardcooked eggs, chopped

Blend the cheese with the juice. Add the sardines, onions, chopped eggs, and salt. Blend thoroughly.

SALTED NUTS

nut meats—pecans, almonds   butter
  (peeled or unpeeled), or walnuts   salt

Heat 2 tablespoons butter or salad oil per cupful of nuts in a heavy skillet. Don't let it get too hot. Add the nuts and stir constantly until they are just browned. Drain on paper toweling, and sprinkle with salt. These nuts keep their crispness well when stored in a tightly sealed jar.

TOASTED SALTED NUTS

Spread nuts in a shallow pan adding 1 tablespoon of butter or olive oil for each cup of nuts. Salt well. Bake in a 400° oven stirring occasionally until just done. They will darken as they cool. Drain on paper towel and serve while still warm.

SESAME ROLL-UPS

Mrs. A. M. Charlton
Cambridge, Mass.

12 slices white bread, crusts   butter
  trimmed   sesame seeds

Flatten the bread slices with a rolling pin. Spread both sides of each slice with soft butter. Roll up and sprinkle with sesame seeds. Bake the rolls in a preheated 300° oven for 20 minutes until golden brown.

SPORTSMAN'S APPETIZER

As served at buffet suppers at One Louisburg Square, Boston.

2 large tomatoes   6 tablespoons butter
two 6-ounce cans tuna   1/2 cup mayonnaise
2 hardcooked eggs   4 slices white bread, crusts
1 green pepper   removed
1/4 cup Worcestershire sauce

Combine the tomatoes, tuna, eggs, and pepper, and chop coarsely. Add the Worcestershire sauce, melt 2 tablespoons of the butter, and sauté the mixture in it until the peppers are tender. Add the mayonnaise and blend. Melt the remaining butter and sauté the bread on both sides until brown. Spread with the mixture. Place on a cookie sheet and heat in a 350° oven. Cut into triangles and serve hot.

16 pieces

Chapter 5.
Soups & Chowders

In all the branches of cookery, I don't think there is anything more *fun* than making soups. Because the flavor builds up gradually as the elements cook together and blend, it is usually a fairly slow process, but one which leaves room for much experimentation and invention. You must taste as you go along and probably will want to correct the seasoning with a touch or two of your own. Personally, I find an open cupboard with a large selection of herbs, spices, and seasonings ranged in full view a wonderful source of inspiration in cooking. And when making soup, it is often interesting to add vegetables, herbs or bones you may have on hand to the basic recipes given here.

Among the soups that follow, there are many that, served with good bread, will make a complete lunch or suppertime meal. For instance, soups are especially good for small children's supper. By the end of the day, they are often too tired to manage anything but a cup and spoon.

On the other hand, addition of a soup course can make a festive and leisurely occasion out of a family or party luncheon or dinner, well worth the extra effort. It enhances the flavor and texture of the repast and pleasantly prolongs the time at table. Conversation thrives, and appetites can be whetted or whittled, as you please, by your choice of soup. A soup tureen is a great help to keep soup hot on the table.

The basis of most good soups (and of many other dishes as well) is soup stock, also called bouillon, or broth. Some vegetable soups create their own uniquely flavored stock, as the vegetables cook in water or cream, while others require meat, fish or chicken stock. Chicken stock is commonly used as the base for delicate soups, while beef stock is needed for the more full-bodied soups. There are very good meat concentrates on the market that may be used to make stock, and commercial beef and chicken consommés or bouillon cubes should be kept on hand; they too are of fine quality. Nevertheless, homemade stock is easy to make, economical, and far better. And for homemade *bouillon cubes*, see our box on "Portable Soup"!

PORTABLE SOUP

A recipe included in The Emigrant's Handbook, *published in 1845 as a "complete guide for the Farmer and the Emigrant," tells how to make your own bouillon cubes.*

"*To make Portable Soup.*— Take a leg or a shin of beef, weighing about ten pounds; have it from a bullock recently killed; break the bones, and put it into your soup pot; just cover it with water, and set it on the fire to heat gradually, till it nearly boils. It should boil for nearly an hour. When scum rises, it should be carefully skimmed off, and a little cold water be poured in once or twice, which will cause more scum to rise on the surface, which must again be removed. When the scum has ceased rising, let it boil for eight or nine hours, and then strain through a hair-sieve into a stone jar, and place it where it will quickly cool.

"The next day, after removing every particle of fat, pour it quite through a very fine sieve, or tamis, into a stew-pan, taking care that none of the settlings at the bottom go into the stewpan. After adding a quarter of an ounce of black peppercorns, let it boil briskly, the pan uncovered, until it begins to thicken and is reduced to about a quart. All scum that rises must be removed as in the preceding process, but without adding water to it. When it begins to thicken, withdraw it from the brisk fire, and place it where it can continue to boil gently, until it becomes a very thick syrup. Great care must be taken to prevent it burning, which would in one instant destroy the whole.

"Pour out a little in a spoon to ascertain if it will jelly. If it does not, then boil it longer, and at length pour it into a little potting jar, about an inch and a half in depth and perfectly dry. These pots are recommended if the soup is intended for home consumption, and is sufficiently concentrated to keep for six months. If to be longer preserved, it may be put into bladders such as are used for german sausages: or it may be dried in the form of cakes, by pouring first into a dish until cooled. When cold enough to turn out, weigh the cake, and divide it into pieces of an ounce, or half an ounce each; place them in a warm room, and turn them twice a day for a week or ten days, by which time they will be thoroughly dried. If kept in a dry place, they may be preserved for years."

SPICE BAG

A spice bag is useful in making soups and sauces and in cooking meats or stews. Its ingredients lend their flavor to the dish and may then be easily withdrawn. A good general rule for its contents includes:

1 bay leaf	1 sprig thyme
6 peppercorns	1 sprig parsley
4 cloves	

Tie them together in a square of cheesecloth or nylon net.

BEEF STOCK

5 pounds beef bones with lots of meat and marrow	3 fresh tomatoes, or canned tomatoes and their juice
giblets of a chicken	mushroom stems, if at hand
2 onions, sliced	salt and peppercorns
1 carrot, sliced	spice bay—bay leaf, parsley, thyme, as available
1 small turnip, sliced	
1 stalk celery, sliced	Worcestershire or soy sauce

Cover the ingredients with cold water (about 3 quarts) and simmer gently for about 2 hours, skimming from time to time. Strain and cool. The next day, skim off the fat, and the stock is ready for use.

About 2 quarts

VEGETABLE BEEF SOUP

Pick the meat from the bones which made the beef stock described above. Return to the stock with new vegetables, finely minced (carrot, onion, celery, turnip, tomato), and a few peas or beans and cook until tender. Season to taste.

Serves 6-8

CHICKEN STOCK

4 pounds chicken backs, necks, and giblets	1/2 bay leaf
	2 sprigs parsley
1 onion	tarragon
1 carrot	salt and a few peppercorns
1 stalk celery	

Rinse the chicken, cut up the vegetables, and cover all of the ingredients with cold water, about 2 quarts. Simmer gently for about 2 hours, skimming occasionally. Strain the stock, cool, and remove any fat. This stock will keep in the refrigerator for 3-4 days, or it may be frozen.

Or, of course, you can use the leftover bones of a roast or fowl as the base of your stock. Here are some hints for soup-making from turkey, duck, or goose bones.

TURKEY BONE SOUP

bones of 1 turkey and any leftover gravy	1 stalk celery, sliced
	1 sprig each of parsley and thyme
1 onion, sliced	1 bay leaf
1 carrot, sliced	salt and a few peppercorns

Place all the ingredients in a large kettle; cover with 3 or 4 quarts of cold water, and simmer, covered, for 2 hours, skimming as necessary. Strain, cool, and remove fat. This soup may be used as is, or a hearty soup can be made by adding some of the vegetables left over from the turkey dinner (mashed potatoes, creamed onions, celery, carrots, or mushrooms). If there is stuffing left too, it can be puréed and added to the soup. Either way, most New Englanders maintain that the soup is the very best part of the turkey.

GOOSE SOUP

When you are lucky enough to have a goose carcass, a distinctive and wonderful soup can be made by the method described for Turkey Bone Soup. Remove any bits of meat and set them aside to add to the soup later. Add a handful of lentils to cook with the soup (they will absorb some of the goose's fat), and in the end add some sliced mushrooms to the soup—they are particularly good with goose.

DUCK SOUP

Duck makes an especially rich and flavorful soup.

1 duck carcass, with any leftover gravy, stuffing, and drippings	peppercorns
	1 to 3 tablespoons mashed potato or potato flour
1 onion, sliced	parsley, chopped
1 carrot	Worcestershire or soy sauce
1 small turnip, diced	5 or 6 mushrooms, sliced (raw or canned)
1 or 2 stalks celery	
1 bay leaf	
salt	

Cover the duck carcass, gravy, drippings (after removing as much fat as possible), and stuffing with water. Add onion, carrot, turnip, celery, the bay leaf, salt, and peppercorns. Simmer all together for an hour or more until the meat remaining falls easily from the bones. Remove the carcass from the pot, pick off the meat, and return the latter to the soup. Cool the soup and skim off the fat. Reheat the soup and thicken with mashed potato or potato flour (amount used will depend on thickness desired). Correct the seasoning, adding Worcestershire or soy sauce if needed, sliced mushrooms, and chopped parsley.

Serves 4-5

THREE *DIFFERENT* SOUPS—"A" IS FOR APPETITE!
ALMOND SOUP

This soup is delicate and unusually pleasant.

4 tablespoons butter
4 tablespoons flour
1 and 1/2 cups blanched, slivered almonds
1 shallot, or 1 scallion, minced
1 quart chicken stock

pinch of tarragon
juice of half a lemon
salt and pepper
1/2 cup cream
1 scant teaspoon almond extract

Melt the butter and stir in the flour, part of the stock, and all the other ingredients except the almond extract and the cream. Cook, stirring, for about 10 minutes. Purée, return to the stove and add the cream and the almond extract. Serve garnished with whipped cream and watercress.

Serves 6

APPLE SOUP

3 large green apples
1 large onion
4 stalks celery
2 tablespoons butter
2 cups beef stock

2 cups chicken stock
1 teaspoon curry powder
1 teaspoon paprika
juice of half a lemon
1/2 cup thick cream

Chop the onion and celery and cook gently in the butter until golden brown. Peel, core, and slice the apples and add to the vegetables. Cook them in the oven for 20 minutes in a covered iron pan. Add the beef and chicken stocks, curry powder, paprika, and lemon juice. Season to taste and stir. Strain and bring to a boil. Take off heat and finally add the cream. Chill in the refrigerator if the soup is to be served cold. It is a pleasant surprise on a hot summer day when served chilled, and equally intriguing offered piping hot when the leaves begin to turn.

Serves 6

AVOCADO SOUP

1 ripe avocado
2 cups chicken stock
2 tablespoons white rum
1 teaspoon curry powder

juice of 1 lemon or lime
salt and pepper
1 cup light cream

Combine the ingredients in the container of a blender and mix thoroughly. If you do not use a blender, sieve the avocado and beat all together. Chill the soup and serve with a sprinkling of finely chopped chives or a sprig of watercress.

Serves 4-5

BELLEVUE BROTH

5 cups chicken broth (stock)
3 cups clam broth

1/2 pint heavy cream, whipped
salt and pepper

Combine and heat the broths. Whip the cream and season lightly with salt. The soup may need no seasoning at all. Taste to see. Pour it into heated bouillon cups and garnish with the whipped cream.

Serves 8

BUTTERBALL SOUP

Mrs. Walter C. Hanke
Adams, Mass

3 eggs
1 tablespoon melted butter
22 saltine crackers, rolled fine

2 quarts chicken stock
pinch of nutmeg

Beat the eggs well, then add the melted butter, saltines, and nutmeg. Mix all together and let stand 5 minutes. Then form mixture into little balls. Drop balls into hot chicken stock. Cook 5 minutes, or until puffed up. Garnish the soup with something green—finely chopped parsley, watercress, or chives.

Serves 6-8

CHICKEN VICTORIA SOUP

This recipe is one of the specialities of a famous New England inn, the Yankee Pedlar, in Holyoke, Massachusetts. Perhaps the name derives from the High Victorian architecture of the inn.

1/2 cup flour
1/2 cup butter
2 quarts rich chicken stock
1 cup fresh mushrooms, sliced

1/2 cup diced pimiento
1 small onion, chopped
1 cup cooked chicken, diced
salt and pepper

Mix butter with flour over low heat to make a smooth paste, or roux. Bring stock to boil and stir into the roux. Sauté onions and mushrooms for 5 minutes. Mix with pimiento and diced chicken, and add to chicken stock. What makes an inn famous? Well, now you know!

Serves 8

CREAM OF CHICKEN SOUP

Use the recipe for chicken stock (p. 92), including some chicken wings with the backs, necks, and giblets. When the broth is done, cut the meat from the wings and reserve.

3 tablespoons flour
3 tablespoons butter or chicken fat
1 carrot
1 stalk celery } cut up fine
4 or 5 mushrooms

3 pints chicken stock
meat from chicken wings
1 cup cream beaten with the yolk of one egg
salt and pepper to taste

Melt the butter, add the flour and some chicken stock, stirring to keep the mixture smooth. Add the vegetables and the rest of the stock. Cook until the vegetables are tender. Add the chicken meat and cream, then season to taste. This soup may be whirled in the blender to a purée, but it is almost better with the chicken and vegetables left diced. Garnish it with minced parsley, sprigs of watercress, or toasted almonds.

Serves 6

CURRIED CHICKEN SOUP

1 can concentrated cream of chicken soup
1 can concentrated chicken consommé
1 cup light cream or milk
1 teaspoon fresh onion juice
1 tablespoon lemon juice

2 tablespoons orange juice
1 teaspoon curry powder
1/2 teaspoon ground ginger
1 clove garlic
1 apple peeled, cored and quartered, or fruit of half a cantaloupe

Mix all ingredients together, and whirl in the blender with 4 or 5 cubes of ice until light and very cold. Add salt if necessary. Serve the soup in chilled bowls. Several garnishes are good with this soup—grated orange rind, chopped chives, toasted almonds, chopped green pepper, or garlic croutons. This is a great taste teaser on a hot day.

Serves 4

BRIGHT RED SOUP

A light, tangy soup from the autumn garden.

6 small beets, cooked and diced
  (canned beets may be used)
1/2 cup of the water in which they
  were cooked
2 large ripe tomatoes, skinned,
  seeded, and diced
2 cups beef stock

2 teaspoons onion juice
juice of half a lemon
1 cup red wine, port or Bordeaux
salt to taste
3 cloves
6 peppercorns

Simmer these ingredients together until they are well blended. Then serve very hot, topped with cold sour cream and a green herb—parsley or chives.

Serves 6

VERMONT CABBAGE SOUP

3 cups cabbage, chopped fine
1 and 1/2 cups water
3 cups milk

1 cup cream
juice of half a lemon
salt and freshly ground pepper

Cook the cabbage in water for about 15 minutes, until soft but still green. Add the milk and the cream, lemon juice, salt and pepper. Reheat and serve garnished with finely chopped parsley and a small pat of butter.

Serves 6

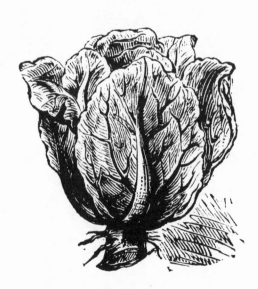

CREAM OF YOUNG CARROT SOUP

This creamy, golden soup with satisfying flavor may be transformed into party fare by liquidizing in the blender. A large bowlful with garlic croutons makes a good main dish for lunch or supper.

4 tablespoons butter
the white part of 2 leeks, sliced, or
   1 bunch scallions
1/2 onion, sliced
1 stalk celery, sliced
1 bunch (1 pound) young carrots
   (if older carrots are used, discard the core and cut into narrow
   strips)

1 large potato, peeled and sliced
1/2 clove garlic, crushed
salt and white pepper
a little sugar
spice bag (p. 92)
1 tablespoon cornstarch
2 cups milk
4 tablespoons cream

Melt the butter in a heavy saucepan; add the sliced leeks (or scallions), onion, and celery, cover pan, and cook gently for 10 minutes. Uncover and add carrots, potato, garlic, salt, pepper, sugar, and herbs. Mix well, add water to cover and simmer until the vegetables are perfectly tender (about 40 minutes). Liquidize in the blender (or purée), then return puréed mixture to the same saucepan. Add cornstarch and milk and simmer for 3 minutes. Taste for seasoning. Just before serving, stir in cream. Garnish with a good quantity of finely chopped parsley or mint and tiny croutons fried in butter (and garlic, if desired).

Serves 6

CAULIFLOWER SOUP

1 cauliflower
2 onions
1 tablespoon oil
2 tablespoons butter
1 small clove garlic

3 tablespoons flour
1 bay leaf
2 and 1/2 cups milk
1/2 cup cream

Cut the cauliflower and onions in pieces; cook them with the oil, butter, and garlic for 2 or 3 minutes. Then add enough water to cover the vegetables and cook until they are soft. Over low heat, stir in the flour, and slowly pour in the milk. Stir until the soup comes to a boil, then add the bay leaf. After simmering for a few minutes, whip the soup in a blender until light. Add the cream, reheat the soup, and serve garnished with finely chopped chives and fried croutons.

Serves 6

ESSENCE OF CELERY

6 large stalks celery   1 slice onion
2 quarts well seasoned chicken
    stock

Dice the celery quite fine. Simmer it in the chicken stock, uncovered, for 30 minutes. Rub through a very fine strainer. Serve hot or cold, garnished with thin slices of celery heart.

Serves 6

CHERRY SOUP

1 pound red cherries, pitted   1/4 teaspoon salt
1/2 cup sugar   1/2 cup orange juice
2 teaspoons cornstarch   1 cup red wine
1/4 teaspoon cinnamon

Chop the cherries very fine, and mix with the sugar, cornstarch, cinnamon, and salt. Stir in the orange juice, and bring the mixture to a boil, stirring constantly. Remove from the heat, and stir in the wine. This soup may be served hot or cold.

Serves 6

CHERRY SOUP II

If cherries aren't in season when you feel like cherry soup, here is a quick good recipe that uses canned pie cherries.

1 can cherry pie filling whirled   cinnamon, cloves, lemon juice,
    in a blender with: and salt to taste
      1 cup white wine
      1/2 cup orange juice
      1/2 cup beet juice

In the summer, serve cold, garnished with yoghurt and fresh mint leaves. This is a good winter soup, too, served hot with cold yoghurt and grated orange rind.

Serves 6

FRESH CORN CHOWDER

6 ears fresh corn   1 tablespoon flour
2 tablespoons butter   3 cups rich milk
1 small onion   salt and pepper

Score each row of kernels with a sharp knife, and scrape them and the milk from the cobs. Cook the onion in the butter until soft but not brown. Add the flour and the corn, and stir until the mixture starts to thicken. Transfer the mixture to a double boiler and gradually add the milk— stirring until cooked—then season to taste with salt and pepper. Serve hot, garnished with lots of finely chopped parsley and a small additional pat of butter.

Serves 6

Here are two soups to make when cucumbers are ripening so fast in the garden that it is hard to use them all.

CUCUMBER SOUP

4 cucumbers   1 egg yolk
4 scallions   1 cup cream
1 quart chicken stock   salt and pepper
1 tablespoon flour

Peel, seed, and thinly slice the cucumbers, peel and thinly slice the scallions, and simmer both with 1 cup of the stock until soft, about 15 minutes. Stir in the flour, cook for a few minutes, then add the rest of the stock and simmer 10 minutes longer. Stir in the cream and egg yolk and heat without boiling. The soup may be served hot or cold, garnished with finely chopped dill, watercress, parsley or mint, or a combination of these.

Serves 6

CUCUMBER YOGHURT SOUP

4 cucumbers   1 pint yoghurt
2 cloves garlic, crushed   salt and pepper
1 pint chicken stock

Peel, seed, and *thinly* slice the cucumbers. Add the other ingredients and chill for several hours. Serve iced, with finely chopped chives.

Serves 6

YOGHURT

Yoghurt is easy, and much more economical if you make it at home. Mix 2 tablespoons of commercial yoghurt (plain) with a cup of milk in a small bowl and leave overnight in a warm place. The pilot light of a gas stove is an ideal spot. In the morning, you will have yoghurt. The process can be repeated indefinitely.

GREENS SOUP

A tantalizing and elusively flavored soup can be made from greens left over from a salad or culled from the garden—the fresh outside leaves of lettuce, green tops of scallions, celery tops, a bit of watercress or spinach, pot herbs.

1 quart chicken stock
salad greens as available
1 shallot or a clove of garlic,
    minced

2 tablespoons butter
salt, white peppercorns, and a
    pinch of mustard
1 cup light cream

Cook all the ingredients except the cream together until just soft and still green. Whirl in the blender. Add the cream, reheat, and serve, garnished, if you wish, with whipped cream and chopped chives. This soup is best served hot.

Serves 6

PORTUGUESE KALE SOUP

Mrs. Margaret H. Koehler
Orleans, Mass.

Thoroughly wash a pound of kale, and cut it into very small pieces. Parboil 5 cubed potatoes. Add to the potatoes and water in which they have been cooked two chopped onions, 1 pound sliced chourico (two tablespoons bacon drippings may be substituted, if necessary), the kale, salt and pepper to taste, and let simmer for an hour or a little longer, adding more water if necessary. A second version of this famous soup calls for soaking a cup of pea beans overnight and cooking them with the above mixture.

ESSENCE OF MUSHROOM

1 quart chicken stock   1 cup water
1 pound mushrooms   sherry

Clean the mushrooms, chop them fine, and simmer in the stock and the water for 30 minutes. Pass through a fine sieve and add sherry to your taste. Serve garnished with thinly sliced mushroom caps.

Serves 6

MUSHROOM AND SCALLION SOUP

4 tablespoons butter or chicken
   fat
2 bunches scallions
1 clove garlic
salt and pepper
4 tablespoons flour

1 quart chicken stock
1/2 pound mushrooms, sliced fine
pinch of tarragon
juice of half a lemon
1/2 cup cream
1 or 2 egg yolks

Slice the scallions (both the green and the white parts), mash the garlic and cook slowly in the fat until soft, but still green. Add flour, seasoning, and part of the chicken stock and cook until thick. Purée in the blender, if desired. Return to the heat and add the mushrooms, the rest of the stock, cream, tarragon, and lemon juice, and cook for just a few minutes. Stir some of the soup into the egg yolks, and add the egg to the rest of the soup, being careful to stir quickly so that the egg will not curdle. Serve at once.

Serves 6

GREEN ONION SOUP

1 bunch scallions—bulbs and
   fresh leaves, chopped together
1 quart chicken stock
2 tablespoons butter
2 tablespoons flour

1 sprig thyme
1 shallot, minced
salt and white pepper
pinch of mustard
1 cup light cream

Cook the scallions and shallot with the thyme in the butter until soft but still very green. Add the flour and seasonings and part of the stock, then cook a little longer. Reheat with the rest of the stock and the cream. This soup is good served with finely chopped parsley, fried croutons, and grated cheese, accompanied by melba or hot buttered toast.

Serves 6

ONION SOUP

One of Mrs. Anne Gibbons Gardiner's Receipts from 1763

Take half a pound of Butter, put it into a Stew pan & set it on the Fire, & let all the Butter melt, and boil until it is done making a Noise; then have ready ten or a Dozen middling sized Onions, peeled and cut small, which throw into the Butter, and let them fry for a Quarter of an hour; then shake a little Flour and stir them round; shake your Pan and let them do a few minutes longer; when you must pour in a Quart or three Pints of boiling water; stir them round, and throw in a good piece of the upper Crust of the stalest Bread you have. Season with Salt to your palate. Let it then stew or boil gently for ten Minutes observing to stir it often; after which take it off the Fire, and have ready the yolks of two Eggs beaten fine in a Spoonfull of Vinegar, and then stir it gently & by Degrees into your Soup, mixing it well. This is a delicious Dish. (Indeed it is, and the substitution of beef stock for half of the water gives this soup the fillip it needs today. Serve with grated Cheddar cheese).

MAINE POTATO SOUP

Marcia Bonta
North Vassalboro, Me.

4 medium potatoes
water
4 slices bacon
4 tablespoons bacon fat
1 onion, diced
2 tablespoons flour

1 and 1/3 cups dried skim milk
3/4 teaspoon salt
1/4 teaspoon pepper
1/4 teaspoon paprika
1 teaspoon dried chives
dash of garlic salt

Wash and scrape the potatoes and boil them in a covered pot until thoroughly cooked. Drain off and reserve the cooking water. When the potatoes are cool, dice them and set them aside. Fry bacon slices until crisp. Put bacon fat into a heavy pot and sauté the onion in it until soft. Add the flour and cook until bubbly. Add the potato water to the dried skim milk and enough additional water to make a quart. Stir milk mixture quickly into the flour mixture, cooking until thickened. Flavor with salt, pepper, paprika, chives, and garlic salt. Add the potatoes and cook slowly for 10 minutes. Crumble bacon on top and serve.

Serves 6

SORREL SOUP

Sorrel speaks of spring. Then and all summer long, it grows freely as a weed in most New England pastures and gardens. When picked young and fresh, it is ideal for cooking.

2 cups sorrel leaves	3 cups chicken stock
2 tablespoons butter	2 egg yolks
2 teaspoons cornstarch	dash of salt
1 sprig parsley, minced	1 cup light cream

Wash the sorrel leaves and cook them in the butter until just wilted. Purée the sorrel and add other ingredients, dissolving the cornstarch first in a little stock, or whirl all together in the blender. Then cook the soup over gentle heat until slightly thickened. Serve hot or chilled, garnished with sour cream and chives, or with thin slices of lemon.

Serves 6

FRESH TOMATO SOUP

Canned tomato soup is one of the great blessings of modern life—beautifully smooth, zesty, comforting, and cheap—available anywhere, infinitely adaptable. *But* in August, September, and October, when your garden burgeons with fat, ripe fruits, you should consider this fleeting, perfect, homemade soup.

4 tablespoons butter	2 heaping tablespoons flour
5 or 6 large ripe tomatoes	2 cups (or more) milk
1 clove garlic, crushed	herbs

Melt butter in a soup pot. Rinse tomatoes and cut in pieces. Discard the seeds that are easily removable without losing too much juice. Put tomatoes into the pot and simmer gently as you add the garlic and flour, then gradually stir in enough milk to make a cream soup of medium thickness. Cut in the herbs which are abundant in late summer—basil, parsley, chervil, chives—and serve with the tomatoes still in big pieces and tasting of the garden. This is good hot or cold.

Serves 6

WATERCRESS AND SPINACH SOUP

1 bunch watercress
1 cup cooked spinach
1 small potato, boiled or baked
2 small slices Bermuda onion

4 cups well seasoned chicken
  stock
1/2 cup cream
pinch of mace

If the watercress is a little wilted, it will still do. Pick it over, discard any yellow leaves and trim the stems. Put the vegetables, the potato peeled, into the blender; purée, adding the stock and the cream and the mace. Heat together for 5 minutes and serve. This makes a very piquant soup.

Serves 6

WHITE TURNIP SOUP

4 medium-sized white turnips
1 large onion
3 tablespoons butter
salt and pepper

3 slices bread
2 egg yolks
1/2 cup cream
parsley

Peel, slice, and coarsely chop the vegetables and cook them slowly in the butter for 5 minutes. Add 6 cups of boiling water, salt and pepper, and bread, which you have first dried out in a slow oven and crumbled. Simmer the soup for a half hour and purée it. Reheat over low heat. Stir in the egg yolks beaten well with the cream. Serve at once, garnished with finely minced parsley.

Serves 6

WATERCRESS SOUP

This lovely bright green soup is as refreshing to look at as it is to taste.

1 small onion
1 potato, sliced
1 bunch watercress
1 big sprig parsley
1 big sprig dill

2 cups chicken broth
1 egg, or 2 egg yolks
1 cup heavy cream
salt

Cook the onion and potato slowly in butter until a little soft, but not brown. Add water to cover, about 1/2 cup, and cook until very soft. Mix with the chopped greens, the broth, egg, and half of the cream, then purée in the blender until light and frothy. Serve hot or iced, garnished with the remaining cream, whipped and salted, and a small sprig of watercress. Cheese sticks are a nice accompaniment.

Serves 6

WINTER SOUPS

These hearty winter soups are the perfect meal after a long day on the slopes, ski-mobiling, coasting, or shoveling snow. They are warming, nourishing, and just plain soul-satisfying. Serve them with a loaf of good bread, and perhaps a salad and some cheese for a complete and delicious dinner.

BAKED BEAN SOUP

Mix left-over baked beans with an equal quantity of beef stock, some grated onion, tomato paste, butter, and flour. The quantities will depend upon the quantity of baked beans. Add enough to make the soup piquant and to bind it. Purée all together or whirl in the blender, and then simmer for 30 minutes. Serve with left-over brown bread toasted under the broiler and fresh butter.

BERKSHIRE CORN AND TOMATO CHOWDER

1 onion, finely chopped	2 cups water
4 tablespoons butter	2 cups canned corn
1 bay leaf	salt and freshly ground pepper
2 tablespoons flour	1/2 cup cream
2 cups canned tomatoes	1 or 2 egg yolks
2 tablespoons sugar	

Cook the onion and butter until the onion is soft but not brown. Add the bay leaf and flour, and mix well. Add all the other ingredients except egg yolks and cream, and simmer for 30 minutes. If you wish, strain the soup, or whirl it in the blender. Just before serving, add the egg yolks beaten into the cream. Garnish with croutons.

Serves 6

BOSTON BLACK BEAN SOUP

1 pound dried black beans	4 tablespoons flour
3-4 quarts water	1 onion, minced
2 tablespoons salt	1/4 teaspoon black pepper
1 ham bone	1/4 teaspoon dry mustard
4 tablespoons butter	2 cups cream

Cover the beans with water and soak overnight. In the morning, drain, and put in a large pot with the water, salt and ham bone. Cook for about 2 hours until the beans are soft. Remove the ham bone and skim the soup. Purée the mixture. Melt the butter in a saucepan, gradually add the flour, onion, pepper, mustard and the cream. Stir until slightly thick, then add to the bean purée. Simmer together for a few minutes and serve garnished with thin slices of lemon and hardboiled egg, or covered with Boola-Boola Topping (see below) and run under the broiler until golden.

Serves 8-10

BOOLA-BOOLA TOPPING

This topping will transform a number of soups into a very special affair. It is good on split pea soup, or split pea soup mixed half and half with canned green turtle soup, Boston black bean soup, lentil or tomato soup. This amount of topping will garnish six bowls of soup.

1 egg yolk	1 cup whipped cream
3 tablespoons grated Parmesan cheese	

Combine egg yolk and cheese and mix to a smooth paste. Fold in the whipped cream. Swirl on top of soup in ovenproof bowls and brown quickly under the broiler. A tablespoon of Madeira or sherry added to the soup will make it even more festive.

NEW ENGLAND CORN CHOWDER

A hearty chowder that can be made in winter from canned corn. Served with corn bread and pickles or relish, this is a familiar New England supper.

1/2 cup salt pork, diced	1/2 teaspoon salt
4 tablespoons onion, chopped	2 cups water
1/4 cup celery, chopped	2 tablespoons flour
2 tablespoons green pepper, chopped	2 cups warm milk
1 raw potato, peeled and diced	1 No. 2 can creamed corn
	chopped parsley

Sauté the salt pork, then add to the pan and sauté the onions, celery, and green pepper. Add the potatoes, salt, and water, and simmer until the potatoes are soft. Add the flour, milk, and corn, and heat all together thoroughly. Sprinkle with finely chopped parsley.

Serves 6

LENTIL SOUP

A number of wonderful soups can be made when you have a nice ham bone with bits of meat on it. The spicy ham, dried legumes, and fresh vegetables make filling and tasty fare.

1 pound lentils	1 stalk celery, sliced
1 ham bone	1 bay leaf
3 quarts water	1 sprig thyme
2 carrots, sliced	cloves, salt and pepper
2 onions, sliced	

Soak the lentils overnight. In the morning, put them with the ham bone, vegetables, and the seasonings in water and cook for 2-3 hours. Remove the ham bone, the bay leaf and the thyme. Skim the soup if necessary. Cut pieces of meat from the ham bone and return to the soup.

Serves 8-10

SPLIT PEA SOUP

1 pound green split peas	peppercorns
3 quarts water	bay leaf
1 meaty ham bone	1 carrot, sliced
2 medium onions, sliced	1 parsnip, sliced
1 clove garlic	1 rib celery, sliced
parsley and thyme, 1 sprig each	1 cup white wine
2 teaspoons salt	

Soak the split peas overnight and drain. (If you are in a hurry, the peas may be cooked in a pressure cooker in 2 cups of water for 10 minutes.) Put the peas in a large pot with the water, the ham bone, and all other ingredients except the carrot, parsnip, celery, and white wine. Simmer on the back of the stove for 2 hours or so, stirring occasionally. Remove the bone, cut off the meat and return meat to soup. Add remaining ingredients and simmer for 15 minutes, or until vegetables are done. Sprinkle a pinch of mace atop each serving, and serve with common crackers, saltines, or baking powder biscuits. This soup is splendid with Boola-Boola Topping (p. 108).

Serves 8-10

OLD-FASHIONED POTATO SOUP

4 potatoes	1 tablespoon flour
3 cups milk	celery salt
1 tablespoon chopped onion	salt
2 tablespoons butter	cayenne pepper

Boil the potatoes and mash them. Brown the onion in butter, add the flour, then the potatoes, milk and seasonings. Stir and heat until smooth. Serve sprinkled with grated cheese and chopped parsley.

Serves 6

INSTANT VICHYSSOISE

Marion Ormsbee
North Haven, Conn.

4 cups water
2 chicken bouillon cubes
1 tablespoon dried onion flakes
  softened in a little water
1 tablespoon butter

1/3 cup (more or less) instant
  potato
1 cup milk
salt

Boil the water and dissolve the bouillon cubes in it. Add the onion flakes and butter. Remove from heat and add instant potato to thick soup consistency. Add milk, then salt to taste. To serve soup as vichyssoise, chill and serve very cold, garnished with chopped chives. To serve as potato soup, reheat.

Serves 5-6

ESAU'S POTTAGE

From an old cook book, here is the lineal descendant of the soup for which Esau sold his birthright—the kind of soup to come home to on a winter's night.

1/2 pound green split peas
1/4 pound red lentils
2 tablespoons pearl barley
4 tablespoons white beans
1 good soup bone
1/2 pound shin beef
2 carrots, diced

2 stalks celery, diced
1 onion, thinly sliced
2 quarts water
salt and freshly ground pepper
large sprig of parsley
extra parsley to garnish

Put the peas, lentils, barley, and beans into a large bowl, cover to twice their depth with cold water and leave to swell overnight. Next day rinse well. Put the bone and the meat (in one piece) with salt and water into a soup kettle. Bring slowly to the boil, skim, then add the other ingredients. Cover and simmer as slowly as possible for 2 or 3 hours, stirring occasionally. When the soup is ready the legumes will have dissolved into a purée, and sieving will be unnecessary. Before serving taste for seasoning, remove the bone, and serve a little of the meat with each serving. Garnish with scissored parsley.

Serves 6-8

CLAM CHOWDER

Grace Louise York
Harwich, Mass.

1 quart shucked clams and their
   liquor
1/4 pound salt pork, diced
2 onions, finely sliced
6 medium-sized potatoes, sliced
   thin

1/2 teaspoon salt
1/8 teaspoon pepper
4 cups milk
2 tablespoons butter

Rinse the clams in clam liquor. Remove the black caps. Strain, and reserve 1/2 cup clam liquor. Chop the clams and set aside. Fry the salt pork until brown and crisp. Drain on paper. Sauté the onion slices, then add the potatoes. Sprinkle with salt and pepper. Sauté for 10 minutes. Add the chopped clams and 1/2 cup clam liquor. Cover with water and cook for 20 minutes. Add the fried pork and fat to the clams and vegetables. Then heat the milk and add to the chowder. Add butter, season to taste, and serve.

Serves 8

CAPE COD QUAHOG CHOWDER

This is best made several hours ahead of serving time, for this allows it to "season." The next day it tastes even better.

1 pint quahogs (shelled and
   coarsely ground)
1/4 pound salt pork
2 medium onions
4 medium potatoes

liquor from quahogs
evaporated milk (tall can)
1 tablespoon butter
salt and pepper

Try out (fry) salt pork cut into tiny squares. Reserve the bits of salt pork. Fry onions in the fat, being careful not to burn. Peel the potatoes, cut in cubes, and add to the onions. Cover with water, and simmer gently until potatoes are cooked through. Add the ground quahogs and their liquor, and bring to a near boil. Let simmer (but do not boil) for 5 minutes. Add evaporated milk, undiluted. Scald, but do not boil. (This is important, for if it boils after the milk is added, the chowder will curdle). Add butter, salt and pepper, and the reserved pork scraps. Serve steaming hot.

NAUSET/EASTHAM
FISH CHOWDY

Albert E. Snow
Orleans, Mass.

A favorite soup of President John F. Kennedy's that is quick to prepare, nourishing, and easy to digest.

1 4-pound haddock
3 cups cold water
1/4 pound fat salt pork, diced in
   1/4-inch cubes
6 onions, sliced fine
2 tablespoons flour

2 cups potatoes, diced in 1/2-inch
   cubes
4 cups rich milk
2 tablespoons butter
salt and pepper
3 sprigs parsley, minced

Skin the haddock. Save the head and the tail. Cut out the backbone. Save same. Cut the fish into 2-inch pieces. Put the head, tail, backbone, and any odd remnants of meat into a saucepan. Add cold water. Bring slowly to the boiling point, then let simmer for 30 minutes. Place pork bits in another saucepan to try 'em out till crisp and browned. Empty pork bits, standing them aside. Into their fat, add the onions, frying them slowly for 5-10 minutes, till browned. Remove onions. Stir in the flour. Slowly add the broth drained from the bones, stirring continuously to avoid lumping. Add diced potatoes, onions, and fish. Cover. Simmer slowly for an hour, until the potatoes lose their stiffness some. Add hot milk, butter, salt and pepper to taste. Add minced parsley. Simmer 5 minutes longer. Serve soup accompanied with warmed pilot biscuits, oysterettes, or common crackers.

Serves 8

CLAM SOUP

YANKEE *Magazine's cookbook would not be complete without a recipe contributed by Miss Hildegarde Halliday of New York City.*

Many a miss has yearned for a magic potion that would make the man of her dreams fall in love with her and in Newport, Rhode Island, Miss Halliday's aunt had had such a romantic talisman before the turn of the century, a recipe for a very special clam soup. Miss Halliday

says, "This is without exception one of the most delicious soups I have ever eaten. Mr. G. F. Downing was already enamoured of my aunt but upon feasting on this soup he felt that a beautiful girl who was also such a beautiful cook should be his without further delay."

W. A. Croffut, of whom nothing is known here except that he favored this soup and was a gifted versifier, wrote the recipe.

First catch your clams along the ebbing edges
Of saline coves. You'll find the precious wedges
With backs up, lurking in the sandy bottom;
Pull in your iron rake, and lo! you've got 'em!

Take thirty large ones, put a basin under,
And cleave with knife their stony jaws asunder,
Add water (three quarts) to the native liquor,
Bring to a boil (and, by the way, the quicker

It boils the better, if you'd do it cutely).
Now add the clams, chopped up and minced minutely;
Allow a longer boil of just three minutes,
And while it bubbles, quickly stir within its

Tumultuous depths, where still the mollusks mutter,
Four tablespoons of flour and four of butter,
A pint of milk, some pepper to your notion,
And clams need salting, although born of ocean.

Remove from fire (if much boiled they will suffer;
You'll find that India rubber isn't tougher).
After 'tis off add three fresh eggs well beaten,
Stir once more and it's ready to be eaten.

Fruit of the wave: Oh, dainty and delicious!
Food for the Gods! Ambrosia for Apicius!
Worthy to thrill the soul of sea-born Venus
Or titillate the palate of Silenus!

MRS. GEORGE WASHINGTON'S CRAB SOUP

Served in the White House by Mrs. Franklin Delano Roosevelt.

1 and 1/2 cups crabmeat	1/2 teaspoon mushroom sauce
1 quart milk	(mushroom catsup)
2 hardboiled eggs	1/2 teaspoon A-1 sauce
suggestion of nutmeg	1/3 cup sherry
1 tablespoon butter	1/2 cup cream
1 tablespoon flour	salt and pepper

Pick crabmeat over for shells and set aside until needed. Mash the hard-boiled eggs to a paste with a fork and add to them the butter, flour, and a little pepper. Bring the milk to a boil and pour it gradually onto the well mixed paste of eggs, etc. Put over a low fire, add the crabmeat, and allow to simmer for 5 minutes. Add the cream, and bring to the boiling point again, then add sherry, salt and sauce. Heat sufficiently to serve, but do not boil after the sherry has been added.

Serves 6

RECIPE WITH A HISTORY

For sixty years my great uncle Albion fished out of New Harbor, Maine, and earned his living from the sale of the hake, haddock, and cod he caught. For his own eating he preferred haddock. Hake, he said, was flat, and for cod he had no use, dismissing it with two words: "Cod, God!"

My Great Aunt Emily would sometimes say, "A corned hake would go good, Albion," or "Couldn't we have a change from haddock?" But Uncle Albion liked haddock, and that was what the family got.

One day when their son was about ten years old, Aunt Emily rebelled. "Fred," she said to her son, "run down to the shore and bring me up a fish, anything but haddock. And, Fred, if your father is on the dock, bring it up the back way."

That evening Uncle Albion sat down to a supper of hot buttered biscuits and what Aunt Emily called a "smother," a new dish that Uncle Albion eyed doubtfully before tasting, but approved after his third plateful.

"Tasty, Emily," he conceded, though I never thought I'd like haddock any way but fried or chowdered, but this mess is really tasty."

Suddenly young Fred squealed: "It's cod, Pa! You been eating cod!"

Uncle Albion looked from Aunt Emily, who nodded, to the tureen holding the fish. Then he poked at it. In that moment Uncle Albion knew as well as Aunt Emily and Fred the kind of fish he had just eaten.

"After all these years, Emily," he said sadly, "and you, too, Fred, not to know a haddock. That," he pointed toward the tureen, "is haddock."

Then in a disgusted voice: "Cod!" he said, "Cod, God!"

The "smother" remained a favorite dish in the family, and it was always tacitly agreed that it was made with haddock.

Iva Reilly
New Harbor, Me.

HADDOCK SMOTHER

3 large slices salt pork
1 small onion, diced
3 pounds haddock (cod, or any white fish)
3 tablespoons flour

salt and pepper
1 pint water
1 quart milk
1 tablespoon butter

Try out the salt pork, and brown the onions in the fat. Cut the fish into pieces convenient for handling, place in a large kettle, and sprinkle with flour, pepper, and salt. Add the fat, onion, and water, and cook until tender. Add the milk and butter, and serve hot.

Serves 8-10

YANKEE LAND
AND SEA CHOWDER

Mrs. A. J. McGuiness
Worcester, Mass.

2 cups raw diced potatoes
1 pound fish fillets, haddock or
   cod
1 cup diced raw onions
1/2 teaspoon salt
3 cups water

1 can cream-style corn (16 oz.)
1 can minced clams (8 oz.)
1 and 1/2 quarts milk
1 tablespoon sugar
1 tablespoon diced pimiento

Cook potatoes and onions with fish in salted water until vegetables are
tender and fish flakes. Add corn, clams, and milk. Heat all to simmer.
Add sugar, salt and pepper to taste, and 1 tablespoon diced pimiento.
Serve topped with buttered crackers (any kind) sprinkled with chopped
chives and/or parsley.

Serves 6

LOBSTER CHOWDER

1 2-pound lobster
1 and 1/2 cups diced potatoes
3 tablespoons butter
1 small onion, minced

2 tablespoons flour
4 cups scalded milk
salt and pepper
6 common crackers

Boil the lobster. Drain and cool. Remove meat from shell, reserving liver,
and cut meat in small pieces. Cover bodies with cold water, and simmer
15 minutes. Strain, add the potatoes to stock, and cook until tender. In
saucepan, melt butter and cook onion until delicately browned. Blend in
lobster liver, then stir in flour. Pour milk in gradually, stirring until
thickened. Add lobster meat, potatoes, stock, and seasoning. Simmer 5
minutes. Split common crackers. Place in hot tureen and pour chowder
over crackers. Sprinkle with parsley.

Serves 6

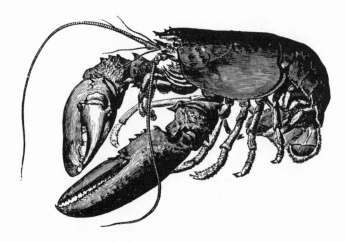

LOBSTER SOUP

a 2 and 1/2-pound lobster
water to cover
1/2 teaspoon salt
white peppercorns
1/2 onion, sliced
1/2 carrot, sliced
large sprig parsley
1/2 teaspoon dried tarragon

1 small bay leaf
3 cups chicken stock
1 cup cream
4 slices white bread, without crusts
sherry or Madeira
1 tablespoon butter

Put about a pint of water in a saucepan large enough to hold the lobster. Add the salt and peppercorns, onion, carrot and herbs tied in a cheese-cloth bag. Bring to a boil and add the lobster and simmer, covered, for 15 minutes. Discard the spice bag, and set the lobster aside to cool. Strain the stock, and return it to the heat with the chicken stock and the bread. Stir together until the bread has dissolved in the stock. Remove the lobster meat from the shell, and cut up, reserving some of the larger pieces to garnish the soup. Mash the liver with the butter and add to the soup, along with the rest of the lobster meat, the cream, and sherry or Madeira to taste. Serve hot.

Serves 6

MOCK LOBSTER SOUP

Mrs. Margaret Walbridge Aikkola, a native New Englander now living in Finland, sent YANKEE this recipe which her father invented to taste like lobster soup. It does. The dill gives the broth its nutty, lobster-like flavor.

1 pound fish fillets (haddock or flounder) or sea scallops
1 quart salted water
a sprig of fresh dill (or a heaping teaspoon of dried dill

1 can cream of tomato soup or tomato bisque
1 tablespoon butter
pepper
fresh parsley

Bring the water to a boil. Add the fish and dill and simmer until tender, about 15 minutes. Remove the dill sprig. Break up the fish with a fork. Add the undiluted soup and simmer for 5 minutes longer. Dot with butter and sprinkle with pepper and parsley.

Serves 6

OYSTER BISQUE

1 dozen oysters	1 bay leaf
2 cups chicken stock	1 tablespoon butter
3/4 cup soft breadcrumbs	1 tablespoon flour
1 sliced onion	2 cups milk
2 stalks celery	salt and pepper
sprig of parsley	chopped parsley or dill

Clean and pick over the oysters, reserving their liquor. Cut the firm part of the oysters from the soft part, and chop separately. Simmer the stock with the breadcrumbs, onion, celery, parsley, bay leaf, and firm part of the oysters for 3 minutes. Then remove the leaves, and purée, Melt the butter, stir in the flour, then add the purée and the oyster liquor. Bring to the boil, and add milk, the chopped soft part of the oysters, salt and pepper, and heat. Purée the soup again, or not, as you wish. Serve garnished with chopped fresh parsley or dill and salted whipped cream. Pass crisp oyster crackers with this delicate soup.

OYSTER SOUP

This delicious old-time recipe, which first appeared in an 1832 cookery book with the very long title "A Boston Housekeeper, *The Cook's Own Book, Being a Complete Culinary Encyclopaedia*", differs from the standard recipe for Oyster Stew used today only in the beneficial inclusion of flour and marjoram.

three pints of large fresh oysters	a bunch of sweet herbs
two tablespoonfuls of butter,	a quart of rich milk
rolled in flour	pepper to your taste

Take the liquor of three pints of oysters. Strain it, and set it on the fire. Put into it, pepper to your taste, two tablespoonfuls of butter rolled in flour, and a bunch of sweet marjoram and other pot herbs. When it boils add a quart of rich milk—and as soon as it boils again take out the herbs and put in the oysters just before you send it to the table. Be sure to let the soup *simmer* for 3 minutes after adding the oysters.

Oyster stew is traditional for Christmas Eve supper when everyone is too busy and excited to linger long at table. Served with toasted oyster crackers (I prefer them to the toast mentioned in the recipe), a salad, and fruitcake or mince pie and cheese, it makes a festive meal, quickly prepared and quickly eaten.

A family recipe well over a hundred years old and vouched for by all those generations.

Oyster Stew

Stew 2 doz. oysters in their own liquor for about 5 min. When coming to a boil take them up and strain off the liquor (reserving it)

Put a piece of butter the size of an egg into a stew pan add 1 teasp flour when the butter is melted stir, then add the oyster liquor and 3 tablesp milk or cream, mace, pepper and salt.

Let boil up for a couple of minutes Remove from the fire.

Put in the oysters and let warm, they must not boil or they will be made hard.

Line the bottom of a dish with slices of toasted bread & pour in the Oysters.

(Mrs Wm C Endicott Sr)
of Danvers - Mass

PUREE OF OYSTER SOUP

4 tablespoons butter
1/4 cup finely chopped onion
1 package tiny frozen peas
1 cup milk
1 pint fresh oysters with their liquor

2 cups clam juice
1/2 cup dry white wine
salt and freshly ground white pepper
1 cup heavy cream

Melt half of the butter in a saucepan, and cook the onions in it until they are soft but not brown. Add the peas and milk. Simmer until the peas are just tender. Add the oysters and clam juice, and simmer over very low heat for 10 minutes. Put in the wine, remaining butter, salt, and pepper. When the butter melts, purée the mixture and beat, or whirl in the blender until light. Return to the saucepan. When ready to serve, preheat the broiler, and whip the cream seasoned with a little salt. Heat the soup almost to boiling, and spoon it into hot, heatproof dishes. Top each dish with a generous amount of whipped cream, and place under the broiler until cream is golden brown.

Serves 4

NANTUCKET SCALLOP CHOWDER

2 onions, sliced
4 tablespoons butter
1 pint scallops
2 cups boiling water

1 cup potatoes, diced
4 cups scalded milk
salt and pepper
chopped dill

Sauté the onions in the butter, and remove them from the pan. Cut up the scallops, and sauté them in the butter. Add the onions and potatoes to the boiling water, and simmer 20 minutes. Add the scallops and scalded milk, and simmer for an additional 15 minutes. Season with salt and pepper, and garnish with a good quantity of chopped dill.

Serves 6

AUNT CLARA'S SHRIMP GUMBO

Mrs. Helen B. Haaland
Woodbury, Conn.

1 pound fresh shrimp
3 medium onions
1 quart water
2 tablespoons tarragon vinegar
1/4 cup raw rice
1/2 pound okra
butter
1 tablespoon flour

4 tomatoes (canned tomatoes may be used)
1 teaspoon Worcestershire sauce
1 teaspoon chopped parsley
2 bay leaves
a pinch each of salt, pepper, and sugar

Boil the shrimp and one of the onions, chopped, in 1 quart of water with the vinegar for 10 minutes. Reserve the water. Peel and clean the shrimp. Cover the rice and okra with one inch of water and cook dry. Fry the remaining onions, finely chopped, in butter over low heat, smooth in the flour, and add the shrimp stock, then the okra, rice, shrimp, tomatoes, and seasoning. Simmer for 20 minutes and serve piping hot.

Serves 6

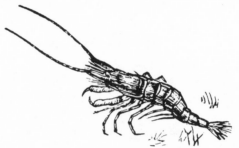

SOUP GARNISHES

Soups may be garnished either with something that hints of what the soup contains—sections of mushroom on mushroom soup, tips of lobster claws on lobster soup, leaves of watercress in whipped cream atop watercress soup, or with some contrasting ingredient— toasted almonds, chives, or watercress sprigs, for instance, on cream of chicken or tomato soup. Grated cheese adds to many hearty soups, and salted whipped cream to delicate ones.

When soup is served as a first course, it may be unaccompanied, or served with one of the light crackers which follow. If the soup is to be used as the main course of the meal, serve cornbread, muffins or popovers with it on a butter plate.

SOUP ACCOMPANIMENTS

CRISP CRACKERS

Spread crackers with a small amount of butter, dust with paprika and bake in 500° oven until lightly browned. Serve hot.

SOUFFLEED CRACKERS

Split New England common crackers and soak them in ice water for 5 or 6 minutes. Dot lightly with butter, dust with paprika, and bake in a 500° oven until puffed. Reduce the heat to 375° and bake until brown, about 45 minutes.

CHEESE STRAWS

Roll out pastry dough (p. 277), sprinkle it with grated cheese (Parmesan and Cheddar are both good) and salt and cayenne pepper. Fold over, press the edges together securely and roll again. Sprinkle with more cheese and repeat, folding a second time and a third. Cut the pastry into 4-inch strips about 1/4 inch wide and bake in a hot oven (450°) until golden brown, about 8 minutes.

SMALL CROUTONS

Cut slightly stale bread into tiny cubes and stir in melted butter in an iron frying pan. Place the croutons in a low oven until browned. Stir them occasionally. If the soup is not a delicate one, some mashed garlic may be cooked with the croutons.

LARGE CROUTONS

Cut rounds of American or French bread and fry them in butter, with or without garlic as you desire, until golden brown. Serve floating on a hearty bowl of soup with minced parsley or grated cheese.

MELBA TOAST

Brush thinly sliced bread with melted butter and perhaps a little grated cheese and bake in a medium oven (350°) until browned on all sides.

OLD FASHIONED SODA CRACKERS

Soda crackers are the usual Yankee accompaniment to chowders, eaten with and crumbled in the soup. If you would like to make your own, here is an old recipe.

sour milk	1 teaspoon butter, softened
1/2 teaspoon soda	1 teaspoon lard
3 cups flour	salt

Mix enough sour milk, in which the soda has been dissolved, into the flour to make a very stiff dough. Knead well, working in the butter and lard, and roll out very thin. Cut, shaping the crackers as you wish, sprinkle with coarse salt, and prick them in patterns with a fork. Bake the soda crackers in a moderate oven (350°) until they are crisp.

Chapter 6.
Fish & Seafood

The cod of Bay State fame was the mainstay of the diet of our earliest American ancestors and a great liking for that fish and fish of all sorts is still peculiar to this part of the country. Fish and seafood were more abundant then than they are now, and ten-pound lobsters were taken with ease from the sea. These giants are still around, though now they are taken from deeper, off-shore waters. New Englanders still enjoy a great variety of seafood, especially during the summer.

As court bouillon plays a large part in the successful boiling or poaching of any fish (it is as important a part of fish cookery as meat or chicken bouillon is for soups) the recipe follows immediately.

Fresh fish should not be kept for any length of time—one day at the most—it is best bought and used the same day. A whole fish if fresh has clear, firm eyes, tight scales and is free of a strong fishy odor or a slimy surface. Cut fish or fillets should be firm and fresh smelling. Use a reliable fishmonger.

The term "mask" as used in this chapter means to cover the surface of—to frost, if you will—the fish with the recommended sauce.

Often fish tastes best served simply with melted butter, a dusting of finely minced parsley or other herbs (dill is good), with lemon halves on the side. Sweet butter is best for the purpose. For a more elaborate dish, fish may be cooked with sliced almonds, or served with Hollandaise (p. 247) or white wine sauce (p. 251). Mask cold fish with mayonnaise or green mayonnaise (p. 243). Fried parsley is excellent served with fish.

COURT BOUILLON

3 tablespoons butter
1 onion, minced
1 stalk celery, minced
1 carrot, chopped
1/2 cup vinegar

2 sprigs parsley, minced
1 quart boiling water
1 bay leaf
8 whole cloves
4 peppercorns

Melt the butter in a skillet, add the vegetables and sauté for 5 minute Add the remaining ingredients and boil for 5 minutes. Strain.

BOILED BROOK TROUT

2 brook trout
water to cover
juice of half a lemon
1 small onion, chopped

2 small carrots, sliced
1 bay leaf
salt and pepper

Boil the trout in the water with the other ingredients for 6 to 8 minutes, or until the fish turns blue and flakes easily when tested with a fork. Remove the fish to a platter and garnish with the vegetables and serve with parsleyed boiled potatoes. Butter the vegetables.

Serves 2

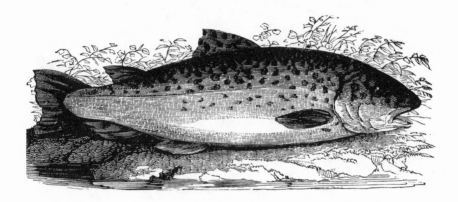

PAN FRIED FISH

Small fresh water fish, perch, trout, pike, freshly caught and cleaned are never more delicate than when simply sautéed in hot butter. Wash and clean the little fish, first removing their scales with a sharp knife and their fins with small scissors. Salt and pepper them and roll them in a little flour.

Heat a frying pan and when very hot drop in butter the size of a walnut for each fish. (Cook only 2 or 3 at a time). Sweet butter is particularly good. Let it get a little brown, then lower the heat and lay the fish in the bubbling butter. Cook for about 2 minutes on each side or until the flesh is flaky. Place the fish on a hot platter and return the pan to the fire. Melt another lump of butter for each fish and add chopped chives or parsley. Scrape the sauce from the pan onto the fish and serve with lemon.

POACHED STRIPED BASS

Poach bass following the recipe for salmon (p. 132). A 5-pound striped bass will serve 8 people. Cook a 5-pound striped bass for 45 minutes. It is good served hot, masked with Hollandaise sauce or cold with mayonnaise and capers, or with green mayonnaise (p. 243). Pass the fish and allow the guests to serve themselves, cutting pieces from the upper half of the fish. Take it back to the kitchen; remove the backbone, which will come out whole; turn the fish, garnish it afresh, and return it to the table.

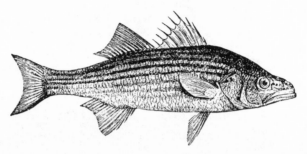

The two following recipes bear a close family resemblance.

DOWN EAST TURKEY

Mrs. Kenneth Dion of New Durham, New Hampshire, inherited this version from her grandmother who was the daughter of a captain of a fishing fleet off Prince Edward Island in the 1870s.

1 pound salt codfish	8 medium potatoes, boiled and
1/4 pound salt pork	peeled

Freshen the cod by covering it with cold water, bringing it to the boiling point in a saucepan, but do not boil. Pour off the water and repeat the process at least 3 times. In the last water, cook the fish over low heat for 10 minutes. Taste it to be sure it is not too salty. While the cod is freshening, dice the salt pork and render over low heat until light brown. Peel and boil the potatoes. Put the hot boiled potatoes in a deep serving dish and place pieces of codfish over them. Pour the salt pork fat and the crisp cubes over them. This dish should be served with pickled beets and a tangy salad.

Serves 4

CAPE COD TURKEY

Mrs. Dewey Boesse
South Yarmouth, Mass.

1 box salt codfish (1 pound)
1/4 pound salt pork
8 medium potatoes, boiled and
   peeled

1 cup medium cream sauce (p. 245)
1 hardcooked egg

Cover the cod with cold water, bring to a boil, drain. Repeat this process 2 or 3 times, then simmer the fish until tender, about 10 minutes. Meanwhile boil the potatoes, cube and try out the salt pork, and prepare the cream sauce and the hardcooked egg. When serving pour the cream sauce over the potatoes and the fish, add the sliced egg and sprinkle with the pork scraps.

Serves 4-6

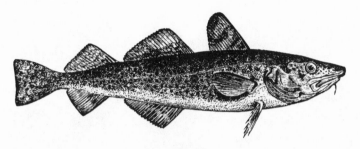

CALDEIRADA A PESCADORA (FISHERMAN'S STEW)

Mrs. Margaret H. Koehler
Orleans, Mass.

2 pounds fish (haddock, flounder,
   halibut, or anything similar)
1/2 cup olive oil
4 large onions, sliced
2 cloves garlic, minced
1/2 bunch parsley, chopped
pepper

1 teaspoon coriander seeds, or 2-3
   sprigs coriander
6 to 8 potatoes, sliced
large can solid-pack tomatoes
1 bay leaf
salt
1 cup dry white wine

Heat the olive oil in a deep pot. Add the sliced onions, garlic, parsley, pepper, and coriander. Cook until the onions are golden. Then place a layer of fish over the onions, then a layer of potatoes, then the tomatoes, bay leaf, salt, and wine. Cover tightly and simmer for about 45 minutes, or until the potatoes are done.

Serves 6-8

FINNAN HADDIE WITH OYSTERS

Finnan haddie is haddock cured with the smoke of green wood.

2 cups finnan haddie	Tabasco sauce
1 pint oysters	paprika
1 and 1/2 cups cream sauce (p. 245)	

Soak the finnan haddie for 30 minutes. Drain and flake the fish, removing any bones. Simmer for 25 minutes in fresh water. Heat the oysters in their own liquor. As soon as the edges curl (5-6 minutes), put them in the cream sauce. Add the finnan haddie and simmer gently for about 5 minutes. Season with Tabasco sauce and paprika, and serve on hot buttered toast.

Serves 6-8

FISH 'N MEAT SUPREME

Henrietta Waite
Sagamore, Mass.

1 and 1/2 pounds haddock or cod fillet	butter
1 jar chipped beef	salt and pepper to taste
2 cups cheese sauce (use canned cheese soup or see below)	paprika

Simmer the fillets till they flake in just enough water to cover the fish. Sauté the chipped beef in butter till its edges curl. In a greased casserole make alternate layers of fish and chipped beef. Make a medium cream sauce (2 cups, p. 245) and add grated cheese to taste. Add salt and pepper. Pour over the fish and beef. Dot with butter, sprinkle with paprika. Bake at 325° for 20-25 minutes.

Serves 6-8

FLOUNDER HYANNIS

2 pounds flounder fillets
2 cups thin cream
1/2 cup sherry
salt and pepper

1 pound shrimp or meat
   of 1 small lobster
1/3 cup buttered breadcrumbs

Trim the fillets, lay them in a frying pan and cover with the cream. Add the sherry, salt, and pepper, and cook 5 or 6 minutes on the top of the stove. Remove to a baking dish and add the shrimp or lobster and bake in a 400° oven until the cream and sherry are thick. Add the breadcrumbs and place under the broiler until bubbly and lightly browned. Garnish and serve.

Serves 6-8

HALIBUT MOUSSE
WITH LOBSTER SAUCE

George P. Stinchfield
Nantucket Island, Mass.

1 pint heavy cream
1 tablespoon butter
2 and 1/2 cups soft breadcrumbs
1 teaspoon salt

1 teaspoon celery salt
1 pound fresh halibut put through
   a grinder or blender
4 egg whites

Scald the cream in the top of a double boiler, add the breadcrumbs, and stir to make a smooth paste. Add the butter, salts and fish, and blend thoroughly. Allow the mixture to cool and carefully fold in the egg whites, stiffly beaten. Pour into a lightly greased mold and place the mold in a large pan with about an inch of water in the bottom. Bake until set, about 1 and 1/2 hours, in a 350° oven. Unmold and serve with lobster sauce (see below). Garnish with parsley or watercress.

Serves 6

LOBSTER SAUCE

3 tablespoons flour
3 tablespoons butter
1 cup court bouillon
1/2 cup heavy cream

2 egg yolks
1/2 cup diced lobster meat
dry sherry
salt and paprika

Mix together the butter and flour over a low flame and add the bouillon gradually, stirring and cooking until the sauce thickens. Add the egg yolks beaten together with the cream and the remaining ingredients. Heat the sauce but do not let it boil.

BAKED MACKEREL

2 small mackerel	chopped chives
1 cup milk	paprika
salt and pepper	melted butter

Split and bone mackerel. Place skin down in a greased pan. Pour over the mackerel milk seasoned with salt and pepper. Bake uncovered in a moderate (375°) oven for 25 minutes. Sprinkle with chopped chives and paprika. Serve with melted butter.

Serves 4

POACHED SALMON WITH PEAS AND POTATOES

This is, of course, the traditional meal for the Fourth of July, combining all the best tastes of early summer. Serve it with freshly baked rolls and strawberry ice cream, or with biscuits and strawberry shortcake.

a 3-pound chunk of salmon	butter
2 quarts court bouillon (p. 126)	chopped parsley
3 cups fresh-shelled green peas	egg sauce (p. 245)
12-16 small new potatoes scrubbed and, if you like, pared	

Wrap the salmon in a large piece of cheesecloth and place it in a pot large enough to let it lie flat. Heat the bouillon and pour it gently over the fish. Simmer, do not boil, the fish over low heat for 25 minutes. While it is cooking, boil the peas and the potatoes separately in just enough salted water to cover. Lift the fish from the pot, remove the skin and place fish in the center of a large hot platter. Arrange the potatoes and peas around it, pour egg sauce over the salmon, butter the vegetables, and garnish all with parsley.

Serves 6-8

COLD SALMON

Cool and elegant hot weather fare.

Poach the salmon as above and chill overnight. Carefully remove the skin, mask it with homemade mayonnaise (p. 243), and serve it on lettuce, surrounded by thin-sliced cucumbers and garnished with lemon halves and parsley. A good side dish is cold cooked garden peas, mixed with a little oil and sprinkled with finely chopped mint.

BROILED SCROD

Scrod is a young codfish weighing about 2 pounds.

1 young fish	breadcrumbs
salt and pepper	parsley
butter	paprika

Split a young codfish, remove bones, and cut into sections for individual servings. Sprinkle with salt and pepper and dip in melted butter. Then roll in a mixture of fine breadcrumbs, chopped parsley, and paprika. Place on an oven-proof platter and broil until tender, about 3 inches from the flame. Baste with melted butter.

Serves 4

BAKED STUFFED SHAD

Have the shad split and the backbone carefully removed. Lay the fish open and sprinkle the interior generously with salt, pepper, and lemon juice. Fill with a well seasoned bread stuffing. Close the fish and place 2 strips of bacon over it, wrap tightly in foil and bake in a 250° oven for 6 hours. The bones will all be edible.

Serves 6-8

SHAD ROE

2 pair shad roe
1/2 cup water

2 tablespoons butter
salt and pepper

Put roe in a frying pan and add the water, salt, and pepper, and cook slowly, covered until the water is gone. Add the butter and brown for about 10 minutes. Serve with crisp bacon and lemon wedges, with or without baked shad.

Serves 4

CAMPFIRE SMELT

3 pounds dressed smelt or other
   small fish
2 teaspoons salt
pepper

1/3 cup chopped onion
1/3 cup chopped parsley
bacon strips, cut in half

Cut six pieces of heavy duty aluminum foil, 12 x 12". Grease them lightly. Place the fish on the foil and sprinkle with salt and pepper, onion, and parsley. Top with a half strip of bacon. Bring foil over fish and seal edges with double folds. Place on the grill 4 inches from the coals. Cook 10-15 minutes.

Serves 6

FILLET OF SOLE IN SHERRY

Evart Andros
Walpole, N.H.

Easy to prepare but very impressive.

1 and 1/2 pounds fillet of sole
2 cups light cream
1/2 cup sherry
salt and pepper

1 4-ounce can shrimp
1/3 cup buttered breadcrumbs
white grapes

Trim the fillets, lay them in a frying pan and cover them with the cream and sherry. Season with salt and pepper and cook about 5 minutes on top of the stove. Remove and arrange in a shallow buttered baking pan. Add the drained shrimp and bake in a hot oven (400°) until the cream and sherry are thick. Add the breadcrumbs and place the dish under the broiler until the sauce bubbles and browns a little. Remove from stove and serve garnished with white grapes cooked in a little butter.

Serves 6

BROILED SWORDFISH, ANCHOVY BUTTER

2 pounds swordfish steaks,
  1 and 1/4 inches thick
6 tablespoons butter

1 teaspoon anchovy paste
freshly ground black pepper
lemon halves

Grease a broiler rack and heat it in the oven. Place the swordfish on the rack and spread lightly with butter. Broil 4 or 5 minutes. Place on a very hot platter. Combine the remaining butter with the anchovy paste in a small saucepan. Melt and pour over the swordfish. Grind the pepper over the steaks and serve immediately with lemon halves.

Serves 4-6

YACHTSMAN'S STEW

The Ocean Point Inn
Ocean Point, Me.

1/2 pound salt pork, diced
2 pounds beef, cut in cubes
2 tablespoons flour
1 teaspoon salt
1/2 teaspoon pepper
1 and 1/2 cloves garlic, minced
1 large onion, chopped
an 8-ounce can tomato sauce

1 bouillon cube, dissolved in
   1 cup hot water
12 peppercorns
3 whole cloves
1/4 cup chopped parsley
1 large bay leaf
3/4 cup sherry or tart white wine

Sauté the salt pork. Sprinkle the beef with flour, salt, and pepper, and brown in the pork fat. Add all the other ingredients except the wine. Cover and simmer for 4 hours. After 3 hours, add the sherry or white wine.

Cook separately:

6 medium-sized potatoes
6 carrots

1 stalk celery, chopped

Cook the vegetables until they are partially tender, then add to the stew for the last 15 minutes of cooking. The stew is thick, so serve it on dinner plates.

Serves 8

CLAM CASSEROLE

Henrietta Waite
Sagamore, Mass.

3 pints clams, in shells
2 cups boiling water
1 small onion, chopped
2 medium potatoes, cubed
salt and pepper

3 tablespoons butter
3 tablespoons flour
1 cup rich milk
4-6 common crackers
paprika

Wash the clams and steam them in the boiling water (cover the pan) just until the shells open. Remove the clams from their shells; snip off and discard the tips of the neck. Rinse the clams in the broth and cut them up. Set aside. Add the potatoes and onion to the broth and cook just until the potatoes are tender. Mix the flour and milk together until smooth. Add to the potatoes in the broth and cook until thick. Then add the clams and pour into a buttered casserole. Crumble the crackers over the dish, dot with butter, and sprinkle with paprika. Bake for 25-30 minutes at 425°. This dish is nice served with beets and whipped potatoes with a grating of cheese on the top.

Serves 4

ESCALLOPED CLAMS

Mrs. John Goold
Camden, Me.

1 quart fresh clams
4 cups common cracker crumbs
1/2 cup butter

1/2 pint whipping cream
paprika

Chop the clams fine (do not grind them). Melt the butter and add to the crumbs. Butter a casserole. Add a layer of crumbs, then a layer of clams and their juices, then crumbs, alternating until all are used up. Now pour over the heavy cream, sprinkle with paprika and bake in a 350° oven for 45 minutes.

Serves 6

CLAM PIE

crust for a 2-crust pie (p. 277)
1 pint clams and their liquor
1/2 pound salt pork, cubed

3 medium raw potatoes, sliced
salt and pepper
butter

Line a 9″ pie plate with half the crust. Try out the salt pork until crisp. Arrange the salt pork, potatoes, and clams in layers in the pie shell. Add the clam liquor, pork fat, salt, and pepper. Dot with butter. Cover with the top crust and bake at 400° for 10 minutes, then reduce the heat to 350° and bake for 20 minutes more.

Serves 4

HAVE A CLAMBAKE

Charles P. Mason
Robert D. Proctor

The ultimate in "garbage can" clambakes, for those with a Paul Bunyan appetite, is lobster, sweet and/or Irish potatoes, hot dogs, eggs, corn on the cob and clams. In the bottom of the can put a limited amount of water depending on the amount of food and seaweed to be above, usually 2 to 3 inches. To this add a cup of vinegar and several tablespoons of salt. Next place a two-inch cake rack in the can, covered well with seaweed. This keeps the lobsters out of water. Place the can over a robust fire and bring the water to a boil. Put the lobsters in back side up, then alternate thin layers of seaweed with potatoes, hot dogs, eggs, corn, and lastly clams. Cover tightly. The potatoes, hot dogs, eggs and corn can be put in cheese cloth, loosely. This makes them easier to remove after cooking. We use a wire basket made for the clams which gives them freedom to open; also you can more readily see when they are open, which is the hour glass indicating the bake is done.

Cooking time varies depending on the amount of food and seaweed from 1 and 1/2 to 2 hours or until the clams open. Never pack the can so tightly with food and seaweed as to prevent the steam from permeating up through all layers, and maintain a healthy fire. As seaweed is not too easy to come by, the bake can be done with only the bottom layer.

You will note we omitted chicken in the above. We used to include it wrapped in cheese cloth with an onion and 2 or 3 links of sausage, but now like it better done seperately over charcoal. For Clambake Sauce, see p. 248.

For those fortunate enough to live right on the coast, a bake may be done right on the shore. Here you start with a large sheet of iron placed over an open fire of driftwood. Cover the plate well with seaweed, then your food and cover all with a large piece of canvas well soaked in water. Keep canvas well wet throughout to hold in the steam and also to prevent it from burning. Cooking time is greatly reduced due to broader base of the fire and the food being spread out more.

Of course nothing compares with the old-fashioned way of doing a bake. Here you started with a pit filled with large round stones to the level of the ground. On this was built a big bonfire of 4-foot cord wood for several hours. The coals were raked off, a good layer of seaweed added covering all the coals, the bakes put on, then covered with wet canvas as above, with the sides sealed to the ground with dirt and stones to hold in the steam. The bakes were contained in wire baskets, one complete bake per person, or, if the baskets would hold it, two bakes serving two people. With our urban life today, this technique is out for most people.

CLAMS, PORTUGUESE STYLE

Use hard-shelled clams (quahogs)—a quart or two. (The quantity can be quite variable.)

Put the clams in a deep kettle, after washing them well. Cut an onion or two in small pieces and scatter over them, and add about a quarter pound of linguica sausage, cut in bite-sized pieces. Cover and steam until tender—about 30 minutes. Serve with melted butter, or with vinegar and olive oil blended.

CRAB STEW

4 tablespoons butter
5 tablespoons flour
red pepper (to taste)
3 tablespoons Worcestershire
  sauce
juice of half a lemon

2 ounces sherry
2 cups milk
1/2 cup cream
1 teaspoon celery salt
4 cups shredded crabmeat

Cream the butter, flour and pepper until smooth, and cook until thick in a double boiler, gradually adding the milk. Blend cream, Worcestershire sauce, and celery salt and add to the mixture. Add the crabmeat and lemon juice to the sauce and keep it hot in the double boiler. Do not boil. At the last moment add the sherry, and serve on white rice.

Serves 6-8

CRAB WITH SHERRY IN SHELLS

2 cups fresh crab meat
2 hardcooked eggs, chopped
1 cup mayonnaise
1 teaspoon grated onion
1 teaspoon chopped parsley

1 cup buttered breadcrumbs
2 teaspoons lemon juice
1/2 teaspoon Worcestershire sauce
1/2 teaspoon dry mustard
3 tablespoons sherry

Mix all the ingredients, reserving a half cup of the buttered breadcrumbs. Spoon mixture into scallop shells or ramekins and top with the remaining crumbs. Bake in a 400° oven for 15 minutes.

Serves 6-8

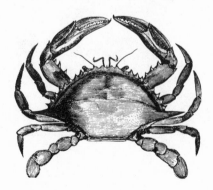

BOILED LIVE LOBSTERS

Giant lobsters weighing 6-10 pounds are just as tender as chicken lobsters and surely the most dramatic dish in the world. Use the enamel vegetable crisper in the bottom of your refrigerator (cover with a breadboard) if you can't find a pot large enough.

Plunge live lobsters, head first, into a large pot of rapidly boiling sea or salted water. Allow enough water to cover them completely. Bring the water to a boil again and cook for 10-20 minutes, depending on size. The lobsters will be a clear, bright red when done. Remove the lobsters from the pot and split. Place each on its back and slit the undershell with a sharp knife. Discard the dark vein, the spongy tissue, and the sac near the head, but save the green liver and the coral, if any. Serve with melted butter and garnish with lemon halves and parsley. Or make Lobster Coral sauce (p. 249).

STEAMED LIVE LOBSTERS

Put only 1-2 inches of water into the pot. Place lobsters in pot, cover tightly and continue as with Boiled Live Lobsters. Steamed, lobsters are if possible even tenderer than when boiled.

LOBSTER IN CREAM SAUCE *Mrs. Mary Ann Adams*
Buffalo, N.Y.

1 boiled lobster	1 cup cream
2 tablespoons butter	2 egg yolks
1 jigger sherry	1 tablespoon melted butter
1 tablespoon flour	3 tablespoons cream

Boil a medium-sized 2 and 1/2 to 3 pound lobster and allow it to cool. When cold, split it in two and dice all of the meat. Heat 2 tablespoons butter and sauté the lobster meat in it for several minutes. Add the sherry, the flour, and the cup of cream. Simmer gently for about 10 minutes, then add the beaten egg yolks mixed with 1 tablespoon melted butter and cream. Mix all thoroughly and fill the lobster shells. Bake in a hot oven until lightly browned, or, while still hot, run under the broiler.

Serves 2

MARJORIE MILLS'S LOBSTER PIE

Marjorie Mills was for several decades New England's First Lady of cookery, Women's Page editor of the Boston Herald-Traveler, author of many books, and radio commentator. A devoted partisan of Nantucket, she lives in a wonderful 17th-century house on the island.

4 tablespoons butter
1/2 cup sherry
2 full cups lobster meat
6 tablespoons butter

2 tablespoons flour
1 and 1/2 cups thin cream
4 egg yolks

Melt the 4 tablespoons of butter; add sherry. Boil 1 minute, add lobster and let stand. Melt the 6 tablespoons butter; add the flour and stir well until it bubbles. Remove from heat. Slowly stir well until cream and wine drained from the lobster are thoroughly blended. Return to heat and cook, stirring all the time, until the sauce is smooth and thick. Remove from heat. Beat egg yolks well. Stir, a tablespoonful at a time, into the yolks 4 tablespoons of the sauce. Add to the sauce, mixing well. Heat over hot (not boiling) water. Sauce may curdle if it boils. (If the sauce *should* start to curdle, quickly add an ice cube or a spoonful of cold sweet or soured cream, and it will become smooth again.) Sauce should be stirred constantly while heating (takes about 3 minutes). Remove from heat, add lobster. Turn into individual casseroles or small deep pie plate. Sprinkle with topping. Bake in a slow, 325° oven for 10 minutes.

Serves 4

LOBSTER PIE TOPPING

1/2 cup cracker meal
2 tablespoons finely crushed
  potato chips

1/2 teaspoon paprika
2 tablespoons Parmesan cheese
4 tablespoons melted butter

Mix first four ingredients. Add butter and blend well. Sprinkle on lobster pie.

STEAMED MUSSELS

Mussels are abundant along our shores, but because there is little demand for them they are often not to be found in our fish markets. They can be specially ordered and are a delectable treat. Inexpensive, too. They make an extremely pretty dish as the inside of the mussel shells are a deep silver blue, the mussels nestling in them bright apricot.

4 pounds mussels
1 bunch green onions, cut up, or
  2 medium onions, sliced
2 carrots, sliced
water to cover

1/2 teaspoon dried chervil
1 bay leaf, crumbled
juice of half a lemon
salt and fresh black pepper

Scrub the mussels, using soapless steel wool if necessary, and rinse in several waters. Steam them with the above ingredients until the mussels open and the vegetables are tender, 8 to 10 minutes. Add to the pot:

1 glass dry white wine
1/2 cup heavy cream

finely chopped parsley

Serve in large soup plates with oyster forks to extract the mussels and soup spoons for the broth.

Serves 4

PARTY OYSTERS

6 large oysters
6 fillets of grey sole
butter
2 tablespoons flour

1 cup light cream
1 cup chopped lobster meat
fresh chopped tarragon
sherry

Wrap each oyster in a ribbon of fillet of sole, secure with a toothpick, and broil in butter. Prepare the sauce in the following manner: brown 2 tablespoons butter in a pan on the stove; add flour to make a paste; then slowly pour in the cream. Pour this sauce over the lobster, let simmer for 3 minutes, add the tarragon and sherry, and pour over the broiled oysters. Cook in the oven for 15 minutes. Serve with white rice.

Serves 6

SCALLOPED OYSTERS

1 cup soft breadcrumbs	pinch of mace
1 cup dry cracker crumbs	1 tablespoon lemon juice
3/4 cup melted butter	2 tablespoons chopped parsley
1 quart oysters, picked over	1/2 cup oyster liquor
1 teaspoon salt	1/4 cup milk or cream

Mix the breadcrumbs, cracker crumbs and butter and spread half of the mixture in a large, shallow pan. A big pie pan does well. Arrange the oysters in two layers on the crumbs, add the remaining ingredients, and top with the rest of the crumbs. Bake in a hot (400°) oven for 30 minutes.

Serves 6

SPINACH OYSTER CASSEROLE
Gretchen Frelinghuysen
Woodstock, Vt.

This dish is quick and good if made with frozen puréed spinach.

1 pound puréed spinach	butter
1 can celery soup	paprika
1 medium onion	white pepper
1 pint oysters, chopped or whole	seasoned breadcrumbs

Thaw 2 packages of frozen spinach and place in the bottom of a buttered casserole. Sauté the onion, sliced, in butter and distribute over the spinach. Arrange the oysters on the casserole, mix their liquor with the soup and pour over. Top with a sprinkling of paprika and white pepper, a thick crust of seasoned breadcrumbs and dot with more butter. Bake for 20 to 25 minutes at 350°.

Serves 4

BAKED SCALLOPS

1 quart scallops
1 cup breadcrumbs
2 tablespoons grated cheese

1 cup cream sauce (p. 245)—
  add mushrooms if desired
salt and pepper

Wash the scallops, cover them with cold water and heat slowly to the boiling point. Line a buttered baking dish with alternate layers of crumbs and scallops; sprinkle each with salt and pepper. Add the sauce, sprinkle with breadcrumbs and cheese, and bake for 30 minutes at 375°.

Serves 4

SEAFOOD IN SHERRY AND CREAM

This is a very good recipe and very useful. You can vary it in many ways. It is best prepared well ahead of time. Festive but not too expensive, it is easy to make. If you want twice as much just use a larger pot and double everything. Serve this dish hot over plain white rice, over patty shells, or over halved baking powder biscuits as a shortcake. It may be put in a buttered baking dish and browned in the oven with a topping of grated cheese, buttered breadcrumbs, or sliced almonds. Curry powder or chopped dill weed added to the dish are good, too. Other ingredients —lobster, shrimp, halibut, scallops, or mushrooms—may be added or substituted. Or mix with rice and bake the whole as a sort of pilaf.

1/2 pound lump crabmeat,
  fresh or frozen
1/2 pound fillet of sole
1/2 pound haddock
4 tablespoons butter
1/2 cup cream
1/2 cup milk
2 tablespoons flour

juice of half a lemon
1/2 teaspoon salt
1/2 teaspoon paprika
several dashes Tabasco sauce
6 oysters, cut in halves
1/2 cup sherry
1 egg yolk
3 whole scallions, chopped fine

Melt the butter in a good-sized saucepan and add the crabmeat, the fish cut in pieces, and the scallions. Cook gently until the fish starts to turn white. Add the cream and milk and the flour and continue cooking over low heat, stirring, until the sauce is thick. Add the oysters, the remaining seasoning, the egg yolk and wine.

Serves 6

BRAUMEISTER SHRIMP

An unusual recipe from a group of Bostonians devoted to good food who meet weekly in Louisburg Square for the "Beacon Hill Wednesday Night Buffet."

3 pounds jumbo shrimp
6 bay leaves
3 stalks celery, chopped
5 sprigs parsley
1/2 tablespoon dried basil or tarragon

1 and 1/2 medium onions, chopped
3 cloves garlic, split
1 and 1/2 tablespoons salt
9 cloves
18 peppercorns
beer to cover

Wash the shrimp, put them in a pot with all the other ingredients above and cover with beer. Boil gently, covered, until the shrimp are pink—15-20 minutes. Cool in the stock, then shell and devein the shrimp. (This can all be done the day before you plan to serve the dish.)

3/4 cup butter
3/4 tablespoon anchovy paste
3 cups scalded heavy cream

1 pound bacon, fried crisp and crumbled
parsley
French bread

Work the butter smooth with the anchovy paste, put in a pan with the shrimp and sauté gently until golden brown, stirring at intervals. Add the cream and stir once more. Serve steaming on thick slices of French bread garnished with bacon crumbs and fine-snipped parsley.

Serves 6

"BOYS"

A curry traditionally is accompanied by a great number of side dishes or condiments. These are called "boys" because in India (ah, me), a different boy was on hand to pass each one. Among the possibilities are the following.

Major Grey's chutney
ginger marmalade
grated coconut
chopped toasted peanuts
chopped hardcooked egg whites
chopped hardcooked egg yolks
chopped sweet onion
chopped green pepper

cucumbers in yoghurt (very cold)
sautéed bananas, hot
crumbled crisp bacon
grated orange rind
candied kumquats
Bombay Duck (available in specialty food stores)
chopped candied pineapple

SHRIMP CURRY

This is a great production, interesting to prepare and dramatic to serve. It is easy, but does take a good deal of time.

3 pounds shrimp
shrimp mix (a blend of herbs packaged especially for this purpose)
2 tablespoons butter
3 onions, chopped
2 apples, peeled, cored, and chopped

1/2 cup raisins, cut in half
curry powder (p. 147) to taste
2 cloves mashed garlic (optional)
4 tablespoons Major Grey's mango chutney
1 quart chicken stock
coconut milk when available
flour if necessary

Sauté the onions, apples, and raisins in the butter until soft. Blend in the chutney. Add the chicken stock. If coconut milk is available, reduce the amount of stock accordingly. Add curry powder and garlic and simmer the sauce, covered, for an hour or more, stirring from time to time. Meantime, peel the shrimp and cook them in butter to which a little shrimp mix has been added. If the sauce is too thin, add a very little flour and cook a bit longer. The sauce is, however, supposed to be a thin one; the vegetables alone are the thickening of a real Indian curry. Add the shrimp and let them sit in the sauce for several hours. Taste again for seasoning, heat, and serve on steaming hot white rice.

Serves 6

LOBSTER, CHICKEN, OR LAMB CURRY

These curries are all made with the same basic sauce as Shrimp Curry, substituting diced lobster, chicken, or lamb for the shrimp, and omitting the shrimp mix.

CURRY POWDER

There are many good curry powders on the market. They vary considerably in flavor, so in choosing one, it is a good idea to sniff it first to make sure it is what you like. Many people like to make their own. It is an interesting procedure. The following combination makes a nice curry but vary the ingredients as you like!

8 pods cardamom (remove seeds from pods and grind)
1 and 1/2 teaspoons ground ginger
1 and 1/2 teaspoons ground turmeric

1/2 teaspoon ground jeera (cumin seed)
1/2 teaspoon ground coriander
1/2 teaspoon cinnamon
1/2 teaspoon nutmeg

Chapter 7.
Poultry & Game

POULTRY

From earliest memory birds have been used for "best" occasions. Chicken every Sunday, creamed chicken for children's birthday parties, chicken salad for Church Supper, turkey for Thanksgiving, goose for Christmas if you are lucky, and ducks and pheasants and squabs for special feasts. These attitudes have hardly been changed by the passage of time, but it is a happy fact that due to the skill of the poultry industry the old, old promise of a chicken in every pot has very nearly become a reality.

ROAST CHICKEN

Choose a plump (4 or 5 pounds) bird. Wash and dry it inside and out and rub well with salt, white pepper, paprika and butter. Herb stuffing, wild rice stuffing, black walnut and white grape stuffing, cornbread stuffing are all excellent with chicken. Truss the bird, place a piece of aluminum foil lightly over it and roast, breast-side up, until tender, about 3 hours in a 325° oven. Remove the foil for the last half hour of roasting. Remove the bird and keep it warm while making a gravy. It will be easier to carve if it rests for 20 minutes or so.

PAN GRAVY FOR CHICKEN, TURKEY, AND OTHER BIRDS

Remove the bird to a warm platter in a warm place. If there is a great deal of fat in the pan, pour part of it off before adding the flour (use 1-2 tablespoons flour to every 3 tablespoons fat). Brown the flour-fat mixture for a minute or so, stirring constantly, then add, a little at a time, boiling chicken stock (and chopped, cooked giblets, if you like them), still stirring. Continue cooking and stirring until the gravy is thick and brown. Add stock, salt, and Kitchen Bouquet as needed. A glass of white wine improves chicken gravy, and a glass of red does much for turkey gravy.

BAKED CHICKEN TARRAGON

3 chicken breasts, halved
flour
salt and pepper
dried tarragon

butter
lemon slices
white wine

Clean and dry the six pieces of chicken. Dredge them in flour seasoned with the salt and pepper. Arrange the pieces in a baking dish (a big Pyrex pie plate is the right size), and shake tarragon over them. Place 1 tablespoon butter on each piece and cook in a hot (400°) oven until nicely browned—about 30 minutes. Remove from the oven, and pour wine over the chicken; baste well with the resulting juices, and place a thin slice of lemon on each piece of chicken. Return to a 300° oven for an additional 10 minutes. Wild rice is good with this.

Serves 4-6

There are a number of attractive ways to vary this easy dish, each with its own special flair.

BAKED CHICKEN WITH PEACHES

As above, but place a clingstone peach half on each chicken piece and add a little peach juice to the dish.

BAKED BREAST OF CHICKEN IN BING CHERRY SAUCE

When the chicken is cooked, remove pieces to a hot platter. Add a 1-pound can of bing cherries, a dash of cognac, and 2 tablespoons cornstarch to the pan. Stir over low heat until thickened to make a delicious sauce.

CHICKEN BREASTS WITH MUSHROOMS AND HAM

Put a large, buttered mushroom cap on each piece for the last 10 minutes of cooking, and place a piece of ham beneath each portion.

CHICKEN PROSCIUTTO

3 chicken breasts, halved, boned, and pounded flat
6 slices Prosciutto or country ham
salt and pepper

6 slices Provolone cheese
butter
cream sauce (see p. 245)
1/2 cup grated Parmesan cheese

With chicken sections flesh-side up, place a slice of Provolone cheese, a slice of ham, and a pat of butter on each section. Roll chicken together tightly and fasten with a toothpick. Place, toothpick up, in broiler and cook at 350° for 45 minutes or until tender. Meanwhile, make the cream sauce, and stir in the Parmesan cheese. When chicken is ready, arrange pieces on a platter and pour the sauce over them. Guests should beware lest the first prick of the fork cause a butter volcano. Else, a delicious dish!

Serves 4-6

CHICKEN IN
OYSTER AND CHAMPAGNE SAUCE

An elegant party dish made with the finest ingredients that still costs less than a dollar a serving!

4 whole chicken breasts, halved
1 and 3/4 cups water
2 teaspoons salt
8 white peppercorns

1/2 teaspoon dried tarragon
1/2 bay leaf
1/2 lemon, sliced
1 stalk celery, cut up

Simmer the chicken breasts in water with the other ingredients until tender—about 35 minutes. Remove the chicken from the stock and allow to cool. When cool, skin and bone the breasts. Cover and keep warm. Strain the stock. Make the sauce (see below). To serve, arrange the warm chicken on a hot platter, surround with fluffy rice, and pour the sauce over the chicken.

Serves 8

OYSTER AND CHAMPAGNE SAUCE

1/2 cup butter
1/3 cup flour
1 and 1/2 cups chicken stock
1 half-bottle champagne
1 pint oysters, picked over

1 pound mushroom caps,
  sliced and cooked in 2
  tablespoons butter
1/2 cup heavy cream
2 egg yolks
1 tablespoon salad oil

Melt the half cup of butter and stir in the flour; add the chicken stock and stir until thick. Add the champagne and simmer very gently until thick and reduced in volume by about a half—approximately 30 minutes. Add the mushrooms and oysters to the sauce and cook 5 minutes. Beat the egg yolks, salad oil, and cream together and stir into the sauce.

CHICKEN PIQUANT

3/4 cup rosé wine
1/4 cup soy sauce
1/4 cup salad oil
2 tablespoons water
1 clove garlic, sliced

1 teaspoon ginger
1/4 teaspoon oregano
1 tablespoon brown sugar
3 chicken breasts, halved

Combine wine with soy sauce, oil, water, garlic, oregano, and brown sugar. Arrange chicken breast sections in baking dish, and pour the wine over them. Cover and bake at 375° about an hour, or until tender. Serve over rice.

Serves 4-6

VEAL-FILLED CHICKEN BREASTS

4 chicken breasts, boned,
  skinned, and halved
1/2 pound ground veal
1/4 pound mushrooms, sliced
4 tablespoons butter
2 eggs, beaten separately

1-2 cloves garlic, crushed
1 tablespoon chopped parsley
salt and pepper to taste
1/2 cup flour
1/2 cup breadcrumbs
1 cup chicken stock

Sauté the veal and mushrooms in 2 tablespoons butter, remove the mixture to a bowl, and add one of the beaten eggs, the garlic, parsley, salt and pepper. Lay the chicken breasts flat, pound them thin with a rolling pin or other blunt instrument, and stuff each piece with some of the veal mixture. Fold them up securely and fasten the rolled breasts with toothpicks. Dip each piece first in the remaining egg, then in flour, then the breadcrumbs. Refrigerate the breaded breasts for at least an hour (this helps to keep the breading on when they are fried). Heat the remaining 2 tablespoons of butter, then fry the breasts over medium heat until well-browned all over. Cover the skillet when they are brown and cook a little longer. When done, remove to a hot platter and remove the toothpicks. Rinse the pan with the broth, scraping it, and pour sauce over the chicken.

Serves 8

BROILERS WITH OYSTER STUFFING

2 broilers, split
1 medium onion
butter
1 cup breadcrumbs
parsley, chopped

tarragon, fresh or dried
lemon juice
1/2 pint oysters and their liquor
salt and pepper

Wash and dry the chickens and season them with salt and pepper. Rub the skin all over with butter. Mince the onion and cook it briefly in butter. Add to the breadcrumbs and season with the other ingredients (except oysters). Cut the oysters in two and then add them and their liquor to the mixture. Spread the stuffing on the inner side of each piece of chicken. Lay the pieces on a rack in the center of the oven, preheated to 400°. Put a large pan in the bottom of the oven to catch the drippings and keep the stove clean. Cook the chicken for 10 minutes, then reduce the heat to 350° and cook for 20 minutes longer. Brush the surface with a little butter and serve.

Serves 4

SOUR CREAM CHICKEN

An easy way to cook moist, perfect chicken.

broilers or fryers, cut in quarters   pepper
salt   sour cream

Put chicken in baking pan skin side up. Season with salt and pepper.
Cover with sour cream. Bake at 350° for one hour.

CHARCOAL-BROILED CHICKEN WITH GARLIC AND HERBS

This barbecue specialty can be prepared equally well using the broiler
and the oven.

2 broilers (2 and 1/2 to 3 and   1 teaspoon chopped fresh
   1/2 pounds each), quartered   tarragon, or 1/2 teaspoon
juice of 2 lemons   dried tarragon
2 teaspoons salt   1 teaspoon chopped fresh parsley
1 teaspoon coarsely ground   (1/2 teaspoon if parsley is dried)
   black pepper   4 cloves garlic, mashed
                                         1 and 1/2 cups salad or olive oil

Stir the seasonings into the lemon juice, and then add the oil, slowly
and stirring constantly to make a thick sauce. Wash and dry the chicken
pieces and place them close together in a shallow pan. Spoon the marinade over them and allow to stand, basting occasionally, until ready to
grill. Grill the chicken over a charcoal fire, basting with the marinade
as it cooks. Meanwhile, slice a loaf of French or Italian bread diagonally to make rather long slices. Spread the slices with the following
mixture.

1/2 cup butter   1 tablespoon mixed herbs (basil
1 clove garlic, crushed   and parsley are good)

Heat the slices near the edge of the fire until hot and partially toasted.
When the chicken is done, serve on the bread (this way, none of the
juice is lost).

Serves 6

NORTHERN FRIED CHICKEN

This recipe produces a very crisp fried chicken that can be successfully reheated.

2 frying chickens, cut up
   (4 drumsticks, 4 second joints,
   4 wings, 4 breast pieces, 4 back
   pieces — use a cleaver)
cooking oil
2 eggs, beaten

pinch of powdered garlic
   or tarragon
salt
pepper
2 cups flour

Wash and dry the chicken pieces. Pour flour into a paper bag, and season with salt and pepper and garlic or tarragon. Beat eggs in bowl. Shake chicken pieces separately in paper bag, dip into egg, and then shake again in flour (replenish egg and flour mixtures if necessary). Meanwhile, heat 4 inches of oil in a heavy pot or Dutch oven. When oil is hot enough to brown a bread cube instantly (350-370°), put in chicken pieces, one or two at a time. Cook until golden brown on all sides, turning once (8-10 minutes). Line baking tin with paper toweling. Place chicken pieces as they are browned on paper toweling, not touching each other. When all pieces have been browned and placed on the tin, bake in an oven preheated to 250° for 1 and 1/2 hours, or until done. To reheat, place pieces in a paper bag and heat through in a low (200°) oven.

Serves 6-8

HONEY-JUICED CHICKEN

1 broiler-fryer, cut in
   serving pieces
1 cup pancake mix
1 teaspoon salt
1/2 teaspoon pepper

1/4 cup shortening
   or salad oil
1/2 cup honey
3/4 cup orange juice
1 orange, peeled and sliced
parsley

Coat chicken pieces in mixture of dry ingredients. In frying pan, shortening ready, brown chicken pieces. This will take 20-30 minutes. Pour the honey and orange juice, mixed, over the chicken. Cook covered at low heat for 45 minutes. Serve, garnished with warm orange slices and parsley.

Serves 2-4

YANKEE *is indebted to Hope J. Heath of Edgartown, Massachusetts, for this recipe, which goes back to the earliest days of our history. It was given to Mrs. Heath by her grandmother, Susan Duke Jones, who had it from her grandmother. The original recipe called for squirrel, but as wild game became scarce, chicken was substituted.*

"Grandmother Jones was raised by her grandparents, Alexander and Evalina Garrett, on their plantation, Oak Hill, outside Charlottesville, Virginia. Evalina was a fourth generation descendant of Pocahontas and John Rolfe. She and her husband are buried in Thomas Jefferson's private cemetery at Monticello.

"Oak Hill was noted for its hospitality. I was fascinated by my grandmother's tales of plantation happenings, ante-bellum customs, parties, visiting neighboring country places and, in return, being visited by friends and relations from all over the state. Sometimes whole families would arrive unexpectedly, confident of their welcome, by carriage or on horseback, to stay for several days, or weeks, or even longer. The problems of a plantation hostess were not acute. Oak Hill was largely self-sustaining. A smokehouse full of hams and bacon, a poultry yard and dairy, gardens and orchards, a mill for grinding corn meal yielded the necessities and some of the luxuries. Only salt, sugar, wheat flour, and wines were imported. Servants were plentiful, so Alexander and Evalina were free to entertain their guests with country pastimes: riding, picnicking, boating on the Rivanna, visiting friends, soirées with music and dancing. There was foxhunting, too, and a favorite main dish for the hunt breakfast was Brunswick Stew."

BRUNSWICK STEW

3 slices bacon
a 5-pound chicken cut up as for
　frying
corn cut from the cobs of 3
　large ears
2 cups fresh lima beans

3 large, ripe tomatoes, skinned
　and cut up
2 teaspoons salt
1 teaspoon sugar
pepper to taste
2 cups chicken stock

Cut the bacon in small pieces and try out in a large skillet. Remove the bacon, and brown the chicken pieces well in the fat. Place the chicken, the fat, and all the other ingredients with the bacon on top in an ovenproof casserole. Cover it and cook for an hour in a 325° oven.

Serves 4-6

ORANGE-ALMOND CHICKEN

Mrs. Nathaniel Underdown
Peterborough, N.H.

1 frying chicken (about 3 and 1/2
   pounds), cut up
1 teaspoon salt
1/4 teaspoon pepper
1 teaspoon paprika

1/3 cup butter
1 cup orange juice
2/3 cup slivered almonds,
   toasted

Wash the chicken and pat it dry. Combine salt, pepper, and paprika. Rub into the chicken until thoroughly coated. Melt butter in a large frying pan with a cover. Sauté the chicken pieces until golden brown on both sides. Cover the frying pan, reduce heat, and cook for 25-30 minutes until the chicken is tender. Remove the chicken to a warm platter and keep it hot in a warm oven. Pour the orange juice into the frying pan. Stir to loosen all the browned particles. Cook over high heat until it is reduced by half. Pour over the chicken. Sprinkle with the toasted almond slivers and serve at once. If you prefer a thicker gravy, blend 1 teaspoon of cornstarch with an equal amount of water; stir into the reduced orange juice and cook until thickened.

Serves 4

CHICKEN PINAFORE

This recipe which was contributed to YANKEE *by Mrs. Catherine T. Smith of Brunswick, Maine, was handed down, she tells us, through the family of General Joshua L. Chamberlain, the hero of Little Round Top at Gettysburg and one of Maine's great men. He was with General Grant when General Lee offered his sword at Appomattox and later served as Governor of Maine and President of Bowdoin College. As becomes a true Brunswick man, he sailed his own yacht,* Pinafore, *which gave her name to this recipe. This is the original version. (Mrs. Smith adds that in the early part of the century, shredded wheat was used in many ways. "It was coarser then and more tasty.")*

Simmer a large meaty fowl for 2 to 2 and 1/2 hours or until done, in a large kettle, the bird covered with water. Put in 1 large onion or several small ones, 2 bay leaves, a handful of celery leaves, and 1 tablespoon salt. Cook steadily until a little less than 1/2 the water remains. Remove carefully from kettle and place on platter, surrounded by 6 or 8 large cakes of shredded wheat, previously heated in a hot oven for a few minutes. Thicken the broth to a medium consistency and serve at table to be carved by the man of the house.

Serves 6

FRICASSEE OF CHICKEN

It is hard to improve upon this old New England favorite, most flavorful if cooked the day before using and left to blend overnight. Correct the sauce next day if necessary, adding Worcestershire sauce, herbs, or lemon juice, at your discretion. Serve the fricassee on a hot platter over baking powder biscuits, or surrounded with fluffy white rice or dumplings. A simple vegetable, carrots or green peas cooked with small onions, and currant jelly are, I think, the most appropriate accompaniment.

2 plump chickens cut for
   fricassee (8 pieces each)
water to cover (about 1 quart)
2 tablespoons salt
16 white peppercorns
1 teaspoon dried tarragon

1 bay leaf
1 lemon, sliced
2 stalks celery, sliced
1 onion, sliced
1 carrot sliced

Simmer the chicken in the water with the above ingredients until tender, about 35 minutes. Remove the chicken from the stock and when cool skin the chicken if you wish (this is not necessary). Strain the stock. Make a sauce with the following ingredients:

1/2 cup butter
1/3 cup flour
3 cups chicken stock

1 pound mushrooms (optional),
   sliced and cooked in 2
   tablespoons butter
1/2 cup heavy cream
2 egg yolks

Melt the butter and stir in the flour; add the chicken stock and stir until thick. Simmer very gently until thick and reduced in volume by about a half, approximately 45 minutes. Add the mushrooms. Beat together the egg yolks and the cream and stir into the sauce. Pour over the chicken.

Serves 8

STEAMED CHICKEN WITH CREAM

a 3-to-4 pound chicken, whole
4 chicken livers
1/2 lemon
salt and pepper
2 cloves
1 stalk celery, chopped

1/2 cup water
1/2 cup dry white wine
1 cup cream
2-3 egg yolks
capers

Skin the chicken, but cook the skin along with it to flavor the sauce. Rub the chicken with the lemon, salt, pepper and place it in a Dutch oven with the cloves, celery, water, and wine. Cook until done, adding more water if needed. This should take about an hour in a 350° oven or over a moderate heat on top of the stove. There should be at least a half cup of broth (stock) left after cooking. Remove the chicken to a hot platter and strain the broth. Add to it the cream. Heat them together, then take from the heat and stir in the egg yolks. Stir until thick, adding some capers. Pour the sauce over the bird and garnish the platter with triangles of toast fried in butter. Place a sautéed chicken liver on each triangle. Garnish the dish with watercress.

Serves 4

MAINE CHICKEN STEW

Prepare this ahead of time; reheat for serving.

2 chickens, 3 and 1/2 to 4 pounds, cut for stewing
6 potatoes, sliced
3 onions, sliced
cold water

2 tablespoons butter
1 cup thin cream
salt and pepper
minced fresh parsley
6-8 common crackers

In an iron kettle, place alternate layers of chicken, sliced potatoes and onions. Cover with cold water and simmer gently until the chicken is tender (45-60 minutes). Add the butter in small bits and cream or milk. Season with salt and pepper and minced parsley. Split the common crackers, moisten in cold milk, and heat in the stew.

Serves 8

PHILADELPHIA MIXED GRILL

Follow the directions for Mixed Grill (p. 194), using quartered chickens instead of lamb chops. Browned chicken livers may be added to the dish.

YANKEE CHICKEN HASH

3 cups coarsely chopped chicken
1 and 1/2 cups cooked sausage
  meat
3/4 cup chopped green pepper
3/4 cup chopped onion
2 and 1/2 tablespoons chopped
  parsley

1 tablespoon chopped chives
1/2 cup coarse bread crumbs
1/2 teaspoon grated lemon rind
1/2 cup rich cream sauce
  (see p.245)
salt and pepper
4 tablespoons butter

Mix the chicken, sausage meat, green pepper, onion, parsley, chives in a large bowl and chop until fine. Stir in the bread crumbs, lemon rind, cream sauce. Heat butter in a heavy skillet and spread the hash evenly. Cook gently over low heat until the bottom is brown and crusty. Fold in half and slide on to a hot platter.

Serves 6

JELLIED CHICKEN PATE

Prepared ahead of time and chilled, this pâté makes an excellent luncheon or buffet dish sliced thick and served on lettuce leaves or other greens. A small slice is pleasant as a first course, or the pâté may be used in sandwiches. Serve it with Dijon mustard.

1 breast of chicken
water to cover, about 2 and 1/2
  cups
1 teaspoon salt
6-8 white peppercorns

1 bay leaf
1 slice onion
half a lemon, sliced

Cook the chicken breast in water with the seasonings over low heat for 20-30 minutes, or until done. Cool the chicken, skin it, and remove the bones. Reserve the stock. Separate the chicken into several parts.

3/4 pound ground veal
3/4 pound ground pork
1 teaspoon salt
3/4 teaspoon tarragon leaves
1/2 teaspoon ground coriander
  seed

1/2 cup almonds, slivered
  (or pistachio nuts)
2 eggs
2 slices white bread, crumbled
1 cup chicken stock
1 envelope gelatin

Combine the first eight ingredients and mix them well. Place a layer of the pâté in a loaf pan, and arrange the pieces of chicken breast evenly on it. Fill the pan with the rest of the pâté mixture and bake in a larger pan of water in a 350° oven, covered for the first 15 minutes, then uncovered for 40-50 minutes in all, until done. Remove from the oven and cool, with a weight (a brick, or a smaller, weighted pan) on top of the loaf. Chill. Remove the loaf from the pan, scrape off any fat, wash the pan, and fill it with 1 cup chicken stock (left from cooking the chicken), mixed with the gelatin. If you wish, arrange fresh herbs in an ornamental design in the gelatin. Return the loaf to the pan and refrigerate until the gelatin has set. Unmold and serve.

ROAST DUCKLING

Duckling should be cooked a long time in order to melt the thick layer of fat that is beneath the skin away completely, leaving the skin very, very crisp with no fat at all left between it and the meat. Rub the duck well inside and out with salt and pepper, adding, if you wish, garlic and lemon juice. Cook it on a rack in an oven preheated to 350° for 2 and 1/2 hours, depending on size. A stuffed duck will take longer than an unstuffed one. Prick the skin before roasting the duck to allow the fat to drain. When the duck is nearly done, take it from the oven and remove all the fat you can from the pan. Baste with its juices and any marinade that you may wish to use. Duck is delicious but wasteful. A 3 to 3 and 1/2 pound duck serves two generously. A larger duck *can* be carved to serve four.

ROAST LONG ISLAND DUCKLING

Mrs. Thomas Quick
Wilmington, Del.

An unusual and interesting way of cooking duck.

1 Long Island duckling	1/4 cup honey
salt	1/4 cup orange juice
1 teaspoon curry powder	1/4 cup lemon juice
1 clove garlic, chopped	1 teaspoon curry powder
1/4 teaspoon Tabasco sauce	kumquats
1 teaspoon turmeric	

Rub the duck inside and out with salt, curry, garlic, Tabasco, and turmeric. Stuff with rice stuffing (p. 166). Roast at 325° for 2 and 1/2 to 3 hours. When the duck is nearly done, skim the fat from the juices and for the last half hour of cooking baste with honey, orange and lemon juices and curry powder, mixed. Serve the duck quartered. Pour the pan juices over it and garnish with kumquats and parsley.

ROAST DUCK WITH BIGARADE SAUCE

Roast the duck according to the rule on p. 160. A generous rubbing of garlic and lemon juice adds greatly to this recipe.

1 glass currant jelly	1 jigger Madeira
4 oranges	1/2 jigger Cointreau
2 lemons	2 teaspoons cornstarch
1 jigger brandy	

Remove the colored rind from the oranges with a vegetable peeler and with a sharp knife cut the peel into long hair-thin strips. Cut all the pith away from the oranges and separate three oranges into sections, discarding membranes and seeds. Leave the fourth orange whole and place in cavity of bird. Reserve any juice that drops, and add it with the juice of the lemons to the currant jelly in a saucepan. When the duck is done, add the juices from the pan, having first skimmed them, the liquor and the cornstarch, and cook, stirring until reduced. A bouillon cube and a little water may be added if more liquid is desirable. Add the orange sections for the last minute of cooking. Pour over the duck.

ROAST DUCK WITH BING CHERRY SAUCE

Roast the duck according to the recipe (p. 160). Do not use garlic. When it is crisp and brown, remove it to a hot platter. To the skimmed juices in the pan, add a 1-pound can of bing cherries and their juices, 2 teaspoons cornstarch, and brandy or cherry cordial to taste. Stir until thick and smooth. This makes enough sauce for one large duck.

BROILED DUCKLING

Very simple and very good.

1 small duck	butter
salt and pepper	flour
ginger	

Split a small duck. If it is a domestic duck, trim off extra fat. Rub the skin with flour and a little ginger. Let stand a couple of hours. Salt and pepper and then broil as you would a chicken. Broil slowly and baste with a little butter now and then.

Serves 2

ROAST GOOSE

The finest possible fare for Christmas dinner.

Choose a young goose of 8-10 pounds, allowing 1 and 1/4 pounds per person. Wash and dry the goose. If you have any doubts as to the youth and tenderness of your bird, it is wise to parboil it in water for an hour before roasting. Turn the goose once if this is required.

Dry the goose and rub the skin with salt and pepper, and, if desired, a clove of garlic. Fill the cavity loosely with stuffing (see section on Stuffings at the end of this chapter), and fasten with skewers or string. Prick the skin well to let the fat run off. Place the bird on a rack in a roasting pan; if you have no rack, prop the goose on two wooden spoons to prevent its sticking to the pan. Put it in a 450° oven for 20-25 minutes to brown, then pour off the fat and reduce the heat to 300°. Pour a cup of hot cider or wine over the bird and cook uncovered, allowing 20 minutes per pound for the total roasting time.

Serve the bird on a large platter garnished with glazed fruit, crabapples, spiced pears or stuffed prunes, with bunches of parsley or watercress.

PIGEON PIE

Either squabs or game hens may be used.

6 pigeons	2 cups chicken stock
6 strips bacon	1 teaspoon Kitchen Bouquet
1 tablespoon butter	pepper and salt
1 and 1/2 tablespoons flour	3 onions, sliced

Put the pigeons in a baking dish, with the strip of bacon over each. Place them in a hot (500°) oven and bake for 5 minutes. Blend the butter and flour over low heat, then add the stock, Kitchen Bouquet, and seasoning and stir until smooth. Add the pigeons and the onions. Let simmer for one hour over very low heat. Then put the pigeons and sauce in a pie dish, cover with a pastry crust (see p. 277), and bake at 500° for about 12 minutes.

Serves 6

ROAST TURKEY

Wash the turkey in cold running water. Pat the inside dry with paper toweling; leave the outside moist. Stuff the turkey and push the drumsticks under the band of skin at the tail or tie them to the tail. Rub the bird with salt, white pepper, and paprika, spread it generously with butter, and place slices of fat salt pork over the breast. Preheat the oven to 325°.

Place the turkey breast side up on a rack in a roasting pan. Cover it with a piece of cheesecloth moistened in butter or a loose tent of aluminum foil. Baste once or twice during roasting period with the fat and drippings in the pan. Remove the cloth or foil for the last half hour of cooking. The turkey is done when the drumstick yields readily when pushed up and down. A meat thermometer should register 185°.

Timetable for Roasting Stuffed Turkey

Weight	Time
6 to 8 pounds	3 to 3 and 1/2 hours
8 to 12 pounds	3 and 1/2 to 4 hours
12 to 16 pounds	4 to 5 hours
16 to 20 pounds	5 to 6 hours
20 to 24 pounds	6 to 6 and 1/2 hours

Remove the turkey from the oven and let it stand on a hot platter about 20 minutes before carving.

BROILED SQUAB TURKEY

1 young 6-pound turkey   butter
salt and pepper

Have the backbone removed from the turkey, slit the bird and crack the leg joints. Pin the legs down with skewers to keep them in place until the bird is partly cooked. Season well with salt and pepper, rub well with butter, and place the split bird skin-side down on a broiler rack about 3 inches from the heat. Broil under moderate heat for 45-60 minutes, turning as needed and adding more butter if the skin becomes dry. Turn skin side up when partially cooked. This turkey is excellent served with wild rice and sautéed mushrooms. The breasts may be sliced into 6 slices each; cut the leg portions as desired.

Serves 6-8

POULTRY STUFFINGS

A good stuffing not only enhances the taste appeal of a roasted fowl, but also improves its appearance, as a stuffed bird looks plump and pleasant on the platter. These days, anyone can make a good *regular* stuffing from the packaged mixes found on the shelves of every supermarket. Here you'll find some delectable traditional stuffings. In the event that you use commercial packaged breadcrumbs in these recipes, read the label carefully, as they usually are preseasoned, and you'll have to adjust the seasoning accordingly.

CHESTNUT STUFFING

Mrs. L. M. Kaul
Newtown, Conn.

Recommended for turkey, chicken, or goose, the recipe makes sufficient to stuff a 15-18 pound bird.

1 pound chestnuts, coarsely chopped	2 tablespoons chopped parsley
1/4 pound salt pork	1 teaspoon poultry seasoning
1 onion, chopped	6 cups breadcrumbs
2 stalks celery, minced	1/2 cup melted butter
	2 eggs, beaten

Cook pork in frying pan until brown. Add onions and celery and simmer for 5 minutes. Pour over the rest of the ingredients. Mix well, and stuff lightly into the bird.

CORNBREAD STUFFING

This quantity will stuff a 15-18 pound turkey. Cornbread stuffing is good for chicken too.

3 cups stale cornbread, crumbled	1 bay leaf, crumbled
3 cups stale white bread, crumbled	1 teaspoon dried thyme
1/2 pound butter	1 teaspoon dried sage
2 onions, chopped	2 cloves garlic, crushed
3 stalks celery, chopped	salt and black pepper to taste
1 apple, cored, peeled, and chopped	giblets of the bird (*or* 1/2 pound sausage meat)
3 sprigs parsley, minced	

Crumble the breads into a large bowl. Chop the giblets (or take the sausage meat) and cook with the vegetables in part of the butter until lightly browned. Melt the rest of the butter and add, with the vegetables, apple, herbs, and seasonings, to the bread. Stir to blend well and stuff into the bird just before roasting.

HERB STUFFING

4 cups dry white breadcrumbs
1/2 cup melted butter
1/2 onion, minced
1 stalk celery, minced
1/4 cup parsley, minced

1/4 cup watercress, minced
1/2 teaspoon dried tarragon
a pinch of dried thyme or marjoram
1/2 teaspoon salt
white pepper

Mix together lightly with a fork and stuff the bird.

4 cups

ROAST GOOSE STUFFING

This stuffing is better prepared the day before use, to give the flavors a chance to blend.

1 pound sausage meat
2 cups stale breadcrumbs
1 large onion, chopped
2 stalks celery, chopped
1/2 cup dried apricots, 1/2 cup
   prunes, soaked in cider or wine
   and cut up
1 cup nuts, chestnuts or pecans,
   cut up

3 apples, cored, peeled,
   and diced
seasoning to taste:
   salt and pepper
   sage
   bay leaf, crumbled
   chopped parsley
      (a generous amount)

Cook the sausage meat until lightly browned, remove to a large bowl; cook the onion and celery lightly in the fat. Add to the sausage meat the breadcrumbs, chopped fruits and nuts, and the seasoning. Store in a cool place overnight. Check the stuffing in the morning for taste, and add seasoning if necessary, or a little cider or wine if it is too dry. Stuff lightly in the bird and roast.

WHITE GRAPE, BLACK WALNUT STUFFING

The elusive flavor of the black walnuts and the juicy grapes contribute to a superior stuffing for a chicken, squabs, or Cornish game hens.

1 and 1/2 cups dry breadcrumbs
1/2 small onion, chopped
1 sprig parsley, chopped
1 teaspoon dried tarragon
1 tablespoon sweet butter

1/2 cup seedless white grapes
1/4 cup black walnuts, chopped
1/2 glass white wine
salt and white pepper

Combine and stuff lightly into the bird.

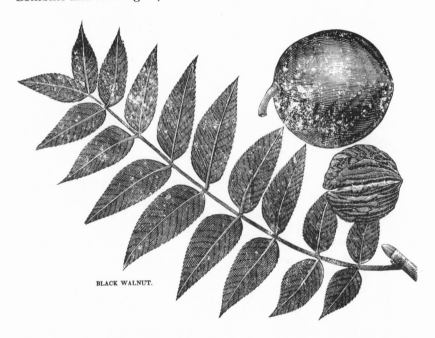

BLACK WALNUT.

WILD RICE STUFFING

*Mrs. Thomas Quick
Wilmington, Del.*

Good for roast duck, chicken, or pheasant.

2 tablespoons butter
3 tablespoons chopped celery
2 cups bread cubes
1 teaspoon salt
pepper
3 tablespoons chopped onion

2 cans mandarin oranges, or
   4 oranges, peeled and sectioned
1 teaspoon poultry seasoning
1 and 1/2 cups cooked wild or
   brown rice

Sauté the celery and onion in the butter. Add the rest of the ingredients, and stuff the duck. Serve with the duck (quartered).

STUFFED WILD DUCK

A 2 and 1/2 pound duck will serve two people well. If the ducks are much smaller, one per person will be necessary.

wild ducks
salt and pepper
lemon juice

apples
applejack
butter or bacon strips

Clean and dry the ducks and sprinkle them inside and out with salt and pepper and lemon juice. Rub the ducks generously with butter, or cover them with strips of bacon. Stuff the birds with quartered apples, tie the legs together and roast them in a 350° oven for about an hour, or until you are satisfied with their doneness, basting with applejack, and pricking the skin. Many people like game rare, in which case ducks need be cooked for only 20 or 30 minutes in a 450° oven.

WILD DUCK WITH MUSHROOMS   *Robert Faxon*
Londonderry, Vt.

Cut your wild duck into pieces, reserving the liver. Brown the pieces in butter. When they are golden, dust them with flour, pour on a glass of very good red wine, one of bouillon, and add some sliced mushrooms. Add salt, pepper, and a spice bag (see p. 92). Cook, covered, over a low flame. A quarter of an hour before serving, add the liver mashed in a little red wine and a spoonful or two of tomato paste; stir the sauce until reduced. Arrange the duck pieces on a hot platter, pour the sauce over them, and surround the platter with croutons of bread fried in butter.

Serves 2-3

WILD DUCK

A Victorian procedure for serving wild duck—a pretty ritual that gives good eating.

When two birds which should have been lightly roasted (*above* , roast wild duck) come to the table, the carver should score the breast three or four times all the way down and sprinkle salt and a little black pepper over it; then he cuts a lemon in two and powders a little cayenne over both halves (half a small teaspoon in all) and squeezes both halves over the birds, adds half a teaspoon of A-1 sauce and a tablespoon of port wine, mixes all with the gravy of the birds, and bastes them well with the sauce before carving.

WILD DUCKS WITH
CARROTS AND OLIVES

Charles J. Wettach
Westminster, Vt.

Mr. Wettach's son-in-law, Ted Williams of baseball fame, supplies the family kitchen with a wide variety of game.

2 large ducks

Clean your ducks and put in them a stuffing made of the following ingredients.

1 tablespoon butter	an equal quantity of
the livers of the ducks	buttered breadcrumbs
2 shallots, chopped	white pepper, salt, and nutmeg
12 black olives sliced	to taste

Brown the livers and cook the shallots (if necessary scallions may be substituted) in the butter. Chop the livers and combine all of the ingredients. Stuff and truss the birds.

2 tablespoons butter	chopped fennel, parsley, and
2 slices of bacon, cut up	thyme, as available
12 small whole onions	1 bay leaf
1 shallot, chopped	1 bunch young carrots
1 clove garlic, crushed	1 cup beef stock
2 tablespoons flour	1 glass cognac
salt and pepper to taste	12 green olives, sliced

Place the butter, bacon, onions, shallot, and garlic in a large casserole and dust them with the flour. Add the salt and pepper and the herbs. Make a bed of sliced carrots and place the ducks upon it. Moisten them with the beef stock and simmer gently with the casserole covered for about an hour and a half. During the last 20 minutes of cooking add the cognac and green olives. Arrange the ducks on a platter surrounded by the carrots and olives. Stir the sauce until thick and smooth and pour it over the birds.

Serves 6

ROAST STUFFED PHEASANTS

This recipe is for two large or three medium-sized pheasants. Lacking pheasants, this interesting stuffing may be used with chicken or capon.

3/4 cup wild rice
1/4 pound chopped mushrooms
1 cup breadcrumbs
1 small can water
  chestnuts (sliced)
1 small can smoked oysters

1 small onion, minced
salt and pepper
fresh or powdered thyme
melted butter
white wine

Soak the wild rice in water for several hours. Drain and combine with the other ingredients, moistening with some melted butter. Stuff the birds, brush with melted butter, truss them, and roast 40-50 minutes at 350°, basting with butter and white wine until done.

Serves 6

PHEASANTS IN CREAM WITH APPLES

2 pheasants, cleaned,
  2 and 1/2 to 3 pounds each
4 tablespoons butter
2 cups tart apples, peeled and
  chopped
1/2 cup, plus 1 tablespoon
  applejack

2 cups heavy cream
1/4 cup lemon juice
salt and freshly ground
  white pepper
1 tablespoon cornstarch

Truss the pheasants and brown them lightly in the butter in a heavy skillet. Remove them and keep warm while you sauté the apples in the remaining butter. Spread the apples in an ovenproof casserole and put the pheasants on top. Add the half cup of applejack to the skillet and stir it over the heat scraping the bottom of the pan. Pour over the birds. Cover the casserole and place it in a 375° oven for 45 minutes. Add the cream, lemon juice, salt, and pepper and cook uncovered for 30 minutes more, basting occasionally, until the birds are tender when pricked with a fork. The drumsticks should move easily. Remove the birds to a hot serving platter. Combine the cornstarch with the remaining tablespoon of applejack and stir this paste into the liquid in the casserole. Cook the sauce on the top of the stove until thick. Strain it over the birds, garnish the platter with bunches of parsley and the birds' plumage, if you have it, and serve with wild rice.

Serves 4

PARTRIDGE IN VINE LEAVES

partridges
salt and pepper
cloves
ginger

lemon juice
bacon strips
vine leaves
red wine

Allow one partridge for each person. Rub the birds with salt, pepper, ground cloves, and ginger, and sprinkle them with lemon juice. Wrap them in strips of bacon and place in a shallow roasting pan. Cover them with grape leaves and bake in a hot (450°) oven for about 20 minutes. Remove the vine leaves and the bacon and return the birds to the oven to brown, having basted them well with red wine. Serve the partridge on a hot platter sprinkled with browned breadcrumbs and surrounded by fresh vine leaves. Make a gravy by browning some mushrooms in butter with the giblets of the birds. Add this, a little cream, and a spoonful of currant jelly to the pan juices.

STUFFED QUAIL WITH OLIVES   *John Davies Stamm*
Walpole, N. H.

6 quail, drawn
1 pound ground meat, beef,
   veal, and sausage
2 large sprigs parsley, chopped

pinch of white pepper
pinch of mustard
2 tablespoons butter

First simmer the quail whole for 1 hour. Combine the ground meats, the parsley and seasonings, and stuff the birds with the mixture. Truss them with string and cook them in a casserole in the butter until they are well browned all over.

2 tablespoons butter
2 slices bacon, chopped
a sprig each of thyme, marjoram,
   and parsley, chopped
salt and pepper to taste

2 tablespoons flour
1 cup beef stock
1/2 cup small green olives, halved
a wine glass of brandy
   or applejack

Place the butter, bacon, herbs, salt and pepper in a casserole, dust them with flour, add stock, and cook covered for an hour in a 375° oven. During the last 20 minutes of cooking, add the olives and the brandy. Arrange the birds on a hot platter surrounded, if you wish, by wild rice. Stir the sauce on top of the stove over low heat until smooth, and pour it over the birds.

Serves 6

QUAIL PIES

These plump little birds make excellent eating, but their flesh is firm and should be parboiled before roasting. Prepared according to this recipe in individual pie dishes, they are easy work for the hostess as the complete meal is contained in the pie.

4 quail	butter
4 carrots, cut in strips and cooked	parsley
1 small can pearl onions	dried tarragon
1 package frozen spinach soufflé	1 recipe flaky piecrust (p. 277)

Parboil the quail gently in salt water for 45 minutes. Defrost the spinach and place a layer on the bottom of each 4 individual baking dishes. Add a few carrots and pearl onions. Brown the quail in butter, breast side up, and place one in each baking dish. Dot with butter, add finely minced parsley and a pinch of tarragon to each dish. Prepare the piecrust, divide it into four parts, and roll out. Cover the pies in such a way as to have the quails' legs protruding slightly through the crust. Ornament the crust with cut-outs, dipped in egg yolk, brush the pies with egg yolk to glaze and bake for 40 to 50 minutes in a 400° oven.

Serves 4

ROCK CORNISH GAME HENS

Culinary Institute of America
New Haven, Conn.

6 Rock Cornish game hens
2 medium carrots
3 stalks celery
10 ounces mushrooms
4 medium shallots
1 small onion
salt and Accent to taste

prepared mustard
flour
chicken stock
red currant jelly
spice bag containing 1/2 teaspoon
    ground fresh oregano, 3 whole
    black peppercorns crushed

Rub the hens with prepared mustard. Mince the vegetables very fine to make what the French call a *mirepoix*. Butter a roasting pan, add the mirepoix to cover the bottom of the pan and place the hens on top of this mixture, and sprinkle with seasonings. Brown them in a hot oven (450°) turning occasionally. When evenly colored, reduce the heat to 350°. Cook breast-side up until tender. When hens are cooked, the leg meat is soft, and the bone will turn with a little pressure. Remove the hens from the pan, add a little flour to the mirepoix and the juice left in the pan to make the roux. Add chicken stock and thicken to the consistency desired. If no chicken stock is available, make some from chicken bouillon cubes. Next add the spice bag and one large tablespoon of good red currant jelly. Allow to simmer 15 minutes, then strain through a fine cheesecloth. Place hens in the sauce in a roasting pan and simmer in a low oven for 10 minutes.   Serves 6

ROAST WOODCOCK

Charles Wettach
Westminster, Vt.

One of these little birds is needed for each serving (only the breasts provide much meat). They are rich, brown, and tender and taste of the seeds and berries of the forests where they live.

Hang the birds for a day or two, then pluck and clean them, reserving the livers. Stuff the birds with pared apples, rub them with butter and pepper and wrap each in a strip of bacon. Roast them in a 375° oven, basting occasionally with a little brandy for about 45 minutes. Serve them with wild rice and carrots and the livers, sautéed in butter.

HUNTER'S STEW

A rich, thick and wonderful stew to prepare for the hunter returning proud and hungry from a successful foray. It can be varied according to the game bagged.

2 wild ducks, or a partridge, or a rabbit, cut in serving pieces
1 cup cubed lean ham
2 onions, chopped
1 carrot, diced
1 turnip, diced
1 soup bone, large
butter

1 stalk celery, diced
2-3 tablespoons tomato paste
1 bay leaf
salt and peppercorns
cloves
sherry or Madeira
Worcestershire sauce
parsley, chopped

Brown the fowl or rabbit pieces in butter along with the ham, onions, carrot, and turnip. Add the soup bone from which all fat has been removed and enough water to cover all. Season with the salt, peppercorns, cloves, and bay leaf, and simmer for several hours until the meat is tender. Remove the meat from the pot and simmer the soup for another hour. Remove the soup bone, return the meat to the pot and add the celery. Simmer until the celery is tender, then add Worcestershire sauce, tomato paste, sherry or Madeira (all these to taste), and the chopped parsley. Serve with fried croutons and add a little cooked wild rice if you wish.

Serves 4-6

FRIED RABBIT

Because of its active life, rabbit has very little fat, so use plenty of shortening and baste frequently, or the meat will become dry.

a 2-3 pound rabbit, cut in serving
  pieces
1/2 cup flour

1 and 1/2 teaspoons salt
pepper
butter or shortening

Wash the rabbit pieces and drain but do not dry. Shake them in a paper bag in the flour and seasoning. Put the pieces in 1/4 inch melted butter in a heavy skillet, turning to brown evenly on all sides. Reduce the heat, cover, and cook slowly for 1 hour or until tender. For a crisp crust, uncover for the last 10-15 minutes of cooking.

Serves 4

COUNTRY FRIED RABBIT

Brown rabbit meat according to the above directions. Remove excess fat, and add 2 cups boiling water. Cover and simmer for 1 hour, or until tender, over low heat. Turn the rabbit once.

LAPIN CREAM GRAVY

Serve with rabbit.

For each cup of gravy desired, use 2 tablespoons rabbit drippings, 1 and 1/2 tablespoons flour, and 1 cup milk. Blend drippings and flour thoroughly in the skillet, add milk gradually, and stir until thickened. Add seasoning to taste, herbs, or a little wine. You'll find a few sliced mushrooms a tasty addition.

BAKED RABBIT

a 2-3 pound rabbit, cut in serving
  pieces
6 tablespoons butter
1 and 1/2 cups finely rolled salt
  crackers

1 teaspoon salt
pepper
chopped parsley

Preheat oven to 350°. Dip pieces of rabbit in melted butter, then roll in cracker crumbs to which seasonings have been added. Place pieces in a shallow baking pan, but do not crowd. Cover the pan with a lid or with aluminum foil. Bake for 1 hour or until tender.

Serves 4

HASENPFEFFER

Sauerkraut is good with this.

a 2-3 pound rabbit, cut in serving
   pieces
1 and 1/2 cups cold water
1 and 1/2 cups cider vinegar
1 teaspoon whole cloves
3 bay leaves
2 teaspoons sugar

1 and 1/2 teaspoons salt
pepper
dash of mace
2 medium onions, sliced
1/2 cup flour
butter

Combine the vinegar, water, seasonings and onion and use to marinate
the rabbit pieces in a covered crock in the refrigerator for a day or two.
Remove and drain the rabbit pieces. Coat them with flour and brown
well in 1/4 inch hot butter in a heavy skillet. Remove excess fat and add
marinating liquid. Cover and simmer for 1 hour or until tender. Remove
the rabbit meat to a hot platter and thicken the gravy with flour or with
finely crushed ginger snaps.

Serves 4

VENISON

Your family hunter has brought you home a deer, and now it's up to
you. Venison may be cooked and served in many of the same ways as
beef, with the difference that butter should be used generously in the
cooking, since venison is much leaner than beef. Meat from the older,
larger animals should be tenderized by marinating in cider, red wine, or
the marinade given below. Steaks will need about 6 hours marinating
time, while the less tender parts—such as those used for pot roast or
stew—may require one or two days. All the following recipes were contributed to YANKEE by Mrs. Pearle M. Goodwin of South Ryegate,
Vermont.

VENISON STEAK MARINADE

2 cups Claret wine
8 black peppercorns
2 cups water

1 bay leaf
1 tablespoon whole pickling spice
1 medium onion, chopped

Rub steaks cut one-half inch thick with a clove of garlic, then immerse
them in the marinade mixture for 6 hours. Fry quickly on a smoking
hot griddle. Serve up hot on a warm ironstone platter, dotted with butter and garnished with parsley and mushrooms.

DELICIOUS HEART OF VENISON

1 deer heart	1 bay leaf
5 strips bacon	1/2 teaspoon sweet basil
2 cups tomato juice	5 whole cloves
2 cups water	pinch of cinnamon

Place tomato juice, water, and spices in the bottom of a steamer kettle. Put the heart with bacon strips over it in the top of the steamer. Cover tightly and steam slowly for 3 hours, or until a fork inserted in the meat comes out easily. Chill the heart thoroughly, then slice thin and serve cold. Strain the cooking liquid and use it as a base for Venison Stew.

VENISON STEW

Cube the less choice and tender cuts of meat and sear over in the bottom of a large kettle in which two tablespoons of bacon fat has been melted. After the meat is browned over, add the liquid (stock) from the Heart of Venison recipe. Add tomato juice and water in equal amounts until the meat is covered. Put in a bay leaf, as it is marvelous for toning down the wild taste the meat may have. Add 4 small whole onions, small whole carrots, potatoes, peas, and wax beans. Simmer for one hour, or until the meat and vegetables are tender.

VENISON ROAST

Good only for small, young deer. This recipe is not recommended for larger animals with big antlers, whose meat will be tougher and more gamey.

1 oven roast of venison	1/2 teaspoon onion salt
1 clove garlic	1/2 teaspoon sweet basil
Burgundy wine	melted butter

Rub the roast with garlic, place in covered roasting pan, and cook 30 minutes to the pound in a 375° oven. When the roast is nearly done, baste it three or four times with the wine, then spread it with the melted butter mixed with the onion salt and basil.

OVEN-BRAISED VENISON

Delicious with sautéed mushrooms.

2 pounds cubed venison	1/2 teaspoon black pepper
1 cup flour	1 teaspoon sweet basil
1 teaspoon onion salt	1/2 teaspoon poultry seasoning

Roll the pieces of venison in the seasoned flour obtained by mixing the other ingredients together. Heat iron skillet to hot, and add 1/2 cup bacon fat. Place cubed meat in the skillet and sear well all over. Add 2 cups water and cover the skillet. Finish by baking in a 375° oven for 50 minutes. The liquid will make a medium thick gravy.

You can even use venison to make such old stand-bys as spaghetti sauce and meat loaf. Mrs. Goodwin showed YANKEE how.

VENISON SPAGHETTI SAUCE

1 and 1/2 pounds ground venison	1 can tomatoes
2 tablespoons bacon fat	1 can tomato sauce
1 large onion, chopped	pinch of cinnamon
1/2 cup chopped celery	1/2 teaspoon sweet basil
1/2 green pepper, chopped	1/2 teaspoon oregano
1/2 teaspoon rosemary	1 cup sharp Cheddar cheese

Sauté the meat in the bacon fat. Add the vegetables and simmer until all are tender. Add the tomato sauce and spices. Simmer until all the flavors are well blended. Turn the heat low and melt the cheese into the sauce. Mix well, and turn over cooked spaghetti, served with grated Parmesan cheese.

DEER MEAT LOAF

1 and 1/2 pounds ground venison	1 teaspoon celery seed
1 box seasoned bread cubes (Croutettes)	2 eggs
	1 can tomato sauce
1 onion, chopped	pinch of garlic salt

Mix the ingredients in a large bowl. Shape into a loaf and bake in a greased loaf pan in a 350° oven for one hour. Garnish with parsley sprigs and tomato slices.

VENISON PATE I

This excellent pâté can be made successfully from the less tender portions of the animal. Serve it hot with brown mushroom sauce (p. 246), or cold with bread and butter and a salad.

2 pounds coarsely ground venison
1 onion, minced
2 sprigs parsley, chopped
grated rind of half a lemon
1 egg
1/2 teaspoon mace
salt and freshly grated pepper

4 slices bacon
1 bay leaf
1/2 cup old-fashioned rolled oats
1/3 cup cider
1/2 apple, peeled and chopped
1 crushed clove garlic
1 jigger applejack

Line an ovenproof loaf pan with the bacon strips and place the bay leaf in the pan. Mix the other ingredients together well with a fork or with your hands. Press firmly into the pan and bake in a 375° oven for 45 minutes. If the pâté is to be served hot, use at once. If it is to be kept to serve cold, remove it to a cool place, and put a brick or other heavy weight on top to pack it firmly.

VENISON PATE II

Similar, but made with chestnuts and port wine.

2 pounds ground venison
1 onion, finely chopped
1 cup roasted chestnuts, chopped
1 stalk celery, finely chopped
2 sprigs parsley, finely chopped
1 egg
1/2 teaspoon dried oregano or
   rosemary

3 slices stale whole-wheat bread
1/2 apple, peeled and chopped
2/3 cup port wine
1 crushed clove of garlic
4 slices bacon
1 bay leaf
salt

Line an ovenproof loaf pan with the strips of bacon and place the bay leaf in the pan. Mix the other ingredients together well with a fork or with your hands. Press firmly into the pan and bake in a 375° oven for 45 minutes.

Chapter 8.
Meats

Meat is the mainstay of the meal. Properly all the other dishes are planned around it, and there is a place in menu planning for both fine cuts of meat and humbler ones. The judgment of meat is, however, a professional job, knowledge not easily acquired by an amateur. Choose a butcher whom you trust and respect and seek his advice freely. A lot of the information in this chapter comes from such a man, Harold Larro, the master butcher in Bill Williams' wonderful country store in Walpole, New Hampshire.

ROAST BEEF

A prime standing rib roast of beef is the joint held in the highest esteem by the Anglo-Saxon school of cooking. A two-rib roast weighing around 4-5 pounds will usually serve six people. However, appetites quicken at the sight of a roast, so it is wise to have at least three ribs if there are several men in the company and four ribs for a larger group. Any leftover beef will make another perfect meal, served cold with a macaroni and cheese casserole.

Have your butcher remove the chine (the backbone), short ribs, and backstrap and tie together the roast. If the meat has been refrigerated, let it stand at room temperature for 2 or 3 hours before roasting. Rub the surface of the meat well with salt and pepper and flour and place fat side up on a rack in a roasting pan. Put a few tablespoons of water in the pan to keep the juices that will fall from sticking to the pan. Insert a meat thermometer in the thickest part of the roast—to be absolutely certain that your meat will be as you like it. Place in an oven preheated to 325° and cook for about 15 minutes per pound for rare beef, or until the thermometer registers 115°. For medium rare beef cook until the thermometer registers 120° to 130°. If you like well-done beef, cook to 150°, but this is a sad waste of a fine piece of meat as it will shrink considerably. Let the roast rest and the juices settle for 20-30 minutes before carving. During this time bake the Yorkshire Pudding (see p.250), roast some potatoes (see p.218), and make the gravy (see p.148) if you want one. Many people prefer just the juices of the meat. Serve the beef on very hot plates.

ROAST BEEF II

Mrs. Richard Lauritzen
Milwaukee, Wis.

This method of cooking roast beef is absolutely care free. A roast of any size cooked this way will be evenly rare right through.

Have the roast at room temperature, rub it with salt, pepper, and flour, and place, fat side up, on a rack in a roasting pan. Cook it in the morning at 375° for one hour. Leave it in the oven all day and do not open the door. 1 hour and 20 minutes before it is to be served relight the oven, still at 375° and cook the roast for 50 minutes for rare, or 1 hour for medium rare. Remove to rest for 20-30 minutes. Set the oven to 450° and bake the Yorkshire Pudding (see p. 250).

EYE ROAST OF BEEF

Harold Laro
Walpole, N.H.

This is a very, very simple and an economical piece of beef that can be presented with much style. Serve it with a mushroom sauce, as below, or with Béarnaise, mustard, or horseradish sauce (see p. 246-7), with an important vegetable—broccoli, asparagus, or stuffed eggplant.

3-pound eye roast of beef   salt, pepper, and flour

Let the roast rest at room temperature for several hours or overnight. Rub it well with salt, pepper, and flour and put it in an oven preheated to 425° in a small roasting pan into which you have put a little water. Roast for 15 minutes; reduce the oven temperature to 325° and cook for 15 minutes longer. Take the meat from the oven and let it rest for 15-20 minutes before serving it. A sauce may be made by adding sliced mushrooms, Worcestershire Sauce, lemon juice, and sherry to the pan in which the roast was cooked, and stirring on the top of the stove. Serve rare and carve *paper* thin.

Serves 6

BREADED BEEF

This recipe may be used for left-over roasts of any kind, rib roast, eye roast, or pot roast.

beef, sliced 1/4 inch thick	2 eggs
salt and pepper	2 tablespoons milk
minced parsley	1 tablespoon salad oil
vinegar	fine dried breadcrumbs
flour	butter

Spread out the slices of beef, season them with salt and pepper and sprinkle each slice with parsley and a few drops of vinegar. Let stand 10-15 minutes. Place flour in one dish; egg, milk and salad oil mixed together in another, and bread crumbs in a third. Dip the slices of beef in the flour, then the egg, then the breadcrumbs. Let stand until the crust dries a little. Heat the fat in a skillet and sauté the slices until a golden brown. Serve with left-over gravy or mushroom sauce (p.246).

CORNED BEEF AND CABBAGE

All New Englanders have grown to love some of the good dishes introduced to our table by New Englanders of Irish background. Corned beef and cabbage is high on the list of favorites. Be sure to rinse the meat well in boiling water first to remove excess salt.

4 pounds corned beef	pepper
cold water	2 onions
1 sprig thyme, several sprigs	1 whole carrot
parsley bound together	1 2-pound cabbage
1 onion stuck with 6 cloves	

Tie the beef neatly, put it into a large pot and cover it with cold water. No salt is needed. Add the other ingredients except the cabbage and bring very slowly to a boil with the lid off the pot so that you can see what is happening. Simmer very gently for 3 hours skimming as necessary. Remove the thyme, parsley, and cloved onion. Now add the cabbage which has been cut in 8 pieces and simmer for a further 15 minutes. Remove the meat and cut the string. Place on a hot platter and surround with the drained cabbage. Dot with butter and sprinkle with finely cut parsley. Serve with horseradish or mustard sauce (see Sauces).

Serves 6-8

PRESIDENTIAL CORNED BEEF HASH

Mrs. Robert L. Henderson
Chestnut Hill, Mass.

This recipe was used at the White House during Herbert Hoover's term.

2 cups minced corned beef (no fat)	2 tablespoons chopped celery
4 medium potatoes boiled and mashed	2 tablespoons chopped green pepper
1/2 cup hot cream	2 tablespoons chopped onion
2 rounded tablespoons butter	salt and pepper to taste

Mix thoroughly and bake for 30 minutes at 375° in a greased pan until rich golden brown.

Serves 4-6

HALF-WAY HOUSE YANKEE POT ROAST

This "Recipe with a History" comes from Muriel Arbeton of Phillips, Maine. "Back in 1835," she says, "Squire James Rangeley's brand-new road ran from the settlement at Madrid, Franklin County, Maine, on the opposite side of the river from the present Highway 104, over Beech Hill, and on to the then brand-new town in the lake country now bearing the famous squire's name.

"To man and beast this seemed a long and tiring trek until it was made to seem shorter by the building of Half-Way House, appropriately at the mid-point between Madrid and Rangeley.

"This Yankee forerunner of today's establishments of rest and refreshment catered to a varied clientele, not excluding wandering Indians. Here, many of the recipes of the region originated, including the delectable pot roast developed by my mother's grandmother who ran Half-Way House in that long-ago time.

"A family of Indians came to Half-Way House one day, seeking a warm meal and an hour's rest and comfort. One of them was a young woman with a baby strapped to a board on her back. Board and baby she removed from her tired shoulders, and leaned against the wall.

"Family reminiscences tell us that the baby, finding himself this much abandoned, gave voice to his disapproval. The tired young mother simply turned the board upside down so that her offspring was given a different view of the situation. This inversion seemed to keep him content for the rest of his visit. (Dr. Spock, please note!) His feelings were further soothed by a rag which Grandmother Ellis dipped into her pot of boiling choke-cherry jelly, and tucked into his little mouth.

"The meal that day was boiled venison, and the young Indian woman, before leaving, explained to Grandmother the Indian way of using wild seasonings.

"The original recipe went like this: 'A hunk of venison or moose meat. Scorch it all over in some grease until it is brown. Put it in a kettle with some water and salt. Dig up some horseradish, and some wild carrot. Put a little of each in the kettle, and boil a long time until the meat is cooked. Then stir in some corn meal to make gravy.'"

HALF-WAY HOUSE
YANKEE POT ROAST

Muriel Arbeton
Phillips, Me.

Interesting seasoning and long, slow cooking transforms a modest cut of meat into one of the most satisfactory of all Yankee dishes. Use a 3-4 pound chuck or tip roast, and you will have enough for six or eight people. If some pot roast is left, it will taste even better the next day.

3-4 pound pot roast	12 whole peppercorns
2 cloves garlic	12 whole allspice
4 tablespoons butter	1 bay leaf, crumbled
salt	1 tablespoon grated horseradish
flour	1/2 cup good rum or dry red wine
1 large onion, sliced	1/2 cup water

If desired:

1 recipe dumplings (see p. 249)   small whole carrots, or larger carrots quartered

Mash the garlic and sauté in the butter. Rub the meat with salt and flour and brown it well on all sides in the butter. Lay the meat on a bed of thin-sliced onion in a large Dutch oven or any pot with a tight-fitting lid. Add the butter, the spices and seasonings and pour the rum or wine over the meat. (A good pot roast will supply most of its own juices, but as it cooks pour the 1/2 cup of water over it to make an ample supply of gravy). Cover tightly and simmer for 3 or 4 hours until the roast is tender. This may be done either in the oven or on the back of the stove. If you want carrots with the pot roast, add them to the pot for the last half hour of cooking and for the last 12 minutes of cooking add the dumplings to steam in the flavors of the pot. When the roast is done, remove it to a hot, round platter and surround with the dumplings and carrots. Stir the gravy until smooth, correcting the seasoning if necessary. Pour it over the roast; if fresh dill is available, cut it over the dish with a lavish hand.

Serves 6-8

NEW ENGLAND BOILED DINNER

A great Yankee favorite, traditionally served on Mondays and Wednesdays throughout the fall and winter.

5 pounds brisket corned beef rinsed in boiling water	6 carrots, unpeeled
4 peppercorns	1 small cabbage, quartered
6 small beets, unpeeled	8 peeled potatoes
	4 medium-sized turnips, peeled

Place the meat in a kettle with the peppercorns. Cover with cold water. Simmer for 3 and 1/2 to 4 hours, until the meat is tender. During the last hour of cooking, remove the peppercorns and add the beets, turnips and carrots. In the last half hour, add the cabbage and the potatoes. When all is ready to serve, remove the skin from the beets. Serve with mustard, horseradish sauce, pickles, and a pepper mill.

Serves 8

RED FLANNEL HASH

Mix the left-over meat and vegetables of a New England Boiled Dinner, chop coarsely, and moisten with a little cream. Bake in an iron skillet in melted butter in a 350° oven for about 40 minutes until nicely browned. Turn out on a hot platter, and serve with the same fixings used for the Boiled Dinner. Connecticut Dabs (p. 26) or Rhode Island Toads (p. 26) are good with this.

CHILI BEEF

This dish is not, of course, of New England origin, but it is so useful and economical (not to mention the fact that it is best prepared a day before it is used) that it has long ago been adopted by New Englanders. It is a favorite dish for church suppers and other gatherings. Good for young people especially.

1 cup white soldier beans	3 bay leaves, crumbled
2 pounds ground beef	1 large can tomatoes
1 pound ground pork	1/2 cup chili sauce
3 large onions, chopped	8 teaspoons chili powder
2 tablespoons cooking oil	1 teaspoon oregano
1 tablespoon salt	1 teaspoon cumin
4 cloves garlic, crushed	1 cup ripe olives, halved

Rinse the beans and soak them overnight in water to cover. Next day cook them in new water and 1 tablespoon of salt until almost soft. At the same time brown the onions and the meat in oil in a very large skillet. Combine the beans, the water that is left from their cooking, the meat and onions, scraping the pan in which they were cooked, and all of the other ingredients, in a large pot. Cover it tightly and simmer over lowest heat, stirring occasionally, for 2 hours. Taste for seasoning. If you like a very hot chili, you may wish to add more of the chili seasonings or add dried red pepper flakes. Serve in bowls with saltines which have been crisped in the oven. Left-over chili may dry out a little the next day. In this case, a can of tomato soup may be added to the sauce.

Serves 8

BEEF STEW

Keep in mind that for some mysterious reason, all beef stews are better if refrigerated overnight (overnight can be expanded to several days too!).

2 pounds top round or chuck steak with all fat and gristle removed, cut into 1 and 1/2-inch cubes
1/2 cup flour
2 teaspoons salt
black pepper
1/2 cup butter
2 cloves garlic, mashed
1 bay leaf, crumbled

1/2 pound mushrooms sliced in thick pieces
2 tablespoons tomato paste
8 medium small onions
1 small turnip, diced
1/2 pound carrots, cut in strips
6 tablespoons butter
1 glass red wine
thyme and parsley

Dredge the meat in the flour mixed with the salt and several big grinds of pepper, coating it on all sides and using up all of the flour. Melt 6 tablespoons butter in a large skillet and brown the pieces of meat in the butter over a brisk heat. Turn the meat to brown on all sides and scrape the pan from time to time to prevent the flour from sticking. This will take 10 or 15 minutes. Toward the end of the time add the mashed garlic and bay leaf to the skillet. When the meat is browned, remove it to a large iron casserole with a tight-fitting lid. Cook the mushrooms in the skillet in the remaining butter and add to the casserole. Rinse the skillet with the red wine and stir wine into the casserole with the tomato paste. Meantime, clean and boil the onions, turnip, and carrots in enough salted water to cover, about 2 cups. When they are nearly soft, about 15 minutes, add them to the meat in the casserole. Stir in the water in which the vegetables were cooked and sprinkle the dish with dried (or fresh) thyme. Simmer gently for an hour. Taste the stew for seasoning, arrange it so that an attractive array of vegetables is on top. Garnish with beef marrow and sprinkle the dish well with parsley or other green herb. Cover it.

Fifteen or 20 minutes before you are ready to serve the stew, turn the heat on and reheat it slowly. Take it to the table and remove the cover there, so that its aroma will be enjoyed by all. A bowl of rice makes a nice accompaniment.

BEEF MARROW

To obtain beef marrow, have the butcher crack marrow bones lengthwise so that the marrow may be easily removed with the point of a small knife. Poach the marrow in a little stock for 10 minutes, until soft and quivery. Drain the marrow and keep it warm.

BEEF MARROW II

Or, get the marrow bones cut to 2" lengths sold in markets today as soup or "dog" bones. Boil the marrow in water or stock until it is soft and can easily be removed from the bone shell (use a table knife to loosen the edges). Then slice the marrow thin and use it on top of your beef stew as a garnish.

STEAK CANTONESE

Dolores Kott
Chicago, Ill.

An interesting change—serve it with dry, fluffy rice.

a 2-pound round steak cut in 1 x
  2" strips
2 tablespoons butter
1 medium onion, sliced thin
2 green peppers, washed, seeded,
  and cut in 2" squares
20 cherry tomatoes, halved, or 3
  medium tomatoes, quartered

1 No. 2 can of pineapple chunks,
  save the juice
1 tablespoon ground ginger
1/2 teaspoon garlic salt
1/2 teaspoon black pepper
3 tablespoons soy sauce

Brown the steak strips in butter in a large skillet. When browned push to one side and brown lightly the green pepper and onion. Add the ginger, salt, pepper, and soy sauce and stir well. Add the tomatoes, pineapple chunks, and juice from the pineapple can. Cover tightly and simmer for 45 minutes.

Serves 6

MEAT LOAF

This meat loaf may be made with beef, or with a mixture of beef, veal, and pork.

2 pounds ground meat
4 slices bread, crumbled
1 onion, minced
4 sprigs parsley, minced
1 clove garlic, crushed
2 eggs

1 cup chili sauce or tomato juice
1 tablespoon salt
freshly ground black pepper
2 strips bacon
tomato catsup (optional)

Mix all the ingredients together (except the bacon and catsup) until thoroughly blended. Pack into a greased loaf pan. For a crisp crust, spread tomato catsup over surface of loaf. Or, if you like a crisp surface all over, pat into a loaf-shaped roll and place on a cookie sheet. Arrange the bacon strips over the meat and bake in a 375° oven for about 45 minutes (if you use pork, allow an hour). The loaf may be served with hot tomato, brown mushroom, or sour cream and dill sauce.

Serves 8

SWEDISH MEAT BALLS

2 pounds hamburger (or 1 and 1/2
   pounds ground beef and 1/2
   pound ground pork)
3 slices bread
2 cups water
1 onion, minced and sautéed

2 potatoes, boiled and mashed
3 teaspoons salt
1/8 teaspoon pepper
2 eggs
butter (or other fat)

Have the butcher grind the meat a couple of times. Soak the bread in water. While it is soaking, mince and sauté the onion and mash the potatoes. Now mix all the ingredients in a large bowl; keep working the mixture until you have a smooth, spongy mass. It is best to work the mixture by hand. Heat butter (or fat) in a frying pan. Shape the balls by using a spoon and the palm of your hand, both wet. Brown evenly in the butter, shaking the pan meanwhile to keep the round shape. Remove to a kettle. Repeat until the meat mixture is used up. Make the gravy.

GRAVY

3-4 tablespoons butter (or other
   fat)
1/2 cup flour

3 cups beef stock
1 cup cream
salt and pepper to taste

Make the gravy in the same frying pan. Heat the butter (or fat) and add the flour, stirring to a golden paste. Add the stock gradually, stirring briskly to avoid lumps. If you prefer a darker gravy, add a few drops of Kitchen Bouquet or brown some sugar for the purpose. Add the cream and season to taste. Simmer the sauce 4-5 minutes.

Pour the gravy over the meat balls and let them cook in it over low heat for 40-60 minutes. Neither overcooking nor reheating will harm this wonderful concoction.

STEAK TARTARE

This dish is a great favorite with its champions, but there are those who will not touch raw meat. Have a frying pan ready and let them retire to the kitchen and cook their portion if they will. The steak should be served within an hour of grinding. Allow 1/3 pound per person.

freshly ground sirloin or top round steak from which all fat has been trimmed
salt, 1 teaspoon per pound
finely minced Bermuda onion

capers
1/2 lemon for each portion
1 egg yolk per portion
black pepper

Add the salt to the ground steak and mound each portion lightly on a chilled plate. Make an indentation in each and carefully slip the raw yolk of an egg into it. Arrange a tablespoon of finely minced Bermuda onion, about 2 teaspoons of capers, and half a lemon on each plate. Garnish with fresh leaves of spinach, parsley, or watercress and serve with fresh melba toast or pumpernickel, spread with sweet butter. Pass a pepper grinder, and let each guest mix his own portion. Some people like Worcestershire sauce or Tabasco on steak tartare, but these strong condiments seem to defeat the point of the dish, which is the fresh sweet taste of the meat. Steak tartare is good on a hot day served with beer.

HEARTY HAMBURGERS

1 and 1/2 pounds ground lean round
2 tablespoons minced onion
1 medium potato, riced

salt and fresh pepper to taste
butter
6 thin slices Bermuda onion
6 thick slices ripe tomato

Mix together the beef, minced onion, potato, salt and pepper. Shape the mixture lightly into 6 patties. Place in a generous amount of hot butter in a large iron skillet and brown on both sides. Brown the onion slices briefly in the same skillet. Arrange an onion slice on a tomato slice, place the hamburgers on top, and serve with Béarnaise (p. 247) or mustard (p. 246) sauce.

My own favorite way to serve hamburgers is to cook the meat, lightly seasoned with onion, salt and mixed with an egg, in a hot pan, browning the patties quickly on both sides. During the last minute or two, add a good-sized piece of butter, some sliced mushrooms, Worcestershire sauce, and white wine. Remove the hamburgers to hot plates, pour the sauce over them, and serve with grilled tomatoes.

ROQUEFORT CHEESEBURGERS

1 and 1/2 pounds chopped beef   Bermuda onion
3 ounces Roquefort cheese   bacon
salt

Shape the meat into 8 patties. Place crumbled cheese on 4 of these, top
each with a plain patty, and press the edges together securely. Lightly
sprinkle a skillet with salt; heat and brown the patties on both sides.
Serve hot on toasted, buttered buns. A thin slice of Bermuda onion and
a sprinkling of crisp bacon may be added.

Serves 4

BAKED HAM

A 15-pound ham will serve 25 or more people, depending on the number of dishes which accompany it. Ham goes well with so many things:
creamed turkey; chicken and oyster pie; baked beans; white beans
cooked with the drippings of the ham; yam pudding; spoon bread;
corn fritters. A fine baked ham makes, in short, a reliable and spicy
focal point of a large buffet meal. Garnish it elaborately and serve it
with a well seasoned fruit sauce. Baking powder biscuits, spinach soufflé, stuffed pumpkin, and corn bread all adapt themselves to the menu.

Remove the rind from the ham with a sharp knife. Spread a piece of
heavy-duty aluminum foil large enough to enclose the ham completely in a large roasting pan. This will keep your oven from getting
stained and will save all of the good juices of the ham. Place the ham
upon the foil, fat side up. Fold the foil carefully upward so that it will
catch all of the juices of the joint. Baste with a cup or so of cider, red
wine, fruit juice, or gingerale (all are good and so is a combination) and
close the foil around the ham. Place in a 300° oven and bake for 20 minutes to the pound. Open the foil occasionally and baste the ham. About
30 minutes before the ham is done, remove it from the oven and score
the fat side diagonally to make small diamonds. Press whole cloves into
the ham at the crossing of the diamonds. Spread it with a cup of brown
sugar mixed with 2 tablespoons of hot mustard. At this time use some
of the juices from the foil mixed with this sauce to glaze the fruit you are
preparing for the ham. Baste and return it to a 400° oven until nicely
glazed.

While the ham is in the last stage of cooking, prepare some attractive
fruit garnish with which to decorate it. Crabapples, kumquats, orange
slices, pineapple slices, and cherries are some suggestions. Glaze them
in a little of the juice, and when the ham is arranged on a large platter,
fix them to the surface with cloves or toothpicks. The bone end of the
leg may be decorated with a large ruffle cut from baking parchment or
stiff shelf paper, or with a bouquet of parsley tied in place with a ribbon of clean white cloth. Place slices of glazed fruit around the ham and
garnish it with more parsley. Serve raisin, cherry, or orange sauce
(see Sauces), or chutney with it.

BAKED HAM IN SOUR CREAM

1 slice ham, 1 inch thick
1 teaspoon dry mustard

1 cup sour cream

Soak the ham in lukewarm water about 1 hour. Drain and sprinkle it with mustard. Arrange it in a baking dish and cover with sour cream. Bake in a 350° oven until tender, about an hour. (If ham has been pre-cooked, soaking will not be necessary.)

Serves 4

BAKED HAM AND PINEAPPLE

a ham slice, cut thick
whole cloves
pineapple slices (canned)

pineapple syrup
molasses

Place ham, studded with cloves, in a greased baking dish. Arrange pineapple slices on top of ham, adding a little of the pineapple syrup from the can. Pour molasses over all. Cover and bake in a moderate (350°) oven for about an hour, basting frequently.

HAM BALLS WITH
SPICED CHERRY SAUCE

Mrs. R. C. Bouse
Port Bolivar, Texas

2 cups ground cooked ham
1/3 cup breadcrumbs
1 egg, beaten
1/4 cup milk

1/2 cup green peppers, chopped
1/4 cup shortening
1/4 cup hot water

Combine ham, breadcrumbs, egg, milk, and green peppers. Shape this mixture into individual balls. Melt fat in a skillet at medium heat. Add the ham balls to brown on all sides, turning occasionally. Remove the skillet from the heat and add hot water. Return the skillet to the heat, cover, and simmer for about 30 minutes. Serve with spiced cherry sauce (see *below*).

Serves 4

SPICED CHERRY SAUCE

1 cup cherry preserve
2 tablespoons prepared mustard

2 and 1/2 tablespoons lemon juice
3/4 teaspoon ground cloves

Combine the cherry preserve, mustard, the lemon juice, and ground cloves. Place the sauce over low heat and bring just to a boil, stirring frequently.

HAM ROLL

Margaret Leatham
Manchester, N.H.

This recipe is useful for the last bit of left-over ham, good served either hot or cold.

1 pound ground ham
1 pound ground beef
3 eggs
5 ounces breadcrumbs

juice and rind of 1 lemon
a dash each of salt, cayenne, and mace

Mix all together and form into a roll shape. Tie securely in cheesecloth and boil for 3 hours.

Serves 6

ROAST LEG OF LAMB

A leg of lamb weighing around 6 pounds will serve six to eight people.

1 leg of lamb
flour

salt and pepper
1 clove of garlic

Trim off any large pieces of excess fat from the lamb to have a nicer gravy. Rub the surface well with flour, salt and pepper and insert a few small slivers of garlic in several places under the surface. (This may be omitted if you do not enjoy a slight garlic flavor.) Place the roast which has rested until it is at room temperature fat side up in a roasting pan in which you have put a little water to keep the juices from burning. Insert a thermometer in the thickest part of the meat. Put the lamb into an oven preheated to 450° for 15 minutes and reduce the temperature to 300°. Roast for 3/4 hour longer or until the thermometer registers 140° if you like pink lamb—15 minutes longer until the thermometer registers 170° if you like lamb well done. Remove from the oven and let the meat rest for 20 minutes (during which time it will cook a little more) before carving. Garnish the shank bone with a bunch of parsley or a paper frill. Serve with roast potatoes, wild rice (p. 220), or white beans.

A leg of lamb is also good served with Béarnaise sauce, and this with fresh asparagus and new potatoes in the spring makes a very special menu, a nice choice for Easter.

BUTTERFLY LEG OF LAMB

This recipe is given for cooking over an outdoor grill. In the winter or in bad weather, it may be cooked in the same way over the coals of a grate fire, or it may be adapted for cooking in the broiler of a stove. In that case, preheat the broiler to 450° and substitute dried herbs rubbed into the meat for the fresh ones. Cook the fell (fat) side first toward the flame, then turn and cook the cut side.

a leg of lamb, boned
salt and pepper
1 or 2 cloves garlic

branches of fresh herbs, parsley,
thyme, marjoram, mint, sage,
green onions, or summer savory,
as available

Have your butcher bone the leg of lamb by making a long cut on the under side. Spread the meat flat. It will resemble an irregularly shaped butterfly. Season it to taste with salt, pepper, and garlic. Place a bed of fresh herbs on the grill and put the lamb upon it. This is a good dish to serve in the summer when your herb garden is yielding bountifully. Cook the meat for about 30 minutes on one side, 15 minutes on the other. It should be deliciously charred on the outside and pink in the center. As the cut is of uneven thickness, there will be pieces of various degrees of doneness to suit a variety of tastes. Carve it as you would a steak and serve with it a green vegetable—asparagus, Brussels sprouts, or broccoli with Hollandaise sauce, and baked or roast potatoes.

Serves 6-8

SPICED BARBECUED LAMB

An interesting way to serve left-over lamb, this recipe was given to my Aunt Emily Thom by Mrs. Nathan Pusey.

1/2 cup sliced onions
1 cup finely diced celery
3 tablespoons butter
1 tablespoon dry mustard
3 tablespoons brown sugar
2 teaspoons salt
1 teaspoon chili powder

2 cups tomato juice
1 small can tomato paste
1/2 cup water
1 tablespoon vinegar
3 cups cooked lean lamb, cut
    into good-sized chunks
18 pearl onions (canned)

Sauté the onion and celery in the butter. Add the mustard, brown sugar, salt, and chili powder. Stir in the tomato juice, tomato paste, water, and vinegar and simmer for 20 minutes. Add the lamb and onions, and simmer for 20 minutes more, or until the sauce is thick.

Serves 6

PINEAPPLE BARBECUED LAMB SPARERIBS

3 pounds lamb spareribs
1 8-ounce can crushed pineapple
1/4 cup vinegar
1/4 cup honey
1 clove garlic, finely chopped

1 teaspoon Worcestershire sauce
1 teaspoon salt
1/8 teaspoon pepper
1/4 teaspoon ginger

Place the spareribs on a rack in a shallow roasting pan. Bake at 325° for approximately 1 hour. Drain off drippings. Combine remaining ingredients and mix well. Pour over the lamb and bake 45 minutes or until tender. Baste lamb frequently during baking.

Serves 4

MIXED GRILL

country sausages
thick-sliced country bacon
loin lamb chops 1 and 1/2 inches
    thick
toast crumbs
chopped basil or parsley

green peppers
large mushroom caps
toast rounds
butter
tomatoes

In a large skillet brown the sausages and bacon—two of each for the number of people to be served if it is a dinner dish. One of each should be enough for lunch. Remove the bacon and sausages to drain on paper toweling. Discard most of the grease in the skillet and brown the required number of lamb chops. Remove them to a large platter which can go in the oven.

Have some fine large tomatoes which are not quite ripe. Halve them and cook them very briefly in the same skillet, then arrange them, cut side up, around the chops. Shake toast crumbs and chopped basil or parsley over the tomatoes. Sauté large sections of green pepper and large mushroom caps very briefly. Arrange them on the platter. Finally garnish the whole with the sausages and bacon curls and some rounds of toast fried in butter.

The platter may now be placed in a 150° oven and will be ready for dinner any time within an hour. Put the plates for the meal in at the same time. When ready to serve, garnish the platter with a large quantity of watercress or parsley.

VANDERBILT GRILL

4 thick lamb chops	tomato halves
butter	4 large mushroom caps
salt and pepper	grated cheese
4 pineapple slices	basil

Place a pan with the lamb chops in the center of the broiler rack. Dot the chops with butter and sprinkle with salt and pepper. Place as near the broiling unit as possible and broil until about half done, about 6 minutes. Remove the pan from the oven. Turn over the chops and dot with butter, salt and pepper. Put 4 pineapple slices dipped in melted butter around the chops, and in the center of each pineapple slice, place a large mushroom cap dipped in melted butter. Place tomato halves sprinkled with salt and pepper between the pineapple slices, return to the oven and complete broiling. Just before taking out the pan, sprinkle the tomatoes with grated cheese and basil.

Serves 2-4

HODGE-PODGE

Dorothy L. Stoddard
Fairhaven, Mass.

2 mutton chops	2 small potatoes
2 slices white turnip	salt
2 small onions	pepper
2 small carrots	tomato catsup

Put the mutton chops (cut from near the shoulder) in a shallow pan which has a tight cover. Pour on boiling water to the depth of one inch. Cover and simmer one hour. Add more water as it boils away, using only enough to keep the meat from burning. Add turnips, onions, and carrots. When the meat, turnips, and onions are nearly tender, add potatoes, which have been first parboiled. Add 1 teaspoon salt and a little pepper. Remove the vegetables without breaking them. Let the water boil nearly away, leaving enough for gravy. Remove the fat, thicken the gravy with flour. Add salt and tomato catsup to taste. Pour it over the meat.

Serves 2

CURRY OF LAMB

One of the finest of all curries is made with lamb.

Three to 4 cups of lamb cut in good-sized chunks will serve 6 people. Make the sauce as you would for Shrimp Curry (p.147), incorporating in it, however, any fat-free pan drippings or left-over juices from the lamb. Add the cut-up meat and season to taste. Serve with an assortment of condiments.

LAMB HASH

Lamb that is left on the roast and the vegetables that remain will provide a splendid hash. Chop together the lamb, potatoes, carrots or spinach, adding a small onion to the bowl. Moisten with a little cream or left-over juices of the meat, from which the fat has been skimmed, and fry to a crisp undercrust in as much butter as is needed. This hash is worth planning ahead for.

STUFFED PORK CHOPS

Mrs. Arvilla Fosdick
Providence, R.I.

6 pork chops, 1 and 1/2 inches
   thick, slit with a pocket
1 cup seasoned breadcrumbs
2 apples, diced
1/2 cup chopped walnuts
1/2 cup chopped celery

1 egg
1/4 cup raisins (optional)
1/2 teaspoon dried oregano or
   thyme
1 cup heavy cream
salt and pepper

Wash and dry the chops and season them with salt and pepper. Combine the other ingredients, except the cream, and stuff lightly into the slits. Place in a baking dish, cover with heavy cream, and bake for 1 and 1/2 hours or until done in a 350° oven. It is convenient to bake sweet potatoes or sweet potato pudding at the same time. Cornbread, too, if you have a hungry family.

Serves 6

ROAST PORK WITH APRICOTS

Marie Wederer
Monroe, Conn.

4-5 pounds pork shoulder
2 and 1/2 tablespoons chopped
   onion
2 and 1/2 tablespoons chopped
   celery
2 and 1/2 tablespoons butter

1 can apricots
2 and 1/2 cups of toasted bread
   crumbs
salt
pinch of nutmeg

Have your butcher bone and cut a pocket in the pork shoulder. Sauté the onion and celery in the butter for 5 minutes. From the can of apricots add 1/4 cup of juice, the breadcrumbs and the seasonings. Stuff this into the shoulder. Roast in a slow oven (325°) for 3 to 4 hours. Add the apricots, and cook for 15 minutes longer.

Serves 6

VEAL CHOPS WITH MUSHROOM SAUCE

This recipe may be used also for scallops of veal.

4 thick veal chops	1/2 pound mushrooms, sliced
2 tablespoons butter	salt and pepper
2 tablespoons olive oil	Worcestershire sauce
2 tablespoons sherry	1/2 cup cream
1 tablespoon flour	a dash of lemon juice

Cook the chops in the butter and oil until golden. Remove them from the pan. Add the sherry and flour to the juices in the pan, then the mushrooms and cook until brown. Add the seasonings, return the chops to the pan and just before serving stir in the cream. Either sweet or sour cream may be used.

STUFFED GLAZED SHOULDER OF VEAL

1 boned shoulder of veal	4 tablespoons butter
12 dried apricots	salt and pepper
1/2 pound sausage meat	1/4 cup port wine or fruit juice
1 pound chestnuts, boiled and peeled	8 or 10 strips of bacon
	apricot jam
5 pears, peeled and diced	

Wipe the veal with a damp cloth. Soak the apricots in water for 30 minutes, then drain and chop. Fry the sausage meat until lightly browned. Chop the chestnuts and combine with the apricots and pears. Sauté slowly in butter until the fruits are tender, about 12 minutes. Combine them with the sausage meat, wine, salt and pepper and pack this stuffing into the cavity of the veal. Roll and sew or tie securely. Place the shoulder on a rack in a roasting pan and cover with strips of bacon. Roast in a slow (300°) oven until done; allow 40-50 minutes to the pound. A half hour before the meat is done, spread it with apricot jam. Bake until a golden glaze is formed.

Serves 8

VEAL VADUZ

2 tablespoons butter
1 medium onion, coarsely
  chopped
1 large can small whole onions,
  drained and rinsed well
2 pounds lean veal, cut into
  1 x 2 and 1/2" strips
1/2 teaspoon salt

2 tablespoons minced parsley
1 and 1/2 tablespoons paprika
2 tablespoons dry white wine
1/2 to 3/4 cup chicken stock
2 tablespoons capers (with juice)
1 small dill pickle, cut into strips
  (optional)
1 cup sour cream

Melt butter in a heavy skillet, add whole onions and sauté gently, turning until evenly browned. Remove onions. In butter remaining, lightly brown chopped onion; add meat and brown lightly. Add salt, paprika, parsley, wine, and about 1/4 cup stock. Cover tightly and cook over low-to-medium heat 45 minutes or until veal is tender, stirring occasionally and adding stock from time to time when necessary. When the meat is tender, stir in the capers, whole onions, pickle strips, and sour cream. Heat thoroughly over low heat. Do not allow to boil. Serve over noodles.

Serves 4-6

CALVES' LIVER

1 pound calves' liver
salt and black pepper
paprika
4 slices bacon

1 tablespoon butter
beef stock
Madeira
chopped parsley

Fry the bacon until crisp and put it in a warm place. Pour off most of the fat leaving just enough to brown the liver. Brown it quickly over a brisk flame, reduce the heat and cook to the degree of doneness you like. Remove to a warm place while you make a sauce by adding the butter, 1/2 cup or so of beef stock, and Madeira to taste to the pan. Simmer 5 minutes until somewhat reduced. Arrange the liver on hot plates. Pour on the sauce, then crumble the bacon on it and garnish with chopped parsley. Good served with asparagus or spinach.

Serves 2

Chapter 9.
Vegetables

THE BIRTHPLACE OF OUR VEGETABLES

Potatoes came from far Virginia;
Parsley was sent us from Sardinia;
French beans, low grown on the earth,
To distant India trace their birth;
But scarlet runners, gay and tall,
That climb upon your garden wall—
A cheerful sight to all around—
In South America were found.
The onion traveled here from Spain;
The leek from Switzerland we gain,
Garlic from Sicily obtain.
Spinach in far Syria grows;
Two hundred years ago or more,
Brazil the artichoke sent o'er,
And Southern Europe's sea coast shore
Beet root on us bestows.
When 'Lizabeth was reigning here
Peas came from Holland and were dear.
The south of Europe lays its claim
To beans, but some from Egypt came.
The radishes both thin and stout,
Natives of China are, no doubt;
But turnips, carrots, and sea kale,
With celery so crisp and pale,
Are products of our own fair land;
And cabbages—a goodly tribe
Which abler pens might well describe—
Are also ours, I understand.

AMICUS.

—Goldthwaite's Geographical Magazine

ARTICHOKES

Artichokes are a great help in winter menu planning as they ship well and are at their best at that time. They are often served as a separate course, either at the beginning of the meal or as a salad course. Serve one for each person on a large plate so that there will be room for the discarded leaves.

Select firm green artichokes, trim off the stem and small tough leaves at the bottom so that they will stand upright. Boil them, covered, in salted water to which lemon juice has been added, for 35-45 minutes, or until an outer leaf pulls off easily. Serve hot, with melted butter or Hollandaise sauce (p. 247), or cold with sour cream sauce (p. 247), or Roquefort mayonnaise (p. 243). If they are served hot, the choke or thistly center is removed after the outside leaves are eaten by each guest. To serve artichokes cold, the inner meatless leaves and the choke should be removed in the kitchen with a sharp edged teaspoon. The artichokes should then be chilled and the sauce spooned into the center of the vegetable.

ASPARAGUS

Snap off and discard the tough ends of the asparagus stalks. Trim them neatly and remove the lower scales with a vegetable peeler. Pour boiling water into a shallow pan which is big enough for the asparagus to lie flat. Add a teaspoon of salt for a quart of water, bring back to a rapid boil, and put in the asparagus spears. Cook briskly, uncovered, until green and tender—about 15-20 minutes. Remove the asparagus to a warm towel to drain. Serve on a hot platter with melted butter and lemon juice, Hollandaise or cheese sauce (p. 247 and p. 245), or covered with breadcrumbs sautéed in fresh butter.

2 pounds serves 4

ASPARAGUS ON TOAST

If you wish to make asparagus a complete meal—and at least once each spring you ought to—serve it with one of the above sauces on hot buttered toast, allowing 2 pounds of asparagus for three people.

ASPARAGUS AU GRATIN

2 pounds fresh asparagus   1/3 cup melted butter
1/4 cup grated cheese   salt, pepper, and paprika

Cook the asparagus for 15 minutes. Drain and place in a buttered, oven-proof dish. Sprinkle with grated cheese, pour on the melted butter and season with salt, pepper, and paprika. Put under the broiler until the cheese is browned.

Serves 4

ASPARAGUS AMANDINE

2 pounds fresh asparagus
1/2 cup melted butter
1 tablespoon grated onion

1/3 cup sliced almonds
1/3 cup breadcrumbs
salt and pepper

Place asparagus which has been cooked for 15 minutes and drained in a buttered, ovenproof dish. Sprinkle with the grated onion, almonds, and breadcrumbs, salt and pepper. Pour the butter over the dish and put under the broiler until the top is browned.

Serves 4

ASPARAGUS TIPS WITH HAM

A nice luncheon or supper dish to serve with hot buttered rolls or popovers. Vary by adding a little curry to the sauce or by sprinkling sliced almonds on top.

2 pounds asparagus
4 large thin slices ham

2 cups cheese sauce (p. 245)

Wrap each piece of ham around 3 or 4 stalks of cooked asparagus. Place in a buttered baking dish and pour the cheese sauce over them. Place dish in a hot oven (400°) for 5 or 6 minutes or until browned.

Serves 4

GREEN BEANS

One of the most wonderful crops of summer, green beans are easy to raise and yield abundantly all summer long. Pole beans may be used in the same recipes. They have a slightly beanier flavor. It is wise to have a couple of rows of each in even the smallest garden. In winter, frozen green beans serve many useful purposes, combining well with almost all other vegetables and vegetable garnishes, and complimenting almost any dish. Green beans frozen whole seem to have the best flavor.

FRESH GREEN BEANS

Remove ends of beans and strings if any. If they are small, leave them whole; otherwise, snap them in 1-inch lengths or French-cut them in long thin strips. Wash the beans, and cook them in a small amount of rapidly boiling salted water until just tender and still green, 10 or 15 minutes depending upon their size. Serve at once with butter.

A pound serves 4

GREEN BEANS COUNTRY STYLE

2 good-sized onions
2 pounds string or pole beans
1 heaping tablespoon flour
3 tablespoons butter

1/2 cup heavy sweet cream *or*
   sour cream
fresh basil
black pepper

Cut onions in slices and boil them for a few minutes in salted water. Add string beans or pole beans—as fresh and young as possible. Cut the larger beans in two but leave the smaller ones whole. Cook briskly for 10-15 minutes, letting most of the water boil away. Add flour, butter, cream or sour cream, fresh basil, and freshly ground black pepper. Turn heat low and stir until the sauce is thick. Very special. (An acceptable substitute may be made with frozen whole beans and dried basil.)

Serves 6-8

GREEN BEANS IN CASSEROLE

1 and 1/2 pounds fresh green
   beans, French cut
salt and pepper, and flour for
   dusting
onion rings

2 tablespoons butter
1 and 1/2 tablespoons flour
1/2 cup cream
grated Swiss cheese
buttered breadcrumbs

Cook green beans until nearly done. Let the liquor in which they cook reduce to a few tablespoons. Place the beans in a shallow casserole, and sprinkle with salt and pepper and a dusting of flour. Cover them with a layer of onion rings shaved paper thin. Make a light sauce of butter, flour, and the bean liquor. Pour over the beans. Add cream and sprinkle with grated Swiss cheese and buttered breadcrumbs and a few dots of butter. Bake in a hot (400°) oven until bubbly.

Serves 6

OTHER SUGGESTIONS FOR SERVING GREEN BEANS

Serve with:

almonds, slivered or sliced, and browned in butter;

water chestnuts, sliced very thin—add a pinch of dill or oregano;

sliced new potatoes garnished with crisp crumbled bacon;

mushrooms and a little cream;

lima beans, with or without almonds.

WHITE BEANS

To accompany roast lamb.

1 pound dried white beans
  (yellow-eye or soldier beans)
1 onion minced

1 crumbled bay leaf
2 teaspoons salt
freshly ground pepper

Wash the beans in several waters, then soak overnight in water to cover. In the morning, set them to simmer slowly in fresh water to which you have added the rest of the ingredients. Cook until tender but not mushy —about 2 hours. Add some of the drippings from the roast lamb, and cover with lots of finely chopped parsley.

Serves 8

DRIED LIMA BEANS WITH CREAM

1 pound dried lima beans
butter
lemon juice

salt and pepper
chopped chives or parsley
cream

Soak lima beans overnight. Boil them in fresh water until soft, but do not allow the beans to burst. Pour off the water, and mix the beans with a good-sized lump of butter, some lemon juice, salt and pepper, and cream. Serve garnished with chopped herbs. Lentils and other dried beans may be prepared in the same way.

Serves 8

HARVARD BEETS

12 medium-sized cooked beets
  whole or cut up
3 tablespoons butter
1 tablespoon cornstarch flour

1 and 1/2 cups beet liquor
1/2 cup brown sugar
1/4 cup vinegar
salt, cloves, and nutmeg

Melt the butter in a saucepan over low heat. Blend in the flour and stir in the beet liquor. Cook, stirring constantly until smooth and thick. Add the sugar and vinegar, then salt, cloves, and nutmeg to taste. When well mixed, add the beets and serve hot.

Serves 6

BEETS IN CREAM SAUCE

12 medium-sized cooked beets, whole or cut up
3/4 cup sour cream
1/4 cup sweet cream
juice of half a lemon

1/2 teaspoon each of dry mustard and salt
white pepper
chopped fresh dill

Heat the beets in the top of a double boiler. Add the other ingredients and mix together—gently to avoid breaking the beets. Serve hot, garnished with fresh dill. (If dill is not available, chopped parsley or chives may be used.)

Serves 4

BEET GREENS

Prepare like spinach (p. 221).

BEETS IN ORANGE SAUCE

Boiled baby beets are good in a sauce made by adding a tablespoon of orange juice and grated orange rind to the butter in which they are served.

BEETS AND BEET GREENS IN CREAM

Here the young savory greens count as much as the beets.

1 bunch young beets, with greens
2 tablespoons butter
1 small onion, minced
salt and pepper

pinch of sugar
1 tablespoon lemon juice
sweet or sour cream
1 hardcooked egg

Dig a few handfuls of very small beets and gather enough leaves to make an equal quantity. A fresh bunch of beets from the market will do, too. Boil the beets separately and skin them. Rinse the greens but do not dry them. Discard all tough stems, then cook slowly in a covered pan to which you have added the sugar, butter, and minced onion. Do not add more water. When tender remove the lid, and boil away any remaining liquid. Add the beets, chopped quite fine; sprinkle with salt, pepper, and lemon juice, and heat through. Add the cream, and serve garnished with the sieved egg.

A pound of beets serves 4-5

BROCCOLI

Broccoli, one of the most delicious of all vegetables, must be cooked immediately before serving to preserve its sprightly green appearance. As it is a rather special vegetable, and also because it does not go well with wine, broccoli is very well suited to be served separately as a first course. Keep the kitchen door closed because of its strong smell.

To prepare the broccoli, slice a little from the bottom of the stems and discard. If the stalks are thick, pare them downward from just below the buds, and gash them lengthwise. Cook the stalks in an inch of boiling, salted water for 10 minutes, uncovered for the first half of the cooking to preserve their color. Serve with lemon butter, breadcrumb sauce, or Hollandaise sauce (p. 247).

A bunch serves 4

PUREE OF BROCCOLI

1 head broccoli or 2 packages   salt, pepper, and mace
  frozen broccoli   1 tablespoon butter
water   3 tablespoons sweet or sour cream
lemon juice

If fresh broccoli is used, clean it and cut up the stems. Cook the broccoli in a large covered saucepan in a small amount of water with the butter, lemon juice, and seasonings until almost tender. Most of the liquid will have boiled away. Purée the broccoli, mixing it with the cream and lemon juice, taste for seasoning, return to the saucepan to reheat, and serve. (This purée is sometimes piped through a pastry tube to form a ring around creamed chicken or fish.)

Serves 6

BRUSSELS SPROUTS
AND CELERY CASSEROLE

1 quart Brussels sprouts
hearts of 1 bunch celery, cut in
   1-inch cubes
2 cups cream sauce (p.245)
1 cup sour cream

1/2 cup breadcrumbs sautéed
   in butter
1/2 cup sliced almonds
chopped parsley

Clean the Brussels sprouts, cutting off the stem ends and removing any wilted leaves. Prepare the celery. Boil the vegetables in salted water to which you have added a little lemon juice for about 15 minutes or until almost tender. Drain, and put the vegetables in a buttered, ovenproof casserole. Combine the cream sauce and sour cream and pour over the vegetables. Combine the sautéed breadcrumbs, almonds, and parsley and sprinkle on top. Bake in a 350° oven for about 10 minutes before serving.

Serves 6

CARROTS AND FRESH MINT

1 pound fresh young carrots
3 tablespoons fresh butter
3 tablespoons water

mint
brown sugar
salt and freshly ground pepper

The carrots may be sliced, or left whole if they are very small. Combine them with the water and butter and cook until tender in a covered saucepan. Add the salt and pepper and a few crumbs of brown sugar; stir without the lid to let any extra liquid steam away. Add three or four small shredded mint leaves. The mint flavor should be elusive, so don't use too much. Heat together and serve.

Serves 4

GLAZED CARROTS

1 bunch carrots
1 cup water

1/2 teaspoon salt
3 tablespoons butter

If the carrots are young and small, scrape them and use whole. Otherwise, cut into peg-shaped pieces. Put them with the other ingredients into a shallow pan or skillet, cover, and cook for 15 minutes. Remove the cover and continue cooking until the water has evaporated. Then shake and toss them over the heat until they are shiny and golden brown.

Serves 4

PUREE OF CARROTS

1 bunch carrots
2 tablespoons butter
2 tablespoons cream

salt and white pepper
pinch of mace

Clean, scrape, and cut up the carrots. Cook them in just enough water to cover until they are very tender and the water has boiled away. Purée them in a ricer or blender with the butter and cream. Season and reheat. Made in the blender, these carrots are light as air.

Serves 4

CREAMED CARROTS IN CHICKEN STOCK

1 bunch carrots
juice of half a lemon
3 tablespoons butter
3 tablespoons flour
2 cups chicken stock

salt and cayenne pepper
chopped parsley and chives
1/2 cup cream
2 egg yolks

Clean the carrots. Leave whole if small, or cut larger carrots as you wish, first removing any tough core. Cook them in 1 cup of chicken stock until just tender. In another saucepan, make a sauce by melting the butter, stirring in the flour and, gradually, the other cup of chicken stock. Add the seasonings, and cook over low heat while stirring until thick. Add the carrots and herbs and the egg yolks mixed with the cream. Reheat but do not boil.

Serves 4

CARROT RING

A very useful recipe and an easy attractive way to offer several vegetables at once for a buffet or large gathering.

1 cup boiled carrots, riced or in
  purée
1 teaspoon grated onion
salt, paprika, and celery salt

1 cup heavy cream sauce (p. 245)
4 eggs, separated
1 teaspoon cream of tartar

Combine the carrots with the seasonings and the cream sauce. Cool, and beat in the egg yolks one at a time. Beat the egg whites until stiff with the cream of tartar and fold into the carrot mixture. Fill a well-buttered ring mold 2/3 full and bake in a moderate oven (350°) in a larger pan of water for about 45 minutes or until firm. This ring may be filled with cauliflower, or Brussels sprouts, or green peas, or filled with one vegetable and surrounded with another. Creamed mushrooms are excellent and the dish may be garnished with chopped parsley or slivered almonds.

CARROTS AND PARSNIPS

A simple but excellent combination.

1 bunch (1 pound) carrots	butter
1 bunch parsnips	pepper
parsley	

Cut equal quantities of carrots and parsnips into shoestring sticks. Start the carrots in boiling salted water; after a minute or two, add the parsnips, which will cook more quickly. When the vegetables are done, serve, garnished with parsley, butter, and pepper.

Serves 6

CAULIFLOWER

For this recipe you will need a large, white cauliflower with fresh, green leaves.

With a sharp knife carefully remove the cauliflower from its green leaves, keeping both intact. Turn the cauliflower over, and cut several large gashes in the stem. Wash it and put it in a large pan containing an inch and a half of boiling salted water. Cover the pan and steam the cauliflower until done, about 20 minutes. Meanwhile, trim the base of the plant so that it will sit flat on a platter. Trim the leaves neatly and steam this part of the plant in another pot just long enough for the leaves to turn bright green. Serve the cauliflower in its leaves on a large, round, hot platter. Pour melted butter, lemon juice, and buttered bread- or nut crumbs over the cauliflower (or Hollandaise or cheese sauce). A fine effect can be made by surrounding the cauliflower with whole buttered carrots or beets, or a combination of the two.

Serves 6

BRAISED CELERY

1 bunch celery
6 tablespoons butter
2 beef bouillon cubes

salt and pepper
parsley
almonds

Clean the celery, and discard the tops and any tough stalks. Cut the stalks, hearts, and root into 3-inch pieces. Heat the butter until bubbling in a large skillet, dissolve the bouillon cubes in the butter, and add the celery, almonds, and seasoning. Cook until the celery and almonds are brown and glazed with the beef-flavored butter. Garnish with chopped parsley, and serve.

Serves 4

CREAMED CELERY HEARTS

4 scallions, minced
1 clove garlic, crushed
3 tablespoons butter
4 cups celery hearts cut in 1-inch
     pieces
salt and white pepper

1/3 cup chicken stock
1/3 cup Madeira
2 egg yolks
2 tablespoons heavy cream
1 teaspoon chopped fresh dill

Sauté the green onions in butter until golden. Add the garlic, celery, salt and pepper to taste, and chicken stock. Simmer, covered, about 15 minutes, or until the celery is just tender. Stir together the egg yolks, cream and Madeira, and add to the celery. Continue to cook over a low flame, stirring constantly until the sauce thickens. Do not let it boil. Sprinkle with the chopped dill.

Serves 6

CREAMED CELERY AND CHESTNUTS

A useful winter dish.

4 cups sliced celery
4 ounces butter
1/4 cup flour
1 cup light cream
1 cup sliced mushrooms

1 (11-ounce) can whole chest-
     nuts, drained
salt, pepper, and cayenne
1 and 1/2 cups half-inch
     bread cubes

Cook the celery in salted water, covered, until tender but still crisp. Drain, reserving 1 cup of the liquid. Melt half the butter, stir in the flour, and gradually the reserved celery liquid and cream. Cook over low heat until mixture bubbles and thickens. Simmer for 5 minutes longer. Add the celery, mushrooms, and chestnuts, and season to taste. Turn the mixture into a serving dish, and sprinkle bread cubes sautéed in the remaining butter over the top.

Serves 6

CORN ON THE COB

Serve the corn as soon as possible after it is picked. If it must wait a few hours, shuck it and cover with cold water. In a large kettle, bring enough water to cover the corn to a rapid boil. Add 1 tablespoon of salt for each quart of water. Boil the corn 3-5 minutes. It will be very tender. Serve with butter and salt.

SUCCOTASH

Scrape the kernels and milk off the cobs of freshly boiled corn. Add to an equal quantity of shelled beans or lima beans. Cook them together in butter, dust with flour, and add light cream. Season with salt and white pepper.

CORN OYSTERS

Ellen Sybil Barney
Walpole, N.H.

An old favorite for winter. Serve with fried chicken, broiled ham, or grilled bacon.

2 eggs	1 teaspoon salt
3/4 cup milk	2 tablespoons melted butter
2 and 1/2 cups flour	1 No. 2 can creamed corn
2 teaspoons baking powder	

Beat the eggs slightly. Add the milk, the sifted dry ingredients, the butter, and the corn. Beat until well mixed. Drop by spoonfuls into hot (375°) deep fat. Fry 3-4 minutes until nicely browned. Drain on absorbent paper, and serve at once.

24 small fritters

FRIED CUCUMBERS

Mrs. Mary B. Kidder
Devon, Penna.

These are excellent for breakfast. They also go well with fish.

Pare the cucumbers, and cut them into pieces as thick as a silver dollar. Dry them in a cloth; season with pepper and salt and sprinkle thickly with flour. Melt some butter in a frying pan. When it bubbles, put in the cucumber slices and fry until a light brown.

FRIED DANDELION BLOSSOMS

Alyce L. Brooks
Jaffrey, N.H.

Very few people realize the nutritious value of dandelion blossoms. This unusual recipe is believed to have originated in Germany, whence it was brought over by the pioneers.

Pick any amount of dandelion blossoms close to the bud (no stem) and soak in salt water for 20 minutes. Rinse well and squeeze out any excess water. Roll well in flour and fry blossoms in enough butter to keep from burning. Keep heat low and brown well, turning blossoms to brown on all sides. Add salt and pepper to taste. Use as a vegetable.

DANDELION GREENS

Wash the greens, keeping only the tenderest leaves. Cover them with cold water until ready to use. Remove leaves from water and shake them to remove most of the water. Cook with a lump of butter in a covered pot until soft. Season with salt, pepper, and lemon juice.

PANNED ESCAROLE

2 heads escarole
2 medium onions, sliced very thin
salt and pepper to taste

3 tablespoons butter
2 tablespoons heavy cream
crushed cornflakes

Wash and pick over the escarole. Cut it crosswise in narrow strips. Melt the butter in a large saucepan, and add the escarole and onion. Cover and cook over low heat for about 10 minutes. Season with salt and pepper, and stir in the cream. Before serving, garnish the top with cornflake crumbs.

Serves 6

FIDDLE FERNS

Fiddle ferns, if you know where to find them, are the first delicacy of spring, appearing even before asparagus. Plunge them briefly in rapidly boiling water, and serve with butter, salt, and if you like, lemon juice. Chopped almonds may be added, or the ferns may be served on hot buttered toast.

BRAISED LEEKS

12 leeks
3 tablespoons butter
2 cups beef stock, or 2 bouillon
   cubes and water

salt and pepper
dried thyme

Wash the leeks thoroughly, trim off the roots and most of the tops (which can be saved for soup), and cook them with the other ingredients in a large frying pan, covered, until tender, about 15 minutes. Leeks make a good first course served hot on buttered toast, or chilled and served with French Dressing. Garnish them with chives if you wish.

Serves 3-4

MUSHROOMS IN CREAM

This may be served as an accompaniment to an entrée, or poured over buttered toast as a lunch or supper dish.

4 tablespoons butter
1 onion, chopped
1 pound sliced mushrooms
salt and freshly ground pepper

paprika
juice of half a lemon
2 tablespoons flour
3/4 cup cream

Melt the butter in a frying pan, and cook the onions until they are transparent. Add the mushrooms, and cook for a few minutes. Add the seasonings and flour. Cook for 5 minutes before stirring in the cream.

Serves 4-6

MUSHROOM PUFFS

Mrs. Edna Beatty
Los Angeles, Calif.

1 pound fresh mushrooms
1/2 cup butter
1 teaspoon salt
3 rounded tablespoons flour

1 cup milk
1 cup cream
1 egg, beaten
breadcrumbs

Wipe the mushrooms, trim the stems, and chop fine. Melt the butter and cook the mushrooms in it. Dissolve the flour and salt in the milk and cream. Add the mushroom mixture and cook until very thick, stirring constantly. Spread the mixture in a flat pan to cool. When cool, form into balls about the size of a walnut. Dip in the beaten egg, then in breadcrumbs, and again in the egg and breadcrumbs. Fry in deep fat (370°) until brown. Serve with meat. Smaller balls may be made to serve as appetizers.

Serves 6-8

TIMBALE OF MUSHROOMS

1 cup chicken stock
1/2 cup light cream
4 eggs
3/4 teaspoon salt
1/2 teaspoon paprika

pinch of mace
1 tablespoon chopped parsley
1/2 pound chopped mushrooms
2 tablespoons butter

Beat together the stock, cream, eggs, salt, paprika, mace, and parsley. Sauté the mushrooms in butter with a little salt and add to the egg mixture. Butter a mold, pour it in, and bake in an oven preheated to 350° for 30 minutes, or until a knife stuck in the center comes out clean.

Serves 6

MUSHROOMS WITH WINE AND DILL

A recipe from the "Beacon Hill Wednesday Night Buffet" group.

3 cups finely sliced mushrooms
6 tablespoons butter
salt and cayenne pepper

3 tablespoons sherry
1 tablespoon chopped dill

Cook the mushrooms in very hot butter for 3-4 minutes. Add the salt and cayenne, then the sherry and finely chopped dill.

Serves 6

GLAZED ONION RINGS

6 large onions, sliced 1/2 inch thick
6 tablespoons butter
3/4 cup Madeira

2 tablespoons chopped parsley
salt and pepper

Melt the butter in a heavy skillet, and toss the onions in the butter. Add 1/2 cup of Madeira and cover the pan. Cook the onions over medium heat until they are tender, 15-20 minutes. Remove the cover and let the wine reduce to a glaze. Stir in the remaining Madeira and the chopped parsley. Season with salt and pepper. Serve with grilled steak.

Serves 6

GLAZED ONIONS

Follow the recipe for Glazed Carrots (p. 207), substituting small peeled white onions for the carrots.

BRAISED PARSNIPS

1 bunch parsnips	nutmeg
3 tablespoons butter	chopped parsley
salt and pepper	

Clean and scrape young, freshly dug parsnips, and cut them in two lengthwise. Melt the butter in a skillet, add the parsnips and the seasoning, and cook covered over low heat until tender. Serve garnished with finely chopped parsley.

Serves 4

PARSNIP GRIDDLE CAKES

6 cooked parsnips	1 tablespoon melted butter
1 egg, well beaten	2 tablespoons flour
3/4 teaspoon salt	

Mash the parsnips, add the egg, and beat until light. Season with salt and butter, and fold in the flour. Drop by spoonfuls on a hot griddle, brown, turn, and brown the other side.

6-8 cakes

GLAZED PARSNIPS

Follow the recipe for Glazed Carrots (p. 207), substituting for the carrots young parsnips, peeled and cut in two.

FRESH PEAS

The recipe of Elizabeth Davies Throne and perfection. A pound of peas in the shell will yield about 1 cup or 2 medium servings. Allow 1 tablespoon of butter for each cup of peas.

Put 2 large lettuce leaves in a double boiler and on them place the butter, then the peas. Salt and pepper lightly and cover with another lettuce leaf. Steam gently for about 20 minutes. In the winter, tiny frozen peas may be treated the same way. Add small pearl onions which have first been parboiled, if you like.

FRESH PEAS IN CREAM

Mrs. James Markham
Hawley, Penna.

The recipe of her grandmother and mine, Ellen Sybil Barney.

3 cups shelled peas	1/2 pint heavy cream
salt to taste	2 egg yolks, well beaten

Cook the peas in just enough rapidly boiling salted water until they are just tender, 10 to 20 minutes depending upon the size of the peas. Drain and cover the peas with the cream and heat together. Have the well beaten egg yolks ready in a hot serving dish. Pour the peas and hot cream *slowly* into the yolks stirring as you do so. Serve at once. For market peas, add 1 teaspoon of sugar to the cooking water.

Serves 6

ROQUEFORT STUFFED PEPPERS

A wonderful dish.

4 medium-sized green peppers	3/4 cup mayonnaise
3/4 cup Roquefort cheese	1/2 cup milk
3/4 cup soft breadcrumbs	1 tablespoon butter

Set your oven at 350°. Cut a half-inch slice from the tops of the peppers and remove the seeds and membrane. Make the filling by mixing the crumbled cheese with the breadcrumbs, mayonnaise, and milk. Fill the peppers and dot with the butter. Set in a baking dish in 1/2 inch of hot water, then bake for 30-40 minutes, or until the peppers are tender when pierced with a fork but still slightly crisp.

Serves 4

BAKED POTATOES

There are a number of ways to embellish the baked potato that find current favor. A little sour cream, chives chopped fine, mashed anchovies, crumbled bacon—all can be good, but don't use them all at once!

Scrub potatoes well and rub with a little butter. Maine potatoes, Long Island, and Idahos, are all good, though we favor the first. Bake on the center rack of the oven at 425° for 45 minutes to an hour, depending upon the size of the potatoes. When the potatoes are light and mealy when pricked with a fork, break them open and put a good sized piece of butter in each, sprinkle with salt, pepper, and paprika, and chopped parsley. Serve piping hot. If your potatoes must be cooked in an oven whose temperature is adjusted to suit some other dish, they may be cooked just as well at a lower temperature, but must cook correspondingly longer.

STUFFED BAKED POTATOES

3 large oval potatoes	salt and pepper
2 tablespoons butter	1/2 cup warm cream

Bake the potatoes in a hot (450°) oven for 40 minutes or until soft. Remove them from the oven, cut in half lengthwise, and scoop out the potato. Mash with the other ingredients and refill the potato shells with the mixture. Bake 5-6 minutes until brown in a hot oven (450°).

Serves 6

VARIATIONS

Add grated Parmesan or Cheddar cheese (1/2 cup) and a tablespoon of finely chopped chives or green pepper to the potato mixture.

Mash anchovies with the potato (one for each portion).

Add 2 tablespoons each of fresh basil, tarragon, and parsley to the potato mixture.

Serve as a main course smothered in creamed dried beef (p. 45) and accompanied by salt pork.

POTATOES HASHED IN CREAM

6 baked potatoes	butter
1 pint heavy cream	grated cheese
salt	paprika

Bake the potatoes in their skins at least 24 hours before using; 36 hours does even better. Keep them in the refrigerator. Peel them, cut in cubes, and put in the top of a double boiler covered with the cream and salt to taste. Cook uncovered for an hour. Place the potatoes and cream in a low casserole and dot with butter, sprinkle with grated cheese and paprika and cook in a 325° to 350° oven for another half hour.

ROAST POTATOES

A marvelously tasty and effortless addition to the main course when you are roasting a joint of meat (pork, beef, or lamb).

8 large potatoes   meat drippings
salt

Cut and trim the potatoes to about the size of golf balls. Boil or steam them in salted water until nearly done. Dry them in a towel. Put in a pan containing drippings (or right in with the meat), brush well with the drippings, and roast in a hot oven for about 15 minutes. (If you put them right in with the meat, which is roasting at a lower temperature, they will take longer to cook.)

POTATO PUFF
Mrs. Margaret Flood
Philadelphia, Penna.

2 cups hot mashed potatoes   whites of 3 eggs (reserve 1 table-
3 tablespoons cream   spoonful)
2 tablespoons butter   salt and pepper, parsley, and
dash of nutmeg   paprika

Add the cream, butter, and seasonings to the hot potatoes, beat until very light, then beat the egg whites to a stiff froth and fold them in. Pile lightly in an ovenproof dish, and brush with some reserved egg white. Brown in the oven 12-15 minutes at 375°. Sprinkle with minced parsley and a dash of paprika.

Serves 6

NEW POTATOES IN CREAM

12 small new potatoes   flour
1 bunch scallions   1 tablespoon butter
1 cup cream   salt and pepper
1 cup milk   chopped fresh dill or parsley

Scrub the potatoes and scallions. Cut the potatoes in quarters and the scallions in 1-inch pieces. Put them in a saucepan and dust with flour. Add the milk and cream, butter, salt, and white pepper. Cook covered over low heat for 20-30 minutes, stirring occasionally, until done. Sprinkle generously with dill or parsley.

Serves 6

AROOSTOOK SAVORY SUPPER

You can use your own judgement as to how much to make of this old-fashioned dish. It is crusty and succulent.

Line the bottom of a buttered baking dish with raw, sliced onions. Fill the dish with thin slices of raw Maine potatoes. Add salt and pepper. Add water to almost cover. Put cubes of salt pork on top. Cook in a slow (250°) oven for 3 hours.

POTATO RIBBONS

Mrs. Arthur K. Emmons
San Diego, Calif.

Even more addictive than potato chips, potato ribbons were a favorite snack of President Garfield's. Mrs. Emmons says: "The recipe is over a hundred years old and was used in the Ballou home in Ohio by Eliza Ballou, President Garfield's mother and my own great-great-great aunt, who fried *her* potato ribbons in the old iron kettle hung in the fireplace."

Cut four pared, medium-sized potatoes in 3/4-inch slices. Pare round and round in very long ribbons. Fry them in hot lard or drippings until crisp and browned. Dry them on paper towels. Some will turn out to look like roses, and are both attractive and delicious filled with creamed chicken, tuna, or peas. Or just pile the ribbons on a hot dish and season with salt.

OVEN POTATO CHIPS

4 potatoes   salt and pepper
butter

Scrub and peel the potatoes and cut them in slices 1/4 inch thick. Soak the slices in ice water for an hour, then drain them well on paper towels. Dip the slices in melted butter and arrange them in large shallow pans. Shake salt and pepper on them and bake for 25-30 minutes in a 350° oven, stirring occasionally until they are nicely browned.

These two wild rice dishes are excellent served with game of all kinds. Today wild rice is almost prohibitively expensive, but there are, fortunately, excellent products on the market which mix brown and wild rice and closely approximate the once plentiful wild rice.

WILD RICE CASSEROLE

1 cup wild rice
4 or 5 strips bacon
3 tablespoons butter
2 onions, chopped
2 stalks celery, chopped
chopped parsley

1/2 cup sliced olives, green
  and black
salt and pepper
marjoram or thyme to taste
buttered breadcrumbs

Boil the rice until done. Fry the strips of bacon until crisp and crumble them. Cook the vegetables in the butter until slightly soft. Combine all of the ingredients except the breadcrumbs. If the dish is not moist enough add a little broth. Cover well with browned breadcrumbs and heat for 15-20 minutes in a 350° oven.

Serves 6

WILD RICE AND MUSHROOMS IN SOUR CREAM

1 pound mushrooms
3 tablespoons butter
1 cup sour cream
salt and pepper
a pinch mace

1/2 cup red wine
1 cup wild rice
parsley
crumbled crisp bacon

Slice the mushrooms coarsely and cook them in the butter. Add salt, pepper, mace, and red wine. When done add the sour cream and heat through. Meantime, cook and season the rice, and cook the bacon. Pour the mushrooms on a large hot platter and surround them with mounds of wild rice, decorate with parsley, and cover with crumbled bacon.

Serves 6

RATATOUILLE

George Mittendorf
Cranbury, N.J.

An excellent dish, particularly useful for a buffet party as it keeps warm for a good time and does not lose in appearance by waiting.

1 large egg plant	1 large can of tomatoes, or fresh
2 green peppers	tomatoes in season
3 onions	basil
1/2 pound mushrooms	oregano
1/4 cup olive oil	Tabasco
	salt and pepper

Cut up vegetables and mix with oil, seasonings, and tomatoes. Pour into a large greased casserole. The juice should just be seen around the edges of the vegetables. Cook for 1 hour in a 350° oven.

Serves 12

SCALLIONS ON TOAST

12 scallions
melted butter
2 pieces buttered toast

Cook the scallions in lightly salted boiling water for 15-20 minutes until tender. Arrange on toast and pour the melted butter over them.

Serves 2

SPINACH AND SOUR CREAM

Freshly picked spinach deserves special treatment.

Trim the stems of the spinach, and wash it in several waters. Lift it from the water, letting it drain a moment in your hands, and toss it into a large pot. Cover the pot tightly and cook the spinach over low heat for 5 minutes. The leaves should wilt but retain their color and shape. Uncover and raise the heat to boil away all the water. Chop the spinach coarsely, just enough so that the leaves are manageable on a fork. Add salt and pepper, a little sour cream, and a few drops of lemon juice.

A pound of spinach serves 3

SPINACH MOLD

2 packages frozen spinach soufflé

Defrost the packages of soufflé until soft enough to spoon. Butter a 1-quart mold and spoon in the spinach. Bake in a 375° oven for about 1 hour, let stand in a warm place for 10-15 minutes, loosen around the edges with a knife, and unmold on a hot serving dish.

Serves 6

BAKED SQUASH

Turban, Hubbard, and Butternut Squash are all traditional.

a 2-pound squash
brown sugar
salt and pepper

lemon juice
butter

Cut the squash into quarters, and remove the seeds and fiber. Place in a pan in which you have put 1/4 inch of water. Sprinkle with brown sugar, salt, pepper, and lemon juice. Dot with butter. Cook covered with aluminum foil in a moderate oven (375°) for 30 minutes. Uncover, baste, adding more butter if necessary, and bake for 30 minutes longer or until tender.

Serves 4

TOASTED SQUASH SEEDS

Spread squash seeds in a shallow pan, add salt and butter, and toast, stirring occasionally until brown.

STUFFED ACORN SQUASH

This makes a nice supper dish.

2 acorn squash
1 and 1/2 cups chopped ham
1/2 cup cooked rice
milk or cream

salt and pepper
butter
bacon strips

Cut squash in half and remove seeds and fiber. Season with salt and pepper, and dot with butter. Bake in a moderate (375°) oven for 30 minutes. Remove and fill with a mixture of ham and rice moistened with a little milk or cream. Spread a strip of bacon cut in two over each half, and return to the oven for 10-15 minutes.

Serves 4

LADY SLIPPER SUMMER SQUASH

6 small summer squash
1 cup sour cream
curry powder
ginger

salt and pepper
2 tablespoons grated Parmesan
cheese

Cut the squash in two, lengthwise. Spread each piece with seasoned sour cream and bake, covered, in a pan containing a little water in a 375° oven for 20-30 minutes, or until done.

Serves 6

BAKED SWEET POTATOES WITH APPLES

3 large apples
3 tablespoons butter
3 large sweet potatoes, boiled
  and skinned

1 teaspoon salt
1/2 cup maple syrup

Core, pare, and slice the apples, and fry them in butter until light brown. Slice the potatoes. Arrange the apples and potatoes in alternate layers in a buttered baking dish. Sprinkle with salt. Pour the syrup over the dish and dot with more butter. Bake in a moderate oven (350°) for about 35 minutes. (Note: Cornflakes may be crumbled over the surface of this dish before dotting it with butter, or it may be topped with a layer of marshmallows.)

SWEET POTATO ORANGE PUDDING

A dish to be served with ham.

1 and 1/2 cups grated raw
  sweet potatoes
3/4 cup orange juice
1 teaspoon grated orange rind
1/4 cup sugar

1/2 teaspoon salt
1/4 teaspoon cinnamon
1/8 teaspoon cloves
1/2 cup melted butter

Mix the ingredients well and pour into a greased casserole. Cover the dish with aluminum foil during the first 35 minutes of baking time in a 350° oven. Then turn the oven to 325° and remove the foil. Bake for 30 minutes longer. When the pudding is done, a knife inserted in the center will come out clean. Children love this pudding topped with marshmallows. (Arrange a layer of them on the casserole for the second part of the baking.)

Serves 6

NOTTINGHAM YAM PUDDING

Dianthe Joylove
Woodbury, Conn.

A family recipe, this light and airy dish is almost a soufflé.

5 medium sweet potatoes, boiled,
   peeled, and mashed
1/3 cup butter
1 and 1/4 cups brown sugar
4 egg yolks, well beaten

1/2 cup sherry
salt to taste
1 teaspoon nutmeg
1/4 teaspoon mace
2 egg whites, stiffly beaten

Cream together the butter and sugar and mix in the beaten egg yolks, the mashed sweet potatoes, sherry, and seasonings. Fold in the egg whites and pour the mixture into a buttered casserole and bake at 350° for 40 minutes.

Serves 8

TOMATOES IN CREAM

6 large tomatoes, peeled and
   sliced
3 tablespoons butter
1 tablespoon flour

1 and 1/2 tablespoons sugar
1 cup cream
salt and pepper
chopped basil, dill, or parsley

Arrange the tomato slices in a shallow baking dish, dust them with flour and sugar, salt and pepper, and dot with the butter. Pour the cream over the tomatoes and cover the dish with a lid or with aluminum foil. Bake in a moderately hot oven (375°) for about 10 minutes, until the tomatoes are tender but not soft. Sprinkle with chopped herbs and serve.

Serves 6

TOMATOES AU GRATIN

Prepare Tomatoes in Cream (above). When done sprinkle the surface with 1/4 cup grated Parmesan cheese; and put under the broiler to brown.

Serves 6

GLAZED TURNIPS

Follow the recipe for Glazed Carrots (p. 207), substituting peeled white, purple-topped turnips for the carrots.

ZUCCHINI WITH ALMONDS

1 pound zucchini (small ones are best)
4 tablespoons butter
1 teaspoon salt

1/2 onion, minced
ground pepper
1/4 cup whole blanched almonds

Roast the almonds in the butter in a large skillet; add the salt, onion, and the zucchini sliced diagonally. Grind pepper over the dish, and cook, stirring, over medium heat until the zucchini is cooked—about 5 minutes.

Serves 4-6

ZUCCHINI CUTLETS

This is a favorite recipe of Mrs. Connie deAngelo, one of the few women regulars on Blackstone Street, Haymarket, Boston.

3 zucchini squash
2 eggs, beaten
2 rounded tablespoons grated Romano cheese
parsley (fresh cut or dried)

3 tablespoons cooking oil
1 and 1/4 cups seasoned breadcrumbs
1/4 teaspoon salt
freshly ground pepper

Cut the ends from the zucchini, peel, and cut into strips about 1 inch wide, 4 inches long, and 3/4 inch thick. Mix salt and pepper with the beaten eggs. Heat cooking oil in a large skillet until hot. Mix the cheese and breadcrumbs. Dip the slices of zucchini in the egg, then the breadcrumb mixture, and brown on all sides. Turn gently to avoid breaking the slices. Add more cooking oil if necessary. Remove to a heated platter, sprinkle with parsley and serve as is, or with a tomato sauce.

Serves 6

Chapter 10.
Salads &
Salad Dressings

A salad of greens is perfect accompaniment to either luncheon or dinner, with meats, hot or cold, chicken, fish, omelets, and various luncheon dishes. Lettuces, chicory, watercress, endive—choose the best available and pick over, wash, and dry the leaves very carefully. Even a little water clinging to the salad leaves can ruin your result. Endive, however, should be wiped clean, never washed.

This chapter includes a number of dressings for greens or for the more elaborate salads using meat and seafood combinations that make the mainstay of a meal served with hot breads. The dressings and often the ingredients of the salads, too, are pretty much interchangeable to suit your taste. A summer garden can yield a tantalizing variety of herbs, lettuces, and tiny fresh vegetables.

GREENS SALAD

When greens are at their best, fresh from the garden or from the Farmer's Market, they should be dressed simply. Remove the outside leaves, wash the salad thoroughly in cold water, and allow it to become bone dry before using it. (First shake it dry and then store it, rolled in a dry towel, in the refrigerator.) Arrange the greens as you choose and add a little chopped herb or herbs, or tomatoes or cucumbers for a change. At the table add to the bowl a few tablespoons of oil, just enough to coat the leaves well, a dash of vinegar or lemon juice. Shake salt and grind pepper over the bowl and mix it all thoroughly. If you like garlic, rub the bowl with a little beforehand. This is a good place to say that, contrary to a frequently voiced theory, a wooden salad bowl should be washed after each using. If not it will become rancid. Use either the finest grade of olive oil or a corn or safflower oil. These delicate oils will not submerge the taste of the greens. For an interesting change we note that the French sometimes dress salad with cream and lemon juice instead of with oil. Splendid!

GREEN BEAN SALAD

Mrs. Frank Savicki
Cranston, R.I.

1 pound fresh or frozen whole green beans	French dressing
1 onion, sliced thin	crisp bacon, crumbled

Cook beans in rapidly boiling salted water—about 10 minutes for frozen, about 15 for fresh beans. Drain the beans, and pour while still hot over onion sliced in a bowl. Moisten with plain or garlic French dressing and refrigerate for at least 2 hours, until very cold. Just before serving, sprinkle the salad with very crisp bacon bits.

CAULIFLOWER SALAD

Sarah K. Wheaton
Darien, Conn.

1 cauliflower	salad herbs
1 jar small stuffed olives	lettuce
Roquefort cheese	

Cut the cauliflower into small flowerlets and marinate in Lemon Salad Dressing (p. 239) for several hours. Slice the olives and combine with lettuce, dressing, and cauliflower. Add a pinch of herbs. Mix well. Serve with Roquefort cheese sprinkled on top.

CUCUMBER SALAD

2 cucumbers
1 small onion
vinegar

salt and pepper
oil
sour cream, if desired

Pare the cucumbers and slice them as thin as possible. If the cucumbers are old enough to have large seeds in the middle, cut that section in two and spoon out the seeds. Cut the onion in thin slices. Sprinkle the vegetables with salt and pepper and marinate them in vinegar for at least 3 or 4 hours in the refrigerator. Drain the salad well and dress it with oil and, if you wish, sour cream. Arrange in a serving dish and return to the refrigerator so that the salad will be icy cold at serving. Finely minced parsley, chives, or mint can be used to lend variety to this dish.

SPINACH SALAD, *PRINCESS LOUISE*

This salad, contributed by Donald Bruce White, was served on the old S. S. *Princess Louise* that used to sail out of San Francisco.

1 and 1/2 pounds spinach
3 hardcooked eggs
3 strips crisp bacon

dressing
chopped chives

Wash, trim, and dry the spinach and tear it into small pieces. Grate the eggs and crumble the bacon over it, add the dressing and chopped chives and mix well.

DRESSING

1 raw egg
1 tablespoon grated Parmesan
  cheese
1 clove of garlic, crushed

1 and 1/2 teaspoons Dijon mustard
1/2 cup oil
1/4 cup lemon juice

Combine the ingredients and chill thoroughly before using.

CHRISTMAS SALAD

Mrs. Robert Mitchell
Swarthmore, Penna.

a head of lettuce, torn in pieces
1 cucumber, sliced thin

1 can mandarin oranges, drained
pomegranate seeds

Toss the ingredients together. Chill, and serve with Onion Dressing (p. 239).

SALADS AS A MAIN DISH

Here are some excellent salads, each of which makes a complete meal with the addition of some interesting toast or bread. They are my favorite luncheon throughout the summer. Combine the ingredients in a quantity sufficient to the size of your group.

BACON AND EGG SALAD

This salad is wonderful combined with Victoria House Dressing (see p. 241).

young spinach leaves, washed and
dried
hardcooked eggs
ham strips
plenty of crisp bacon
chopped pistachio nuts

a fresh pear, peeled, cored, and
sliced
croutons of whole-wheat bread
rubbed with garlic and browned
in olive oil

SALADE NIÇOISE

As written by the contributor, Jay Langdon Gaiser of Dragonwyck, Bermuda.

Rub bowl with garlic
Heavily *oil* and vinegar dressing
& dried basil aplenty or ditto of
chopped fresh
lettuces, endive (watercress, dandelion greens, whatever)
tomatoes (peeled, seeded, eighthed)
scallions—chunked, ringed, however
black olives

tunny fish (or julienne strips of
chicken)
mushrooms, sliced, raw
green or red peppers
hardcooked eggs, chunkily chopped
cucumbers, peeled, seeded, and
sliced
capers
anchovies, if you like

MEAT AND POTATO SALAD

A fine, hearty salad that uses up those choice morsels of left-over beef.

fresh young lettuce, clean and dry
rare roast beef or beefsteak (all fat
removed), cut in julienne strips
cold potatoes (skins on), sliced

chopped cucumbers
oil, vinegar, salt, and pepper to
taste
dill or chives, if available

SALMON SALAD

Helen Haaland
Woodbury, Conn.

2 cups salmon
1 cup chopped cucumber, drained
1 teaspoon chopped parsley
1 teaspoon onion, minced
1/2 cup celery, sliced

1/2 teaspoon salt
1/8 teaspoon pepper
1 cup sour cream
1 teaspoon capers (optional)

Flake the salmon. Add the cucumber, parsley, onion, celery, salt and pepper and mix well. Blend in the sour cream. Place on a bed of lettuce leaves and garnish with capers.

SPINACH SALAD SUPREME

A good hearty luncheon salad.

fresh spinach leaves
garden or iceberg lettuce
hardcooked eggs, peeled and
    quartered
fresh tomatoes, peeled and cut
    into wedges

an avocado (or two), peeled,
    stoned, and sliced
Green Goddess salad dressing
    (p. 242)

Remove the stems from the spinach leaves. Wash the spinach and lettuce thoroughly, dry the leaves, and wrap in a dry, clean towel. Place in the icebox to crisp. Prepare the other ingredients. When you are ready to serve the salad, combine the ingredients by tossing together in a bowl with the dressing.

TROUT SALAD

1 medium-sized trout
herb vinegar
4 hardcooked eggs

lettuce
mayonnaise

Boil trout in slightly salted water. Drain. Remove bones and skin. Break the fish into flakes. Marinate in vinegar for 2 hours. Drain. Serve on lettuce leaves with mayonnaise and hardcooked eggs.

Serves 4

LOBSTER SALAD

Crabmeat Salad and Shrimp Salad may be made by the same rule, substituting crab or shrimp for the lobster meat.

3 cups cooked lobster, cut up
chopped inside part of 1 bunch
  celery
3 hardcooked eggs, chopped
1 teaspoon chopped parsley

1 teaspoon chopped chives
1/2 teaspoon chopped dill
1 cup homemade mayonnaise
  (p. 243)
1 tablespoon lemon juice

Combine the ingredients gently and pile them on a large platter of the finest greens available which have been washed, dried, and lightly coated with French dressing. Garnish the platter as you wish with ripe tomato slices, sprigs of watercress, and stuffed eggs. Serve a cucumber salad on the side.

Serves 6

CHICKEN SALAD

breasts of 3 chickens, or 1 whole
  chicken, cooked as below
inside stalks of 1 bunch celery,
  chopped
1 teaspoon each of chopped parsley,
  tarragon, and chives

2 tablespoons capers
1 cup homemade mayonnaise
  (p. 243)
salt and white pepper to taste
cut up ripe olives, if desired

Cook the chicken in enough water to cover with salt, peppercorns, a slice of onion, and a bay leaf. Cool it, skin it, and cut it in large cubes. Mix with the other ingredients and serve on a large platter on a bed of greens which have been dressed. Garnish as you wish with tomatoes, avocado slices, or bunches of watercress.

Serves 6

VARIATIONS ON CHICKEN SALAD

For these variations you may want to omit the capers and black olives.

HAWAIIAN CHICKEN SALAD

Add a cup of diced, fresh pineapple and about 2 tablespoons of toasted, slivered almonds to the salad.

CHICKEN SALAD SUPREME

Add a cup of white grapes and chopped almonds or pistachio nuts to the salad.

SHRIMP SALAD

Refreshing and satisfying fare with a touch of luxury. Serve it with jellied madrilène for the soup course and hot garlic French bread.

1/2 head lettuce, washed, dried, and crisped
2 tomatoes, sliced thin
1/2 pound cooked shrimp
1/2 pound mushroom caps, sautéed lightly, and cooled
a few stuffed green olives, halved
1/3 cup sour cream

1/3 cup cottage cheese
1/3 cup mayonnaise
2 hardcooked eggs, quartered
salad herb mixture
1 teaspoon sherry
parsley
paprika
salt

Make the salad dressing, using the sour cream, mayonnaise, and cottage cheese. Season with a little salt, salad herb mixture, and the sherry. If you use canned shrimp and mushrooms, rinse them thoroughly before using. Mix them, with the halved olives, into the dressing. Line a shallow, medium-sized salad bowl with lettuce, and place a row of tomato slices around the bowl so that the lettuce shows above them. Spoon the shrimp mixture into the middle. Sprinkle with parsley. Garnish with the hardcooked egg sections sprinkled with paprika.

Serves 3-4

FRUIT SALAD

Fruit salad can be varied greatly according to the season. Oranges, grapefruit and bananas are common in the winter. Marinate the cut-up fruit in French dressing and serve it on the best available greens which have been washed, dried and tossed in French dressing too. Nuts, balls of cream cheese, or maraschino cherries may be used to garnish the salad. In summer, a more interesting salad can be made with sliced peaches and pears sprinkled with lemon juice to prevent discoloration, then marinated in French dressing, bing cherries stuffed with creamed cheese, julienne strips of ham, and again nuts. Pistachio nuts or sliced water chestnuts go well with fruit. The salad may be served with Golden Dressing (p. 242).

APPLE AND CELERY MOLD

Christine Ives
New Harbor, Me.

1 envelope unflavored gelatin
1 cup cold water
1 and 1/2 cups boiling water
1/2 cup lemon juice

1/2 cup sugar
3 tart apples, diced
1 cup celery, diced
1/2 cup pecan meats

Soak the gelatin in cold water for 5 minutes and dissolve in boiling water. Add the lemon juice and sugar. When mixture begins to set, add the apples, celery and broken nut meats. Turn into a mold and chill.

AVOCADO RING

3 avocados
1 envelope gelatin
1/2 cup lime juice
8 ounces cream or cottage cheese

1 and 1/2 teaspoons salt
3/4 cup milk
1/2 bunch watercress

Cut avocados lengthwise into halves; remove the stone and skin. This is done easily by first running a blunt silver knife around the inner skin. Place halves cut side down and slice a thin oval from the outside of each. Sprinkle the ovals with lemon juice and press them gently around the sides of a 6-cup ring mold. Sieve the rest of the avocado or whirl in a blender. Soften the gelatin in 1/4 cup lime juice and dissolve over hot water. Beat the cheese until soft and smooth (or whirl in blender). Remove the tough stems of the watercress only if necessary. Combine and beat all ingredients. Turn into the mold and chill until firm. If you are in a hurry, the process may be speeded by putting the ring in the freezing compartment of the refrigerator for a while. The center of the ring may be filled with chicken, shrimp, or crabmeat salad (p. 231 and p. 232).

Serves 6-8

BEET JELLY RING

Dianthe Joylove
Woodbury, Conn.

2 packages plain gelatin
2 bouillon cubes
1/4 cup cold water
2 cups boiling water
1 cup shredded cabbage
1 cup shredded beets

3 stalks celery, chopped fine
3 tablespoons lemon juice
2 tablespoons tarragon vinegar
1/2 teaspoon salt
few grains cayenne pepper
1 cup sour cream

Soak the gelatin in the cold water. Add the bouillon cubes and pour the hot water over, stirring till dissolved. Add the remaining ingredients, stirring the cream until completely blended. Pour into a ring mold or loaf pan and chill in the refrigerator until ready. To serve, unmold on a platter garnished with lettuce or watercress. If a ring mold is used, the center of the ring may be filled with well marinated sliced tomatoes and cucumbers or a meat mixture.

Serves 4-6

EGG RING SALAD

Phyllis Worcester
Dublin, N.H.

8 hardboiled eggs, put through ricer
1 large onion, chopped fine
2 tablespoons chopped parsley
2 tablespoons chopped pimiento
salt and vinegar to taste
2 tablespoons mayonnaise
1 envelope gelatin

Soak 1 envelope gelatin in 1/2 cup cold water 10 minutes. Add 1 cup boiling water to dissolve. Mix all together. Put in ring mold. Chill until firm. Unmold and fill the center with chopped cucumbers, mixed vegetables or potato salad.

SPINACH RING

A nice change for a summer luncheon or buffet table, this ring may be filled with any cold food that fits the menu—fish or shellfish mixed with celery, egg salad, macaroni salad, quartered tomatoes, or ham and potato salad.

2 envelopes unflavored gelatin
1/4 cup cold water
1 can condensed beef broth
1/4 teaspoon salt
2 tablespoons lemon juice
1 cup French dressing, mayonnaise, or sour cream
1 medium onion, quartered
1 package (10 ounces) frozen chopped spinach, thawed
4 hardcooked eggs, quartered
1/2 pound bacon, cooked crisp and crumbled
pimiento strips

Sprinkle the gelatin over the water and 1/4 cup beef broth in the blender and allow to stand. Heat the remaining beef broth to boil and add to the blender, whirling until all the gelatin is dissolved. Add the salt, lemon juice, and salad dressing and blend well. Stop, add the onion, then the spinach and eggs until eggs are just coarsely chopped. Stir in the bacon and turn into a ring mold or 6-cup mold. Chill for 2-3 hours or until firm. Unmold, garnish with pimiento strips and fill with the desired mixture.

Serves 8

HEALTH SALAD

Marla Joylove
Woodbury, Conn.

2 cups shredded raw carrots
1 cup grated pineapple
1/2 cup shredded cabbage
1 package orange gelatin
2 cups pineapple or orange juice
lettuce

Prepare the orange gelatin, using pineapple or orange juice for the pint of liquid required. Add the vegetables and fruit, and pour into a mold. Refrigerate until the gelatin is set, stirring once before it sets so that the fruit and vegetables do not settle on the bottom of the mold. Unmold and serve on lettuce leaves with salad dressing.

JELLIED ROQUEFORT CHEESE MOUSSE

Mrs. Ruth Skillman
Riverdale, N.Y.

This mousse is particularly good served with the fresh fruits of summer and mixed greens from the garden. It can be used as the main course for luncheon on a hot day or as part of a buffet.

1 tablespoon gelatin
1/4 cup cold water
1 cup whipped cream
1/2 cup Roquefort or blue cheese
1/2 pound cream cheese (or

cottage cheese, whipped smooth)
1/4 teaspoon salt
1 teaspoon onion juice
1/4 teaspoon paprika

Mix the gelatin and cold water and melt over hot water. Mix the cheeses and seasonings with a little cream to smooth them out. Add this to the melted gelatin, then fold in the whipped cream. This amount will fill one 1 and 1/2 quart mold and is very nice in a ring mold surrounded with halved pears or other fruit sprinkled with French dressing. Put watercress in the center of the ring. It can also be molded in a bread tin and sliced or be served to spread on crackers.

1 and 1/2 quarts

CRISP CUCUMBER ASPIC

Mrs. Griswold Frelinghuysen of Woodstock, Vermont, perfected this appetizing summer dish.

2 thin cucumbers, 1 peeled,
    1 unpeeled
2 tender stalks celery, minced
1/2 green pepper, minced
1 tablespoon grated onion
chopped herbs, dill, chives, or
    parsley as available
1 teaspoon salt

1 tablespoon sugar
1/4 cup lemon juice
1/4 cup vinegar
2 packages gelatin softened in
    1/2 cup cold water
2 cups boiling water
2 or 3 drops green food coloring

Slice the seedless end parts of both cucumbers using about half of each. Then remove the seeds from the center sections and dice them. Mix together all of the diced vegetables and the cucumber slices. Add the seasonings, and last the gelatin softened in water, the boiling water, and the food coloring. Pour into a 1-quart mold and chill until set. Serve on greens, with sour cream dressing (p. 242).

FISH IN ASPIC

1 package lemon gelatin
1 and 3/4 cups tomato juice
1 tablespoon vinegar
1 cup celery, diced fine
2 tablespoons minced green
  pepper

1 tablespoon minced onion
1/2 teaspoon salt
dash of pepper
2 cups cooked fish

Boil the tomato juice, dissolve the gelatin in it and all the other ingredients, except the fish. Chill the mixture and when it is about to set combine it with the fish. Brush a mold lightly with oil and pour the mixture into it. Chill until firm and unmold on lettuce leaves which have been tossed in salad oil. Garnish with cucumbers and capers and serve with mayonnaise (p. 243).

Serves 6

CRANBERRY SALAD

Mrs. Ruth B. Phifer
Seattle, Wash.

A tangy, colorful salad which is a traditional Thanksgiving dish of the Phifer family.

3 cups fresh cranberries
2 cups water
2 and 1/2 cups sugar
2 packages lemon gelatin

1 cup crushed pineapple (drained)
1 cup cherries or pink grapes
1 cup chopped walnuts

Cook the cranberries in the sugar and water until the berries pop. Remove from heat. Dissolve the gelatin in this mixture and cool slightly. Add the pineapple, cherries or grapes, and walnuts. Serve with Golden Dressing (p. 242).

CHRISTMAS RIBBON SALAD

Mrs. Walter Choquette
Pawtucket, R.I.

FIRST LAYER

1 3-ounce package lime gelatin
1/2 cup well drained crushed

pineapple
1 and 3/4 cups boiling water

Dissolve the gelatin in the boiling water. When it begins to stiffen stir in the pineapple. Put in a 5 and 1/2 x 4 and 1/2 x 2 and 1/2" bread pan and chill until set.

SECOND LAYER

8 ounces cream cheese (room
  temperature)
1/4 cup salad dressing

1/4 cup soured cream
1/2 cup chopped walnuts

Blend the cream cheese, soured cream and salad dressing until smooth; add the nut meats and spread on top of the stiffened lime layer. Chill.

THIRD LAYER

1 (3-ounce) package of cranberry/
  orange gelatin

1 and 3/4 cups boiling water
1/2 cup raw cranberry relish

Dissolve the gelatin in the boiling water. When it begins to stiffen, stir in the well drained relish. Spread on top of the cream cheese layer. Refrigerate all until firm.

To unmold, run a thin knife around the four sides and dip the pan into hot water up to the top of the gelatin. Wipe the outside carefully. Put a *flat* serving dish on top and invert. Surround with lettuce leaves. To serve, slice at the table. It has a built-in dressing.

HEARTY SALADS

OLD DUTCH COLE SLAW

This excellent cole slaw may be varied from time to time by the addition of white grapes, slivered almonds, or a pinch of dry mustard.

1 young cabbage, finely shredded
1 cup heavy cream
1/2 cup sugar

1/2 cup vinegar
1 teaspoon salt
white pepper to taste

Beat together the cream, sugar, vinegar, salt, and pepper until of the consistency of thin whipped cream. Mix the sauce with the shredded cabbage just before serving. Garnish with sprigs of watercress.

Serves 6

MACARONI SALAD

Mrs. Paul A. Kulkmann
St. Petersburg, Fla.

1 lb. elbow macaroni (cooked)
1/4 cup olives, chopped fine
2 7-ounce cans tuna fish, drained
3 fresh tomatoes, cut up fine
1 large onion, chopped fine

1 cucumber (leave skin on),
  chopped
salt and pepper to taste
mayonnaise

Mix all the ingredients together with enough mayonnaise to moisten the mixture. Refrigerate for several hours before serving.

HOT POTATO SALAD

Carolyn W. Tyler
Fairhaven, Mass.

6 slices bacon
1/2 cup chopped onion
1 teaspoon salt
1 tablespoon sugar
1 tablespoon flour
1 teaspoon dry mustard

dash of pepper
3/4 cup water
1/4 cup vinegar
4 cups sliced boiled potatoes
2 hardboiled eggs, quartered

Fry the bacon until crisp. Remove from the skillet and pour off all but 1/4 cup of fat. Add the onion and cook until lightly brown. Stir in the next six ingredients. Add the water and vinegar. Cook, stirring until thickened. Add the potatoes (mix lightly), the eggs and crumbled bacon. Let stand over heat until warm.

SOUR CREAM POTATO SALAD

6 cups cooked diced potatoes
1 cucumber, seeded and diced
2 hardcooked eggs
1 cup thick sour cream
1/2 cup mayonnaise
1 teaspoon dry mustard
1 and 1/2 teaspoons salt

fresh ground pepper
2 tablespoons vinegar
1 teaspoon celery seed
1 tablespoon minced onion
chopped fresh herbs, chives, dill,
  or parsley as available

Combine potatoes, cucumber, onion, celery seed, salt and pepper. Toss lightly together. Separate yolks from whites of eggs. Chop the whites and add them to the salad. Mash the yolks and combine with the sour cream, mustard, mayonnaise and vinegar. Beat well and toss lightly with the potatoes. Serve on crisp lettuce garnished with tomatoes and sprinkled, if you wish, with crumbled crisp bacon.

Serves 6-8

FRENCH DRESSING

2/3 cup olive oil or any other salad oil

1/3 cup vinegar or lemon juice

1 teaspoon salt

freshly ground pepper, black or white

1 clove garlic, crushed, if desired

Shake ingredients together in a screw top jar and store in the refrigerator.

LEMON SALAD DRESSING

Sarah K. Wheaton
Darien, Conn.

1 cup olive oil

4 tablespoons lemon juice

1 tablespoon onion juice

2 tablespoons sugar

salt and pepper to taste

Combine lemon and onion juice with sugar. Add half the olive oil and shake or blend together, then add the remainder of the olive oil and mix vigorously. This dressing is good with a tossed greens salad or Cauliflower Salad (p. 227).

ONION DRESSING

Mrs. Robert Mitchell
Swarthmore, Penna.

1 large onion

1 cup sugar

1 teaspoon salt

1/2 teaspoon celery seed

1/2 cup vinegar

a little grated lemon rind

2 cups salad oil

Grate the onion on the sugar and allow to stand for 30 minutes. Add the salt, celery seed, and lemon rind. Beat in oil, then vinegar, a little at a time, alternately, until the dressing is very thick. Use with tossed greens salad, cabbage and Roquefort; head lettuce with hardcooked egg, parsley, and crumbled American cheese. This dressing can be made very quickly if you use a blender.

ANCHOVY ROQUEFORT SALAD DRESSING

While the young greens of summer need little adornment in the winter-time, the iceberg lettuce which is sometimes all that is available is improved by having a rather tangy dressing. This one is the recipe of my husband, John Davies Stamm, and it is particularly welcome when salad greens need a little extra inspiration. A half head of iceberg lettuce served with this, cottage cheese, and melba toast makes a splendid lunch that is light on calories.

2 or 3 anchovies
4 or 5 tablespoons of soft
   Roquefort cheese
1/4 cup olive oil

the juice of half a lemon
1 clove garlic
salt

Mash the ingredients together, or whirl in the blender. Pour over the lettuce, adding a few grinds of black pepper and a few chopped pecans.

Serves 2

PARMESAN CHEESE SALAD DRESSING

Mrs. John Whitton
New Canaan, Conn.

1 rounded teaspoon butter
2 slices bread
1 egg, room temperature
1/2 cup salad oil
1/2 cup grated Parmesan cheese

dash of cayenne
salt
vinegar
1/2 clove garlic, mashed

Cut the bread in tiny cubes and stir them in melted butter in an iron frying pan. Place in a low oven stirring occasionally until browned. Beat the egg with salt, garlic, and cayenne and add the oil a few drops at a time, beating until thick. Add the vinegar and beat well, then mix in the cheese. Pour over lettuce and toss. Add the bread cubes at the last moment. This is good with any salad greens, but especially with Bibb or Boston lettuce.

WATERCRESS DRESSING

1/2 cup olive oil
1 tablespoon cider vinegar
1/2 bunch watercress, coarse stems
    removed, washed and thoroughly
    dried

1/2 clove garlic
salt to taste

This dressing must be made in an electric blender. Whirl it until thoroughly mixed and light. The specks of watercress will coat the lettuce and lend their flavor to it. Sliver a handful of blanched almonds into the salad. This makes enough dressing for 2 heads of Boston lettuce. Also good on endive.

Serves 6

COLE SLAW DRESSING

Ellen Ormsbee Warder
Newfane, Vt.

Also very good on sliced tomatoes.

2 tablespoons sugar
1 teaspoon salt
1 teaspoon dry mustard
1 and 1/4 tablespoons flour

1 egg, beaten
5 tablespoons cider vinegar
1 cup sweet whole milk
1 tablespoon butter

Stir together in the order given. Add the milk last. Cook in a double boiler until thick, and then put in the butter and stir well. If too thick, dilute with light cream before using.

GREEN CHEESE SAUCE

This may be used as a thick dressing for greens or other salads, or served to spread on crackers. The color is beautiful.

2 cups cottage cheese
2 ounces blue cheese
2 tablespoons sour cream

1/4 bunch watercress, chopped
1 clove garlic

Whirl all together in a blender at high speed until light and smooth, or if you do not have a blender, mash the ingredients together thoroughly and beat them well with a hand, or electric, beater. Chill before serving.

VICTORIA HOUSE DRESSING

1 egg
1 ounce Roquefort cheese
juice of half a lemon
1/2 teaspoon salt
1/4 teaspoon mustard

1 clove garlic
1/2 cup olive oil
1/2 cup cream (sour cream or
    heavy sweet cream)

Having all of the ingredients at room temperature, place the first six in the container of a blender. Whirl together at low speed and then very slowly pour in the oil. Add the cream and whirl until blended. The dressing should be fairly thick, almost like mayonnaise.

GREEN GODDESS SALAD DRESSING

Said to have been General Eisenhower's favorite salad dressing, this concoction turns a greens salad into a work of art. Add a can of tuna fish or chopped ham and buttered croutons for a light meal.

1 clove garlic, crushed	1 cup mayonnaise
2 tablespoons green onions, chopped	2 tablespoons tarragon vinegar
	1/2 tablespoon lemon juice
1 tablespoon anchovy paste	1 drop green food coloring
1/2 cup sour cream	black pepper

Combine the ingredients and chill for 2-3 hours to blend the flavors.

GOLDEN DRESSING

Mrs. Ruth B. Phifer
Seattle, Wash.

A favorite fruit salad dressing.

2 eggs	4 tablespoons lemon juice
1/4 cup sugar	1 cup pineapple juice
1 tablespoon flour	1 cup whipped cream

Beat the eggs together with the sugar, flour and lemon juice. Add the pineapple juice. Cook the mixture until it thickens, stirring constantly. Cool. Just before serving, fold in the whipped cream.

SOUR CREAM DRESSING

Just as it was written in Newfane, Vt., more than 100 years ago.

Put the yolks of two hardboiled eggs in a soup plate and rub them very smooth. Add a saltspoon of salt and 1/2 saltspoon of pepper. Then rub in sour cream, as much as you would oil. It will get very thick. Now thin it out with vinegar and add a little sugar (this could be put in at the same time as the salt and pepper). Don't have the lettuce wet. The number of eggs depends on the quantity of dressing desired. Chop the whites of the eggs and sprinkle them on top when the salad is ready to serve.

MAYONNAISE

Mayonnaise is often called the mother of sauces. It is easy to make if you remember to have the ingredients at room temperature and move slowly but steadily in adding the oil to the egg yolks. Good store mayonnaise is nice to have on hand for emergency sandwich making, but it bears only a faint resemblance to homemade mayonnaise. It seems to me that a fine salad of chicken or cold asparagus or cold fish deserves only the best of sauces.

1 egg yolk at room temperature	2 tablespoons vinegar or lemon
1 teaspoon salt	juice
1/2 teaspoon dry mustard	1 cup fine olive or salad oil
1/4 teaspoon paprika	

Beat the egg yolk and dry seasonings thoroughly in a small bowl which has been rinsed with hot water and wiped dry; add 1 tablespoon of vinegar and beat again. Beat in oil a few drops at a time until 1/4 cup is used, then add more rapidly. As the mixture becomes thick, add the remaining vinegar.

Note: If the oil is added too rapidly the mayonnaise will curdle. To remedy this, beat the curdled mixture slowly into a second egg yolk.

Mayonnaise may be made in an electric blender or beater. Just be sure to add the oil slowly at first.

About 1 and 1/4 cups

MAYONNAISE VARIATIONS

GREEN MAYONNAISE

Add 1/4 cup of puréed, raw spinach or watercress and a drop of green food coloring.

ROQUEFORT MAYONNAISE

Beat in an ounce of Roquefort cheese and a mashed clove of garlic.

ANCHOVY MAYONNAISE

Beat in anchovy paste or mashed anchovies.

RUSSIAN DRESSING

Add 1/4 teaspoon paprika, an ounce of red caviar and 3 tablespoons of chili sauce.

SOUR CREAM MAYONNAISE

Mix half and half with sour cream and add a teaspoon of horseradish and a tablespoon of capers.

SHRIMP DIP

Mix mayonnaise half and half with sour cream and add curry powder to taste. Serve with cooked fresh shrimp—as a dip.

Chapter 11.
Sauces and Side Dishes

As every serious cook and lucky eater knows, the proper sauce adds the finishing touch of perfection to many an entrée or dish of vegetables. Indeed, certain sauces, such as cream sauce (also known as white sauce) form the basis of numerous recipes. (For dessert sauces, see Desserts.)

CREAM SAUCE

4 tablespoons butter
4 tablespoons flour
1 cup milk

1 cup light cream
salt and white pepper to taste

Melt the butter over low heat and blend in the flour. Add the milk gradually and stir until thick and smooth. Add the cream and simmer for 5 minutes to cook the flour. Season with the salt and pepper. This basic sauce, used in a great many dishes, can be doubled or halved as needed.

2 cups

CREAM SAUCE II

2 tablespoons butter
2 tablespoons flour
1 teaspoon onion juice

1 cup milk or half milk, half
cream
salt and white pepper
a pinch of nutmeg

Melt the butter over a low flame and stir in the flour and gradually add the milk. Add the seasonings and cook over low heat, stirring constantly for several minutes until the flour is thoroughly cooked. A thin sauce may be made by adding a little more milk.

1 cup

CHEESE SAUCE

Stir a cup of diced cheese and a dash of mustard or cayenne pepper into this sauce and cook until the cheese has melted.

EGG SAUCE

Excellent with fish.

4 tablespoons butter
4 tablespoons flour
2 cups milk

juice of half a lemon
salt and pepper
2 hardcooked eggs, diced fine

Melt the butter and blend in the flour. Add the milk gradually over low heat, season and cook for 10 minutes, stirring until thick and smooth. Add the diced eggs.

2 cups

CAPER SAUCE

For lamb or fish.

2 tablespoons butter
2 tablespoons flour
1 cup chicken stock
1 teaspoon dry mustard
1 teaspoon Worcestershire sauce

juice of half a lemon
yolk of 1 egg
1/2 cup cream
3 tablespoons capers

Melt the butter and over low heat stir in the flour. Gradually add the chicken stock, then the mustard, Worcestershire sauce and lemon juice, and stir until thick and smooth. Turn off the heat and add the egg yolk, cream, and capers, and again stir until smooth. Serve at once; if the sauce is to be reheated later, be sure that it does not boil.

1 and 1/2 cups

MUSTARD SAUCE

This sauce is very hot and good on all meats and fish.

2 tablespoons butter
2 tablespoons flour
1/2 cup beef stock

1 cup heavy cream
2 teaspoons dry mustard
1 teaspoon Worcestershire sauce

Blend together the butter and flour over low heat and gradually add the beef stock and the cream. Stir until thick, add the seasonings and serve hot.

1 and 1/2 cups

BROWN MUSHROOM SAUCE

Serve with venison, beef or lamb—even good with hash.

4 tablespoons butter
1/2 pound sliced mushrooms
1 teaspoon onion juice
3 tablespoons flour

1 cup beef stock
salt and paprika
2 tablespoons sherry
dash of Worcestershire sauce

Brown the mushrooms in the butter. Add the onion juice and flour, then stirring constantly, gradually add the beef stock. Stir until thick, and add seasonings and sherry.

1 and 1/2 cups

HORSERADISH SAUCE

1/2 cup heavy cream, whipped
2 tablespoons vinegar

3 tablespoons grated horseradish

Mix together. Serve with roast or corned beef.

3/4 cup

SOUR CREAM SAUCE

Serve with cold asparagus or artichokes.

1 cup sour cream
1 egg yolk
2 tablespoons horseradish,
squeezed dry

juice of half a lemon
salt and pepper to taste

Beat ingredients together and serve cold.

HOLLANDAISE SAUCE

A classic sauce for broccoli, artichokes, asparagus, and cauliflower.

3 egg yolks
1 tablespoon cold water
1/2 cup butter

juice of half a lemon
salt
a dash of cayenne

In the top of a double boiler over hot water (which you must never allow to boil), mix the egg yolks and water with a wire whisk until they are fluffy. Add the butter, 1/3 at a time, stirring after each addition. Finally add the lemon juice and seasoning. Stir constantly until thick.

If, through carelessness, the sauce becomes too hot and curdles, it may be saved if you remove it quickly from the heat and add to the sauce either a tablespoon of cream, cold, or a tablespoon of very hot water, or an ice cube. In the case of the ice cube, remove it when the sauce becomes smooth and use great care in reheating the sauce. Hollandaise sauce is really very easy to make and so, so good.

About 1 cup

BEARNAISE SAUCE

Serve with steaks and chops. Filet mignon and good hamburger are both enhanced by it.

3 egg yolks
3 tablespoons wine vinegar
3 tablespoons dry white wine
2 teaspoons chopped shallot or
scallion

1/2 cup butter
juice of half a lemon
1 teaspoon fresh tarragon (1/2
teaspoon if dried)

Prepare in the same manner as Hollandaise Sauce.

About 1 cup

CLAMBAKE SAUCE

1 pound butter	juice of 1 lemon
1 tablespoon salt	1/2 bottle Worcestershire sauce
1 teaspoon Tabasco sauce	(2 and 1/2 ounces)
1 pint tarragon vinegar	

Melt the butter in a saucepan and stir in the vinegar and seasonings. Cover and let simmer for 5-10 minutes until well blended and thickened.

About 1 quart

BARBECUE SAUCE

This sauce may be stored in the refrigerator. Warm it before using to melt the butter. The sauce may be used successfully with all sorts of meats—steak, spareribs, hot dogs, or chicken.

3 tablespoons butter	1/4 cup soy sauce
1 cup sweet vermouth	1/4 cup Worcestershire sauce
1/3 cup catsup	juice of 1 lemon
1 teaspoon salt	juice of half an onion
1/2 teaspoon celery salt	1 clove garlic, crushed

Melt the butter in a saucepan, add the other ingredients and stir until blended.

About 1 pint

CUMBERLAND SAUCE

For ham.

1 cup ham drippings, free of fat	1 cup red currant jelly
1 lemon	2 tablespoons wine vinegar
1 orange	1/2 teaspoon ground ginger
2 tablespoons prepared mustard	salt, pepper, and cayenne to taste
1 cup port or Madeira wine	

Grate the rind of the lemon and the orange, then squeeze the juice from the fruit. Combine these with all of the other ingredients and cook together until well blended. Season to taste.

3 cups

LOBSTER CORAL SAUCE

For boiled or steamed lobster. When you are lucky enough to have one or two females among your lobsters, seize the opportunity to make this lovely sauce.

2 tablespoons butter	2 anchovies
2 tablespoons flour	lobster coral
1 cup light cream	freshly ground white pepper
1 tomato, skinned and seeded	1 ounce cognac or kirsch

Make a cream sauce (p. 245) with the butter, flour, and cream. Add to this the tomato, anchovies, and lobster roe, puréed together. Add the pepper and cook the sauce until it is smooth. At the last minute, add the cognac or kirsch. The sauce will be a rosy red.

1 cup

LOBSTER SAUCE (see p. 131)

LEMON HERB SAUCE FOR FISH

1/2 cup sweet butter	1/2 teaspoon each, finely chopped chives, basil, and dill
1 tablespoon grated lemon peel	1 teaspoon finely chopped parsley

Cream together and spread on fish.

DUMPLINGS

To be served with stew or pot roast.

2 cups flour	1/2 teaspoon salt
4 teaspoons baking powder	1 scant cup milk

Sift together the dry ingredients and add the milk gradually. Drop by the spoonful and cook with pot roast or stew during the last 12 minutes of cooking.

YORKSHIRE PUDDING

The classic accompaniment to roast beef.

pan drippings
2 eggs
1 cup milk

1 cup flour
1/4 teaspoon salt

Set the oven at 450°. Put some of the drippings from the roast beef in a pan. Mix up the batter of eggs, milk, flour, and salt, and pour into the pan with the drippings. Bake for about 30 minutes. When done, the pudding will be puffy and golden brown. Cut in squares and arrange around the roast.

PRESERVED GRAPE LEAVES

Grape leaves are good to serve with game of various sorts, but as they are nipped by the first frost they should be pickled early in September to be on hand when the birds are.

Tie large perfect grape leaves in firm rolls of a dozen or so, throw them into rapidly boiling salted water (4 tablespoons of salt to 2 quarts of water) and remove them after about 30 seconds. Store them in the brine in sterile jars.

PICKLED WALNUTS

1 pound English walnuts,
   shelled
1/2 cup brown sugar
2 cups maple syrup
1 cup apple vinegar

1/2 teaspoon each of ground
   cloves, ginger, and mace
grated rind of one lemon
2 jiggers dark rum

Boil together all of the ingredients except the nuts and rum until the sauce is well thickened, about 10 minutes. Add the nuts and rum and simmer for 10 minutes longer. Seal in bottles while still hot. Excellent served with game.

WATERMELON PICKLE

Cut watermelon rind in 1/2-inch strips and soak in brine (3 tablespoons salt to each quart water) to cover for several hours. Heat to the boiling point and cook slowly for 10 minutes. Drain, remove the tough skin, and cut into cubes, balls, or wedges. Cover with ice water and let stand for 2 hours. Drain and weigh the watermelon rind. Allow 1 pound sugar and 1 cup water to each pound of rind. Boil the sugar and water with 1 cinnamon stick, 1 tablespoon cloves, and 1 lemon, sliced, for each pound of rind. Add the rind to the sugar water and boil until tender. Seal in clean glass jars.

CRANBERRY SAUCE

4 cups cranberries, washed   2 cups water
2 cups sugar

Boil the water and sugar for 5 minutes. Add the cranberries and cook gently, uncovered, without stirring, until thick. Chill.

Serves 8

WHITE WINE SAUCE FOR FISH

Use this sauce with all kinds of white salt-water fish fillets, sole, flounder, sea bass, and halibut. Pour it over fillets which have been poached in court bouillon. The whipped cream in the sauce causes it to brown quickly when put into a hot oven or under the broiler. This sauce is a culinary masterpiece.

2 tablespoons butter
2 or 3 shallots or scallions, finely minced
2 sprigs parsley
a pinch of dried tarragon
1 bay leaf
1/2 cup dry white wine

1/2 cup court bouillon
1/2 cup cream
1 tablespoon flour
2 egg yolks, beaten
1/4 cup heavy cream, whipped
juice of half a lemon
salt and white pepper

Melt the butter in a saucepan, add the shallots and herbs and cook slowly until the shallots are soft. Add the wine and the court bouillon and cook for about 5 minutes to reduce the liquid by about 1/3. Add 1/2 cup of cream and the flour and beat with a wire whisk. Cook until the sauce is smooth and slightly thickened. Strain the sauce. Mix the sauce with the egg yolks, return it to the stove using very low heat. Beat it constantly until it becomes thick. Do not allow it to boil. Remove it from the fire and carefully fold in the whipped cream and lemon juice and season to taste. Pour over the fish and place in a very hot oven or broiler until the sauce is lightly browned.

2 cups

Chapter 12.
Desserts

Yankees have a tremendous sweet tooth and this chapter is necessarily long. Our files are full of wonderful recipes that our friends have sent us, and it has been a difficult task to decide among them which are the most delicious and the most typical. They are almost all very fattening, but for special occasions, who cares? For everyday, resort to berries, a fine ripe pear, or coffee jelly. They end any meal happily, too, and it is nice to be able to walk away from the table with a light step.

Many of these recipes lend themselves to a variety of interpretations. Blueberry Cobbler can become Cherry Cobbler just as Peach Soufflé can become Strawberry or Raspberry, or Heavenly Pie can be flavored with apricot instead of lemon. Here is a sampling of the kinds of desserts that YANKEE's readers love.

FRUIT DESSERTS

From the time that the first pink rhubarb stalks are pushing up in your garden 'til the last red cranberries are picked, Yankees have a dozen homely, heavenly ways to prepare the fruits of the garden or berry patch. Most of them involve plenty of sugar and thick cream!

RHUBARB-CHERRY CRUNCH

CRUST

1 cup quick oatmeal
1 cup brown sugar
1 cup flour and a pinch of salt
1/2 cup (1 stick) butter

Mix together all of these ingredients and press half of the mixture on the bottom of a 9 x 13" pan.

FILLING

4 cups diced fresh rhubarb
1 cup sugar
1 cup water
2 tablespoons cornstarch
1 teaspoon almond flavoring
1 can cherry pie filling mix
1/2 cup chopped nuts

Spread the diced rhubarb on top of the crust. Boil the sugar, water, and cornstarch until thick. Add the almond flavoring, then the pie filling, and spoon the mixture over the rhubarb. Sprinkle the remaining crust mixture over it, then the nuts. Bake for 45 minutes at 350°. Serve warm with whipped cream.

Serves 12

RHUBARB CREAM

1 pound rhubarb
1 and 1/3 cups water
1 cup sugar
2 tablespoons potato flour or cornstarch

Clean the rhubarb and cut in pieces. Bring water to a boil, add rhubarb and sugar and boil until tender. Mix potato flour with a small amount of water, stir in and bring again to a boil. Cool, cover and serve with cream.

CHERRY SLUMP

2 cups cherries	1 cup flour, sifted
2/3 cup sugar	2 teaspoons baking powder
1/2 cup water	1/4 teaspoon salt
1 teaspoon cinnamon	1/2 cup milk

Remove stems and pits from cherries and combine them with the sugar, water and cinnamon. Bring to a boil. Mix and sift the flour, baking powder, and salt and add the milk gradually. Drop this dough by spoonfuls into the boiling fruit mixture. Cover and cook for 25 minutes. Remove the cover and cook 10 minutes longer. Serve with cream.

Serves 4

STRAWBERRIES IN A BARREL

Who can help being thrilled by the idea of a barrel that spurts out strawberries at every angle of the compass? Picture a barrel practically clothed in strawberries!

Here's how to have one of your own. Get hold of a good-sized barrel and paint the entire outside with a reliable wood preservative. Drill holes an inch or two in diameter in the barrel, leaving 12 or 14 inches. from one to another.

Irrigation of the barrel is provided by centering in it a length of stovepipe, four to six inches in diameter, fixed vertically and filled with gravel or crushed stone. Fill in all around the stovepipe with earth—a sandy loam is best. Now ease out the stovepipe leaving the porous material as a means of feeding water into the barrel.

Put your strawberry plants into the drilled holes, giving them a firm tucking-in and cheering the young plants by the addition of liquid plant food.

Your barrel should be established where it will benefit daily from a full charge of sunlight, and you must do your part by frequent watering of the central column of gravel. Rotate the barrel from time to time so that all of the berries enjoy sunshine. Plant before the end of June.

REAL OLD-FASHIONED
STRAWBERRY PRESERVES

2 pounds white sugar
2 pounds strawberries

1/4 teaspoon cream of tartar

Combine the sugar, strawberries, and cream of tartar. Let simmer slowly until the sugar melts, then cook briskly for 15-20 minutes. Let stand 24 hours, pack in sterile jars, and seal cold.

SUN-COOKED STRAWBERRIES

1 and 3/4 pounds sugar per
pound of strawberries

Bring slowly to a boil and turn over carefully six times with a wooden spoon. Then spread in shallow platters—not more than one layer of strawberries in each platter. Place the platters in a protected place outdoors in the direct rays of the sun for 3 days. Bottle and seal.

STRAWBERRY SHORTCAKE

A very old shortcake recipe. A tablespoon of sugar may be added to the ingredients.

2 cups flour sifted with:
  3 teaspoons baking powder and
  1/2 teaspoon salt

1/3 cup shortening (scant)
3/4 cup milk
strawberries (sweetened to taste)

With forks or fingers, blend the shortening into the dry ingredients and little by little stir in the milk to form a soft dough. Turn on a floured board and pat into one large layer. Bake for 15-18 minutes in a 425° oven. Split carefully and butter the halves. Put the prepared fruit (1 quart) between the layers and on top of the shortcake. Garnish with whole berries and serve warm with thick cream or, if you prefer, cover with lightly whipped, unsweetened cream.

Serves 6

STRAWBERRIES FOR SHORTCAKE

Reserving a few perfect berries to garnish the cake crush the rest of 1 quart of berries slightly, sweeten to taste and serve at room temperature.

RASPBERRY OR PEACH SHORTCAKE

Raspberry and peach shortcake are made the same way as strawberry shortcake and are just as good.

STRAWBERRY SOUFFLE

1 tablespoon butter
1 tablespoon flour
a 10-ounce package frozen strawberries or 1 and 1/2 cups sliced,
  sweetened fresh strawberries

1 and 1/2 ounces Cointreau or kirsch
4 or 5 eggs, separated
few drops red food coloring

Place all ingredients at room temperature. Preheat the oven to 400°. Over low heat mix together the butter and flour, add the strawberries and stir together to make a thick sauce. Add the liqueur and food coloring. Separate the eggs, adding the yolks one by one to the strawberry sauce. Beat the whites in a clean dry bowl until stiff, then fold them gently and lightly into the strawberry mixture and turn into a buttered soufflé dish. Place in the oven and immediately reduce the heat to 375°. Bake for just 30 minutes; serve with whipped cream and, if you wish, fresh strawberry sauce.

Serves 4

STRAWBERRIES JUPITER

Constance Turner
Ponte Vedra Beach, Fla.

A simple concoction, but for the gods.

1 and 1/2 quarts fresh strawberries
1/4 to 1/2 cup sugar
a 10-ounce package frozen
  raspberries

1 tablespoon orange liqueur
1 teaspoon lemon juice
chopped pistachio nuts
fresh mint sprigs

Wash and hull the strawberries and dry them on paper toweling. Slice them, cover with sugar, and chill for several hours. Purée the raspberries in the blender and strain them to remove the seeds. Add the orange liqueur and lemon juice and chill. Just before serving, ladle over the strawberries and garnish with pistachio nuts and sprigs of mint.

RASPBERRY CRUMBLE

Mrs. Ernest Miller
Lansing, Mich.

2 cups crushed raspberries
juice of half a lemon
1/4 cup butter

3/4 cup flour
1 cup sugar
a pinch of salt

Sprinkle the raspberries with half of the sugar and add the lemon juice and stir well. Place in a buttered baking dish. Blend the butter with the rest of the sugar, the flour, and salt and cover the raspberries with this mixture. Bake in a moderate (350°) oven for 40 minutes.

Serves 4

BLUEBERRY COBBLER

1 recipe shortcake (p. 255)
2 tablespoons milk
1 quart blueberries

1 cup sugar
1 teaspoon grated orange rind
butter

Make a soft shortcake dough, adding the milk. Wash and shake dry the berries and mix them with the sugar and rind; place in a buttered 2-quart casserole. Cover the berries with the dough and dot with butter. Bake at 375° for 35-40 minutes and serve hot with whipped cream or ice cream.

Serves 6-8

BLACKBERRY COBBLER

Use the same recipe, substituting blackberries for blue and adding 1 teaspoon of cornstarch.

PEACH SOUFFLE

2 cups peach pulp
2 tablespoons lemon juice
1/2 cup sugar

8 eggs, separated
1/4 teaspoon salt

Add to the peach pulp the lemon juice, sugar, beaten egg yolks, and salt. Fold in the stiffly beaten egg whites and bake in a soufflé dish for 40 minutes in a 350° oven. Serve with whipped cream.

Serves 6

BROWN BETTY

Betty Babbit
Devon, Penna.

8 tart apples, peeled and sliced
1/4 cup sugar, brown or white
fresh grated nutmeg to taste
juice and grated rind of half a lemon

buttered homemade bread,
    crumbled, about 4 slices
1/2 cup hot water

Sprinkle the apples with the sugar, nutmeg, lemon juice and rind. Place alternate layers of apple and breadcrumbs (ending with a crust of crumbs) in a well buttered baking dish. Pour the hot water over the dish and bake for an hour in a slow oven (325°); uncover the dish for the last 10 minutes. Serve hot with a pitcher of rich cream or with hard sauce (p. 287).

APPLE PANDOWDY

white bread
melted butter
4 large green cooking apples

1/2 cup dark brown sugar
1/2 teaspoon cinnamon

Line the bottom and sides of a baking dish with fingers of bread (crusts removed) which have been dipped in melted butter. Fill the center with the apples, peeled, cored, and sliced. Sprinkle the apples with a mixture of the sugar and cinnamon. Add 1/2 cup of water and cover the top with a layer of well buttered fingers of bread. Sprinkle top with additional sugar. Cover and bake 1 hour in a 350° oven. Serve hot with whipped cream.

Serves 6

APPLE OATMEAL CRISP

Good with blueberries too (use one quart).

3 or 4 tart cooking apples
1/2 cup butter
3/4 cup firmly packed brown
sugar

3/4 cup quick cooking oatmeal
1/2 cup flour
1 teaspoon powdered cinnamon

Arrange apples, pared, cored, and thinly sliced in a well buttered shallow baking dish. Melt the butter and stir in the sugar, oatmeal, flour, and cinnamon until well mixed. Sprinkle over the apples. Bake in a moderate oven (350°) for 45 minutes until the crust is golden brown and the apples are soft. Serve the crisp warm with whipped cream, vanilla ice cream, or cheddar cheese.

Serves 6

CRUNCHY APPLE PUDDING

6 cups sliced apples
2 tablespoons brown sugar
1/2 cup orange juice
1/3 cup brown sugar
1/2 cup cornflakes, crumbled

1/3 cup butter
1/2 cup sifted flour
1/2 teaspoon nutmeg or cinnamon
2 tablespoons butter
grated peel of the orange

Arrange the apples in a buttered baking dish. Sprinkle with the 2 tablespoons sugar and pour half of the orange juice over them. Work the 1/3 cup butter and 1/3 cup brown sugar together until creamy. Add the cornflakes, flour, spice and orange rind. Mix well and spread over the apples. Pour on the remaining orange juice and dot with butter. Bake in a 375° oven for about 45 minutes. Serve warm with cream or hard sauce (p. 287).

Serves 6

AUTUMN DELIGHT

Mrs. Marlene Couturier
Thorndike, Me.

DOUGH

2 cups flour
3/4 cup milk
6 tablespoons shortening

4 level teaspoons baking powder
1 teaspoon salt

Combine the above ingredients and roll as for biscuits. Place on the dough:

FILLING

4 apples, sliced
3 tablespoons sugar

1 teaspoon cinnamon
1 teaspoon nutmeg

Roll up like a jelly roll, then slice and place in a buttered 2-inch-deep pan. Make a syrup.

SYRUP

2 cups water
1 tablespoon butter

1 and 1/2 cups sugar

Bring to a boil and pour over the pan. Bake at 375° for about 40 minutes. Serve warm with or without whipped cream.

Serves 6-8

OLD-FASHIONED APPLE ROLLS

Elmer Whittaker
Taunton, Mass.

1 and 1/2 cups flour
1/2 teaspoon salt
1/2 cup shortening

5 apples, cored, peeled, and
chopped
sugar and cinnamon to taste

Work flour, salt, and shortening together until evenly mixed, using a pastry cutter or two knives. Stir in 2 and 1/2 tablespoons of cold water well and roll the pastry out on a floured board. For the filling, mix the chopped apples, sugar and cinnamon to taste. Spread the filling on the pastry and roll up as you would a jelly roll. Cut the roll into 1 and 1/2 inch pieces and place in a 9 x 9" pan. Pour boiling water over the rolls —enough to almost cover them and bake at 400° for 1 hour.

9 rolls

CRANBERRY CRUNCH

Henrietta Waite
Sagamore, Mass.

2 and 1/2 cups old-fashioned oatmeal
1 cup flour
1 cup butter
1 cup light brown sugar
1 can whole cranberry sauce

Mix all the ingredients except the cranberries together in a large bowl, working the mixture with your fingers until it is well blended and crumbles to about the size of peas. Pat half of this mixture firmly on a cookie sheet and spread the cranberry sauce over it. Sprinkle the rest of the crumbs over the top and to the edges. Pat gently but firmly. Bake in a 375° oven for 30-40 minutes. Cut in squares while still warm, and serve with ice cream or whipped cream.

16 squares

CRANBERRY ROLY-POLY

2 cups sifted flour
3 teaspoons baking powder
1/2 teaspoon salt
4 tablespoons shortening
2/3 cup milk
2 tablespoons melted butter
2 cups cranberry sauce, drained

Sift together the dry ingredients and cut in the shortening. Add milk and stir until the mixture forms a soft biscuit dough. Roll out on a lightly floured board to 1/4-inch thickness. Brush with melted butter and cover with cranberries. Roll up like a jelly roll and place, seam side down, on a buttered pan and bake in a hot oven (425°) for 25-30 minutes. Serve warm with hard sauce (p.287) or lightly whipped cream.

Serves 6

CHESTNUT CREAM

This recipe was contributed by Mrs. Pauline McConnell, who wrote: "I wish someone would revive the chestnut dishes of long ago. We always had baskets of chestnuts in our root cellar at home. One of our favorite dishes was Chestnut Cream. This dish is approximately 150 years old and is one which has been passed down from generation to generation in my family." Puréed chestnuts may be bought in cans. They are imported from France and Italy.

1 and 1/2 pounds chestnuts
1 cup granulated sugar
1 cup water
1 cup heavy cream whipped
1 teaspoon vanilla extract
milk

Remove the outer and the inner skins of the chestnuts and boil until soft with just enough milk to cover. Run through a sieve. Combine the sugar and water and cook for about 10 minutes. Mix the chestnut purée and the sugar syrup and, when cool, add the vanilla and the whipped cream. Pile on a dish and chill before serving. If you wish, the cream may be garnished with chocolate curls.

Serves 6

CHOCOLATE CURLS

Place a square of chocolate in a warm place (a gas oven with pilot light burning is very satisfactory) until the chocolate has just slightly softened. Shave it with a vegetable peeler or small sharp knife—longer strokes make longer curls. Use to decorate cakes and desserts.

WINTER PUDDINGS

Some of these desserts are light, some lusty. When the snow piles higher and higher and the days are short, a rich sweet warms the ending of the day as much as a roaring fire.

ANGEL PIE

4 egg whites, beaten stiff
2/3 cup sifted white sugar
1/2 cup confectioners' sugar

1/2 pint heavy cream
cooking chocolate
1 teaspoon vanilla

Beat the confectioners' sugar into the egg whites, pour into a well buttered deep pie plate, and bake at 325° for 45 minutes. Cool. Whip the cream, flavor it with sifted white sugar and vanilla, and spread on top of the Angel Pie. Grate cooking chocolate over the whipped cream, or make chocolate curls.

FORGOTTEN TORTE

Lisa St. Anne
New York, N.Y.

An absolutely magic meringue dish baked by the good fairy.

6 egg whites at room temperature
1/2 teaspoon cream of tartar
1/4 teaspoon salt

1 and 1/2 cups sugar
1 teaspoon vanilla
1/4 teaspoon almond extract

Set the oven at 450° and butter the bottom only of a 9" tube pan. Beat the egg whites with the cream of tartar and the salt until they are foamy. (If you use an electric beater, turn it to medium speed.) Gradually add the sugar, beating the mixture well as you do, and beating until the meringue forms stiff, glossy peaks. Beat in the vanilla and almond extract. Spread the mixture evenly in the pan, place in the oven on the center rack, and turn off the heat immediately. Let stand, with the door closed, of course, overnight. Next morning the torte will be done. Loosen the sides with a sharp knife and unmold it onto a serving platter. (It will settle a bit.) Serve the cake frosted with whipped cream. If you wish flavor it with cocoa and sprinkle it with chocolate curls (p. 261) or slivered almonds. Or a lemon custard may be made with 4 of the egg yolks as in the recipe for Heavenly Pie (below). There are many possibilities. The center may be filled with any fruit you choose mixed with whipped cream.

Serves 8-10

HEAVENLY PIE

Heavenly it is.

1 and 1/2 cups granulated sugar
1/4 teaspoon cream of tartar
4 eggs, separated
3 tablespoons lemon juice

1 tablespoon finely grated lemon rind
1 pint heavy cream

Sift 1 cup of sugar with the cream of tartar. Beat the egg whites until stiff but not dry, gradually adding the sugar mixture as you beat. Spread in a well buttered 9-inch Pyrex pie plate and bake in a 275° oven for 1 hour. Cool. Beat the egg yolks slightly, stir in the remaining 1/2 cup of sugar, the lemon juice and rind, and cook in the top of a double boiler until thick. Cool. Whip the cream. Combine the lemon mixture with half of the whipped cream. Spread on the pie and cover with the rest of the whipped cream.

Serves 6

MARMALADE PUDDING

This pleasant dessert cooks itself while you are eating dinner and makes a light but warm conclusion to the meal.

6 egg whites
6 tablespoons sugar
3 large tablespoons orange marmalade

1 teaspoon orange extract or Cointreau

Beat the egg whites with the sugar (adding the sugar very gradually) until stiff but not dry. Fold in the marmalade and the orange extract. Pour into a well buttered 2-quart double boiler and steam for 1 and 1/4 hours over constantly boiling water. Serve with this sauce:

6 egg yolks beaten until thick and lemon colored
1 and 1/4 cups powdered sugar

a jigger of sherry or Cointreau
1 cup whipped cream

Just before serving, mix well in the top of another double boiler all of the ingredients except the whipped cream. Add that at the last moment and pour over the pudding.

Serves 8

BLITZ TORTE

M. Rowen
Bangor, Me.

1 cup sifted cake flour
1 teaspoon baking powder
1/8 teaspoon salt
1/2 cup shortening
1 cup sugar
4 tablespoons milk

3 eggs, separated
1 teaspoon vanilla
1 teaspoon sugar
1/2 teaspoon cinnamon
1/2 cup almonds, blanched and sliced

Sift the flour, baking powder, and salt together. Cream the shortening with 1/2 cup of sugar until fluffy and add the well beaten egg yolks, vanilla, milk, and the sifted dry ingredients. Beat the egg whites until stiff but not dry and add the remaining sugar gradually, beating until the whites hold a sharp peak. Put the first mixture in two buttered layer cake pans and spread the egg white mixture over them. Sprinkle with the sugar and cinnamon mixed and then the almonds. Bake the layers in a 375° oven for 25-30 minutes. The cake may be assembled and served as is, or with strawberries and whipped cream on top and between the layers.

BOSTON CREAM PIE

2 cups sifted flour
2 and 1/2 teaspoons baking
  powder
1/2 teaspoon salt
1/3 cup butter

1 cup sugar
1 teaspoon vanilla
2 eggs
1/2 cup milk

Sift together the flour, baking powder, and salt. Cream the butter until light and gradually add the sugar; beat in the vanilla and eggs alternately with the milk. Beat well. Turn into buttered round 8-inch layer cake pans and bake for 30 minutes in a 350° oven. Put together with Cream Filling and sprinkle with powdered sugar. Serve in pie-shaped pieces.

Serves 8

CREAM FILLING

3/4 cup sugar
1/3 cup flour
1/8 teaspoon salt

2 eggs or 4 egg yolks
2 cups scalded milk
1 teaspoon vanilla

Mix the dry ingredients and gradually add the scalded milk. Cook in a double boiler, stirring constantly until the mixture thickens, about 15 minutes. Add the slightly beaten eggs and cook for 2 or 3 minutes longer. Cool and add the vanilla. If you wish a richer filling, add 2 tablespoons butter.

BANANA CREAM PIE

Put the layers together with cream filling to which has been added one thoroughly mashed banana.

WASHINGTON PIE

Make like Boston Cream Pie, putting the layers together with cherry jam.

VELVET CHEESECAKE WITH SOUR CREAM TOPPING

The ancient Greeks made very good cheesecake, the best of all was said to be from the Isle of Samos. Today every country has its own version. This American adaptation is creamy, light, and smooth.

1 6-ounce package zwieback,
  rolled into fine crumbs
1 pound cottage cheese
1/2 cup sugar
4 tablespoons melted butter
2 large eggs, separated
2 tablespoons cornstarch
  mixed with:
  2 tablespoons light cream

juice and rind of half a lemon
1/2 teaspoon vanilla
pinch of cinnamon
1 cup sour cream blended with:
  1 tablespoon sugar and
  1/2 teaspoon vanilla

Butter a 9-inch springform pan and press the crumbs onto the sides and bottom. Bake for 5 minutes and cool. Beat the cottage cheese until smooth and add to it the egg yolks, sugar, butter, lemon rind and juice, cinnamon, vanilla, and the cornstarch mixture. Beat well and fold in the egg whites, well beaten. Spoon the mixture into the pan and level it with a knife. Bake in a 350° oven for 25 minutes, or until the cake feels firm to the touch for an inch round the edge. The center will firm up as it cools. Remove the cake from the oven and cool for 10 minutes. Turn the oven to 400°, spoon the sour cream topping over the cake and return it to the oven for 8 minutes. Cook the cake in a place that is free from drafts. When cold cover with aluminum foil and chill in the refrigerator for several hours. (This cake may be glazed with melted strawberry or apricot jam.)

Serves 8

NO-BAKE CHEESECAKE

3 tablespoons melted butter   1/4 teaspoon cinnamon
3/4 cup graham cracker crumbs   1/4 teaspoon nutmeg
2 tablespoons sugar

Combine the ingredients and press 1/2 cup of the mixture into a buttered 9-inch springform pan.

2 envelopes plain gelatin   1 tablespoon lemon juice
1 cup sugar, divided   1 teaspoon vanilla
dash of salt   3 cups (24 ounces) creamed
2 eggs, separated   cottage cheese
1 cup milk   1 cup heavy cream, whipped
1 teaspoon lemon rind

Combine the gelatin, 3/4 cup of sugar and salt in a saucepan. Beat the egg yolks and milk together and stir into the gelatin mixture. Place over low heat and stir constantly until the gelatin dissolves and the mixture thickens slightly, 3-5 minutes. Remove from the heat and stir in the lemon rind and juice and the vanilla. Chill, stirring occasionally, until the mixture mounds slightly when dropped from a spoon. Beat the cottage cheese until smooth and stir into the gelatin mixture. Beat the egg whites until stiff; gradually add the remaining 1/4 cup of sugar and beat until very stiff. Fold into the gelatin mixture. Fold in the whipped cream. Turn into the prepared pan and sprinkle with the remaining crumbs. Chill until firm, 2-3 hours.

Serves 10

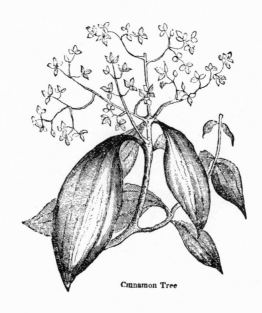

Cinnamon Tree

COUSIN CARRIE'S
CHOCOLATE PUDDING

Frances Fancher
Rutland, Vt.

The old saying, "The sauce makes the pudding," is true in this case. The cake is on the dry side; the sauce is the "drencher." I found an almost identical recipe in the files of Elizabeth Throne Stamm. She says it came from an old Indian squaw in Brule, Wisconsin, who called it Pig Pudding—presumably it had the same effect on northern woodsmen that the celebrated enchantress, Circe, had on the men of Odysseus.

1/2 cup granulated sugar	1/2 cup flour
butter the size of an egg	2 squares chocolate
1 egg	1/2 cup milk
1 teaspoon baking powder	pinch of salt

Cream together the butter and sugar. Add the well beaten egg, the chocolate melted in the milk, then the sifted dry ingredients. Spoon into a well buttered bread loaf pan and bake in a moderate (350°) oven for 20 minutes. Serve hot with Pig Pudding sauce.

Serves 6

PIG PUDDING SAUCE

2 eggs	1 cup whipping cream
1 cup sugar	2 teaspoons vanilla

Beat the egg yolks and whites separately. Add the sugar to the yolks, then the beaten cream. Fold in the whites and the vanilla. You will need three bowls for this.

CHOCOLATE
CORN FLAKE PUDDING

Mrs. Robert Weeks
Brookline, Mass.

2 cups milk	4 teaspoons cocoa
1/2 cup sugar	3 cups corn flakes
2 teaspoons butter	1 egg well beaten

Scald the milk. Remove from heat and add the sugar, butter, and cocoa. When the mixture has cooled, add the cold cereal and the egg. Stir together, pour into a buttered baking dish and bake for 1 hour at 350°. Serve with hard sauce (p. 287), vanilla ice cream, whipped cream or heavy cream.

Serves 4

DR. ZABDIEL BOYLSTON'S HONEYCOMB PUDDING

Dr. Zabdiel Boylston, who braved the threat of mob violence in 1721 in order to get Bostonians inoculated against smallpox, favored this excellent pudding.

1/2 cup flour
1/2 cup sugar
1/2 teaspoon each: cloves, cinnamon, allspice
1/4 teaspoon salt

1/2 cup butter, melted
1/2 cup warm milk
4 eggs, beaten
1 tablespoon soda in 1 cup molasses

Stir together the dry ingredients, add the rest of the ingredients, and pour the mixture quickly into a buttered baking dish. Bake in a moderate oven (350°) about 30 minutes. Turn out on a hot plate. When the pudding is sliced, the honeycomb will show.

HONEYCOMB PUDDING SAUCE

1 cup sugar
1/4 cup butter
juice of 1 lemon
1 egg, beaten

1/4 teaspoon salt
3 teaspoons cornstarch
1 cup boiling water

Cream the sugar and butter, add the rest of the ingredients and cook over low heat, stirring constantly until thickened. Serve the pudding and sauce warm.

COTTAGE PUDDING

A nice, old-fashioned dessert that is good served a little warm.

1 and 3/4 cups sifted flour
2 and 1/2 teaspoons baking powder
a few grains of salt
1/4 cup melted butter

1 cup sugar
1 egg, well beaten
1/2 teaspoon lemon extract
2/3 cup milk

Sift the dry ingredients together 3 times. Beat together the butter, sugar, egg, and lemon extract. Add the flour and milk alternately, beating well after each addition; pour into a buttered 8 x 8" pan and bake in a 375° oven for 30 to 40 minutes. Vanilla sauce, lemon sauce, or strawberry sauce go well with Cottage Pudding. (p. 289)

9 squares

DATE PUDDING

A fine party dessert, this is best prepared in the morning and served at room temperature, covered with cold whipped cream. It is chewy and rich, and the recipe never fails.

1 cup sugar	1 cup nuts, coarsely broken
2 and 1/2 tablespoons flour	1 cup dates, chopped
1 teaspoon baking powder	2 tablespoons sour cream
2 egg whites, beaten stiff	2 egg yolks, beaten

Mix the ingredients, adding the egg yolks last, and bake in a large buttered Pyrex pie pan set in another pan of water at 400° for 40 minutes. Serve with sweetened whipped cream.

Serves 8

DATE APPLE TORTE

4 cups diced tart apples	1 tablespoon melted butter
1 cup sugar	1 teaspoon vanilla
1/2 cup sifted flour	1/2 cup chopped nuts
2 teaspoons baking powder	1/2 cup chopped dates
1 egg	

Combine all of the ingredients in a bowl and stir until thoroughly mixed. Do not beat. Turn into a greased pan and bake for 40 minutes at 400° or until the apples are tender. Serve hot or cold with whipped cream or ice cream.

As in the 1800's our new country became more and more prosperous, it attracted certain groups of wanderers who brought with them an atmosphere of mystery, a flair for colorful clothing, and a sorcerer's skill in extracting money from the pockets of the yokels.

These were the gypsies following a path that had started somewhere in northern India and that led them to the farm of the mother of Minnie Smith of West Franklin, New Hampshire. Among their gifts to her were a recipe and a story.

"When I was a small girl, my mother consented to let a band of gypsies pitch their tents on the lower part of her land.

"Toward morning a young gypsy came to our door. He begged Mother to let him bring his young wife to our barn, as she was already in labor, and their tents leaked. My mother told him to bring his wife to the house.

"The gypsy girl was tucked up in Mother's bed, warm and comfortable, and tenderly cared for. Mother was obliged to act as both midwife and doctor. When daylight came, there was one more gypsy to join the band.

"The gypsies were so grateful to Mother for her kindness that they tried to do all kinds of helpful things. One of them brought her a dish of their own wonderful Indian pudding, made over their campfire. When they asked her what else they could do for her, she said that if they would give her the pudding recipe, that was all she could ask. So, years ago, she wrote down the rules given her by a grateful gypsy:"

BAKED INDIAN PUDDING

1/3 cup corn meal	1 cup raisins
1/2 cup molasses	1/4 teaspoon ginger
pinch of salt	1/4 teaspoon cinnamon
3 cups scalded milk	1/4 teaspoon nutmeg
1 egg, beaten	1 cup cold milk

Mix well the corn meal, molasses, and salt. Pour over the mixture 3 cups scalded milk. Let stand 5 minutes. Add the well beaten egg, spices, and raisins. Put in baking dish, and place in oven. In 10 minutes, after it starts to bake, add 1 cup of cold milk. Stir. Bake 2 hours.

Serves 6

INDIAN PUDDING II

A somewhat lighter contemporary version of the old favorite.

3 cups milk
3 tablespoons butter
1/2 cup cornmeal
1/2 cup brown sugar
1/2 cup molasses

4 eggs, well beaten
1/2 teaspoon each: ground
    ginger, cinnamon, and mace
1/4 teaspoon salt
1/2 cup sour cream

Scald the milk, add the butter and gradually beat in the corn meal. Stir until slightly thickened. Remove from the stove and add the other ingredients, beating well after each addition. Pour into a well buttered casserole and bake in a slow (275-300°) oven for about 2 hours. Serve warm with cold whipped cream or a scoop of vanilla ice cream.

Serves 8-10

PRUNE ICE BOX CAKE

Mrs. P. W. Stewart
W. Hartford, Conn.

2 egg yolks, beaten
a 15-ounce can sweetened
    condensed milk
1/2 cup lemon juice
1/4 teaspoon salt

1 and 1/2 cups cooked chopped
    prunes
2 egg whites, beaten stiff
18 graham crackers

Beat the egg yolks until light and stir in the condensed milk, lemon juice, and salt. Fold in the prunes and beaten egg whites. Put in a buttered dish in layers with the graham crackers and chill overnight.

Serves 6

STEAMED CRANBERRY PUDDING

1 cup sifted flour
2 teaspoons baking powder
1/2 teaspoon salt
1/2 cup breadcrumbs

1/2 cup brown sugar
2/3 cup finely chopped suet
1 cup cranberries
1/3 cup milk

Sift together the flour, baking powder, and salt. Combine the breadcrumbs, sugar, suet, and cranberries with the milk. Add the flour mixture. Pour into a greased mold, filling it only 2/3 full. Cover tightly. Place the mold on a rack in a kettle over 1 inch of boiling water and steam for 2 hours, using high heat at the beginning and, as the steam escapes, lowering the heat. Add water if necessary. Serve with hard sauce (p.287).

Serves 6

HOW TO MAKE BAG PUDDING

Our recipe came from Grandma Lane, who lived in Midlands England without suspecting her progeny would migrate to a place called "New England" and be known as Yongsees. And her basic instructions are simple, because she never dreamed there would come a time when housewives would need to be told how to tie off a pudding bag.

Assuming that somebody will care to revive this lost and ancient delight, the precepts should begin by urging great care and attention. The first time around is critical—in after years the process will be routine. Go, first, to a department store (Grandma Lane, of course, went to the draper's shop) and buy a square yard of unbleached cotton cloth. (At Christmas time in 1970 this cost 17 cents.) Harder to find, but it can be done, is a length of stout cord—not ordinary grocer's twine which grocers no longer use, but something like a boy's top whip, if you can remember what that was. It needs to be a hard-twist string that will support 8-10 pounds, at least. You now own a pudding bag.

CHRISTMAS BAG PUDDING

8 eggs
1 pound beef suet (ground)
1 pound white flour
1 pound raisins, seeded or seedless
1 pound currants

1 cup white sugar
1 tablespoon grated nutmeg
1 teaspoon ginger
1 tablespoon salt

Use an extra cup of flour to flour the fruits well—this will hold the fruits in suspension in the mixture while cooking. Break the eggs into a bowl and whisk them. Don't beat them and don't whisk them to a froth. Just make them smooth in the bowl. Because the eggs are the only rising material in the mixture, this maneuver is better underdone than overdone.

Then mix everything together well in a big container. As the mixture may be difficult to combine with a spoon, there is no objection to going in with your hands and really giving it a larruping. This done, turn your attention to the pudding bag.

Soak the cotton square in warm water and wring it relatively dry. Lay it flat on the kitchen table and flour the top side well. This will form a moist coating of flour on the cloth which is essential to removing the pudding from the bag later. Shake off excess flour. Now dump the pudding mixture in the center of the cloth. The mixture will not be too "loose" and will remain pretty much upright in a blob.

Gather the corners and edges of the cloth up around the mixture to form the "bag" around the pudding, and while somebody holds the folds, tie off the pudding-bag string. Make allowance for some rising (the eggs) and some swelling during cooking. In short, don't tie the bag completely tight about the mixture, but leave a small emptiness between the string and the pudding. If you do it right, the ultimate pudding will have the form of a flattened orb, swelling to the precise size you have left in the bag. If you leave too much space, the pudding will sag.

(continued overleaf)

Breaking the eggs is easier than whisking them . . .

Really give it a larruping!

Dump the pudding on the floured cloth.

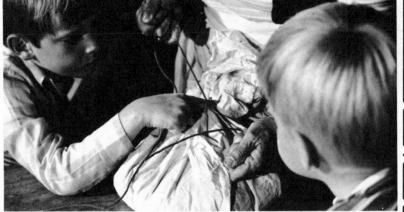

Tying is tighter with a finger-on-the-knot man.

Leave a loop in the string so you can thrust in the handle of a long wooden spoon to retrieve the finished pudding from the boiling water. Everything is going to be wicked hot when the time comes, and the loop is a must. Also, tie the knot around the bag so it can be easily untied (I suggest a bowline on the end of the cord and a clove hitch around the bag).

An ordinary canning kettle is ideal—you are dealing with a pudding nearly the size of a basketball. Make a judgement as to how much water will last 4 hours and have it boiling when you lower the pudding by its loop. It is all right to add water during the cooking, but don't let the boiling stop at any time. After the pudding has absorbed the heat, you can lower the burner, but keep the boil going all 4 hours. You will want a "kivver" on the "kittle."

If possible, plan so that the 4 hours will be up just as the family sits down to dinner. The pudding is now removed from the heat and left to linger in the hot water until time for the final dessert. When that time comes, lift the bag from the big kettle and lower it onto the platter. Best way is to have two people lift on the wooden spoon handle through the loop, and have a third shove the platter home as soon as the kettle rim is cleared. Untying the pudding needn't be difficult if 'twas tied right at first. The pudding will roll forth all fine and dandy. Top it with a sprig of holly.

Serve the pudding with brandy poured over it and set alight, or not, as you choose. Slice it, and pass around hard sauce and soft sauce *(both are on page 287)*—both should be available, and those who take both are what we know as the Wise Men. And what they do not eat that Christmas night will last sometimes into March (unless, of course, it is eaten sooner), which is pretty good mileage for Christmas.

Be careful tying the string, and don't fret the eggs too much.

John Gould
Lisbon Falls, Me.

Use a wooden spoon to lift it out.

The cloth should roll away nicely.

Hard sauce, soft sauce, or both?

YANKEE CHRISTMAS PUDDING

1 loaf stale bread with crusts
1/2 pound chopped mixed candied
   fruit peel
1/2 pound suet, chopped
1/3 cup finely chopped pecans
   or walnuts
2 cups currants
2 cups raisins
grated rind of 1 lemon
1 tablespoon cinnamon

1 and 1/2 teaspoons ground
   ginger
1/2 teaspoon allspice
1/4 teaspoon mace or nutmeg
1 cup sugar
1/2 cup cherry jam
1 teaspoon salt
1/2 cup brandy or rum
6 eggs, well beaten

Crumb the bread and in a large bowl combine the ingredients in the order given. Turn the batter into a well greased 2-quart mold, or two 1-quart molds. Place in a kettle in 1 inch of boiling water. Cover and steam for 4-5 hours, adding more water if needed. Remove mold to a wire rack, uncover, and allow to cool. Invert on wire rack and wrap the cold pudding in plastic film or foil. It may be stored for several weeks in the ice box.

When you are ready to use the Christmas pudding, return it to its mold, cover it, and steam for half an hour. Unmold the pudding again on a hot platter, decorate it with holly and pour heated brandy or rum over it. Touch a match to the pudding and serve it encircled with blue and orange flames. Pass hard sauce or French hard sauce (*p. 287 for both*) with it.

Serves 16

PIES

A few versions of New England's *very* favorite food. Eaten hot or cold, with cheese, thick cream or ice cream, pie is good from breakfast to bedtime.

BASIC PIE CRUST

Mrs. Armande Madore
St. Johnsbury, Vt.

The dough should be carefully rolled, very lightly from the center to the edges to a size somewhat larger than the pie pan it is to fill.

2 cups flour   1 teaspoon salt
3/4 cup shortening

Sift together the flour and salt upon a board or marble surface and cut in the shortening with a pastry blender or 2 knives until thoroughly mixed and like coarse sand.

Make a paste of 1/4 cup flour and 1/4 cup cold water and add to the above mixture quickly and lightly with a fork. Shape into a ball, cover the dough and chill thoroughly. When chilled roll the dough out on a lightly floured surface. This makes enough pie crust for one two-crust (9-inch) pie or two 9-inch shells.

With a little practice it is easy to make good pie crust, but if you are inexperienced, or in a hurry, the commercially prepared sticks make excellent pie crust too.

RHUBARB PIE

So welcome because it is the first fruit pie of spring, rhubarb pie stands with cherry, blueberry, and apple as one of New England's permanent favorites.

pastry for a double crust pie
1 and 1/4 cups sugar
1/4 cup cornstarch
1/4 teaspoon salt
1 bunch (1 pound) rhubarb
     cut in 1 and 1/2 inch lengths

2 teaspoon grated orange rind
     (or 1 teaspoon grated lemon
     rind)
juice of one orange
a drop of red food coloring
2 tablespoons butter

Divide the pastry (*above*) into unequal halves. Roll out the larger por - tion and fit into a 9-inch pie pan. Trim the pastry 1/2 inch beyond the rim of the pan. Roll out the remaining pastry to 1/8-inch thickness and cut into strips about 3/4 inch wide. Mix the sugar, cornstarch, and salt. Add the rhubarb, rind, and juice and toss until well mixed. Tint pink if desired and turn into the pastry shell. Dot with butter. Arrange the pastry strips over the pie in a lattice pattern securing it to the pie-shell firmly and fluting the pieshell and strips together to form a high rim. Brush the pastry with a little milk and sprinkle sugar over it. Bake in a 400° oven for 50-60 minutes, or until the filling has bubbles that do not break.

a 9-inch pie

STRAWBERRY PIE

Jeanne Galloway
Christian Hollow, N.H.

1 flaky pie shell, baked
1 and 1/2 quarts strawberries
an 8-ounce package cream cheese
2 tablespoons sour cream

3/4 cup sugar
3 tablespoons cornstarch softened
  in a little water
1/2 pint whipped cream

Wash, hull and dry the strawberries. Soften the cream cheese with the sour cream and spread in the pie shell. Reserving a few to decorate the finished pie, arrange the rest of 1 quart of berries whole on the cream cheese. Cook the other 1/2 quart of berries over low heat with the sugar, bring to a boil, sieve, add the cornstarch softened in water and cook a few minutes until clear. Cool and pour over the fresh berries. Cover with lightly whipped cream and garnish with the reserved berries and mint leaves.

FRESH FRUIT PIES

This recipe may be used for making blueberry, raspberry, cherry, peach and other fruit pies. Use the pastry recipe on page 277. If you wish a lattice top, cut the second half of the pie dough in narrow strips, fit them over the pie, and secure the ends by moistening and crimping them firmly to the bottom crust.

3 to 4 cups prepared fruit
1 to 1 and 1/2 cups sugar
1 or 2 tablespoons cornstarch

1/4 teaspoon salt
1 tablespoon butter
milk or sugar

Prepare the fruit, and add the combined dry ingredients adjusting the amount of sugar and cornstarch according to the sweetness and juiciness of the fruit. Mix thoroughly, fill a pastry-lined pie pan with the fruit and dot with butter. Arrange top crust or lattice and brush with milk and sugar. Bake for 10 minutes in a 450° oven; reduce the heat to 350° and bake 20-30 minutes longer.

SOUR CREAM ELDERBERRY PIE

Mrs. E. Kathryn Jones
Penn Yan, N.Y.

A recipe which has been handed down for several generations, this pie can be made with fresh or home canned berries for a summer picnic table or Thanksgiving feast.

1 cup elderberries
2 tablespoons flour
1 cup sugar

1 cup sour cream
pastry for a two-crust pie (p. 277)

Stir the filling together and bake in a two-crust pie.

APPLE PIE

Mrs. Armande Madore
St. Johnsbury, Vt.

Gravensteins, Rhode Island Greenings, Roxbury Russets and Cortlands are among the traditional Yankee cooking apples. The familiar McIntosh is as good as any of these.

4 to 5 cooking apples, depending
on size
3/4 cup sugar, if you like a tart
pie

nutmeg or cinnamon, optional
pastry for a 9-inch pie (p. 277)

Pare, core, and slice the apples and arrange them with the sugar in an unbaked pie shell. Cover with pastry for the top. Make several slits in the top crust for steam to escape and crimp the edges firmly. Brush the top crust with milk and sprinkle a teaspoon of sugar on it. Bake at 400° for 10 minutes, reduce the heat to 350° and cook 50 minutes longer. Serve hot with Vermont cheese.

HOT APPLE DUMPLINGS

1 recipe pastry (p. 277)
6 cooking apples
6 tablespoons sugar

6 teaspoons butter
raisins (optional)
cinnamon, sugar, and butter

Roll the pastry 1/8 inch thick and cut into 6 squares. Pare and core the apples and place one on each section of dough. Fill the hollow of each apple with 1 tablespoon of sugar and 1 teaspoon of butter and, if you like, a few raisins. Fold the pastry over the apples pressing the edges together. Place in a shallow pan, sprinkle with cinnamon and sugar. Dot with butter. Bake in a 400° oven for 30 to 40 minutes. Serve while still warm with heavy cream or with hard sauce (p. 287). With the hard sauce you may, if you have strong guests, also pass Brandied Apricot Sauce (p. 287).

BLUEAPPLE PIE

This Rapture of Delight was invented through Necessity by Alton Weagle, an ingenious Fire Tower Guard on Mt. Monadnock. Finding he lacked apples enough to fill the 9-inch pie he was whipping up for expected company, he gathered blueberries on the mountain and spread them over the apples to the required depth. The resulting creation, served hot from the oven was a huge success. Here is his recipe.

CRUST

1 and 1/2 cups flour
1/2 cup shortening

1/2 teaspoon salt
3 to 5 tablespoons water

Cut the shortening into the flour, and stir in the water to form a soft, but not sticky dough.

FILLING

sliced apples
blueberries (if frozen berries
    are used, thaw first and drain
    off the juice)
1/2 to 3/4 cup sugar (3/4 if
    apples are tart)

1/8 teaspoon salt
1/4 teaspoon cinnamon
1/8 teaspoon nutmeg
1 tablespoon butter

Place the sliced apples so that they nearly fill a pastry-lined 9-inch pie plate. Add blueberries over the apples to a depth of at least one-half inch. If the apples are a juicy variety, mix a tablespoon of flour with the sugar. Sprinkle the filling with the other ingredients, and dot with the butter. Cover the pie with the top crust or lattice, and bake 20 minutes at 450°. Lower the heat to 350° and continue baking for 25 more minutes.

DEEP DISH PEAR PIE

A delicate change from apple pie. Very good indeed.

6 large pears, sliced
3 tablespoons lemon juice
1/2 cup sugar
2 tablespoons flour

1/2 teaspoon cinnamon
1/2 teaspoon nutmeg
1/2 cup butter
pastry crust (p. 277)

Select pears that are not too ripe. Plunge them in boiling water. Their skins will peel off easily. Slice them into a buttered ovenproof dish, preferably Pyrex, alternately with the sugar, flour, spices, rest of the butter, and the lemon juice. Cover with pastry crust that has been slashed in a few places and bake in an oven that has been preheated to 400°, placing the casserole on the lowest shelf of the oven. Bake for 45-50 minutes, until the pears are tender and the syrup surrounding them is caramelized. If the crust browns too quickly, cover it with foil. Serve warm with cold whipped cream flavored with a little sugar and a drop of kirsch.   Serves 6

COOLIDGE LEMON CUSTARD PIE

This was the favorite custard pie of the late President Coolidge.

2 eggs, separated	4 teaspoons flour
1 lemon, juice and grated rind	1 teaspoon melted butter
1 cup sugar	1 cup milk
1/8 teaspoon salt	1 7-inch pastry shell

Beat egg yolks until thick and lemon colored. Add lemon juice and rind, sugar, salt, flour, butter, and milk. Fold in egg whites, beaten stiff. Pour into unbaked pastry shell (with edges fluted) and bake in hot oven (450°) 10 minutes; reduce heat to moderate (350°) and bake 20 minutes longer.

LEMON MERINGUE PIE

Mrs. Helen Shed
Dublin, N.H.

1 baked pie shell (good if baked a day or two before filling)	1 and 1/2 cups boiling water
	2 eggs, separated
1 cup granulated sugar	rind and juice of 1 lemon
1/2 cup flour	1 tablespoon butter
1/2 teaspoon salt	4 tablespoons sugar

Mix the cup of sugar with the flour and the salt in a heavy-bottom sauce pan or double boiler. Add the boiling water. Stir and cook over low heat until the mixture boils and looks clearer. Beat the egg yolks slightly with fork. Spoon a little of the hot mixture over them and stir—then add the yolk mixture to the filling in the pan and cook 2 minutes. Add the lemon rind and juice and the butter. Stir and cool slightly. Pour into the pie shell. Make meringue from the egg whites, adding the 4 table-spoons sugar gradually until the whites are beaten stiff. Bake in a 400° oven 3-4 minutes until the meringue is light brown.

CHESS PIE

1 and 1/3 cups firmly packed
   light brown sugar
1/3 cup melted butter
3 eggs, lightly beaten
1/3 cup water

1 teaspoon vanilla
1/2 cup coarsely chopped nuts,
   pecans or walnuts
2/3 cup raisins
1 unbaked 9-inch pastry shell

Beat together the sugar and butter until well blended. Add the eggs, water, and vanilla and beat again. Stir in the nuts and raisins. Pour into the pastry shell and bake in a moderate oven (375°) for 45 minutes. Cool to room temperature and serve with whipped cream.

MILLIONAIRE PIE

Kate Kosman
Hiawatha, Ks.

1/2 cup soft butter
2 cups confectioners' sugar
1 large egg
1/4 teaspoon salt
1/2 teaspoon vanilla

2 baked 8″ pie crusts
1 cup heavy whipping cream
1 cup drained crushed pineapple
1/2 cup chopped pecans

Cream together the butter and sugar and add the egg, salt, and vanilla. Beat well. Spread this mixture in the two crusts. Chill. Whip the cream and pile it, the fruit and the nuts on top of the chilled filling. If you wish to make only one pie, halve the above ingredients and use one small egg.

2 pies

ARUNDEL RUM PIE

A recipe from the late Kenneth Roberts.

2 tablespoons gelatin
1/2 cup cold water
6 well beaten egg yolks
3/4 cup sugar

1 pint cream, stiffly beaten
1/2 cup New England rum
   (Caldwell's or Medford)

Bake a large-size graham-cracker pie shell according to the directions on the package and let it cool. Soak the gelatin in the water, then bring it to a boil and stir it into a mixture of the egg yolks and sugar. Fold in the whipped cream and the rum, pour the mixture into the baked pie-shell, and chill. Serve topped with more whipped cream: (This does seem, really, to be gilding the lily!)

A PAIR OF PUMPKIN PIES
FOR THANKSGIVING

Pumpkin Pie is as traditional as turkey for Thanksgiving, so here are two, a little different. Line two 9-inch pie plates with pastry. Build up and flute the edges. Into the bottom of one pie scatter finely chopped dates (3/4 cup). Into the other slice two crisp McIntosh apples very thin. Mix the pumpkin filling as follows·

a 14 and 1/2-ounce can
  stewed pumpkin
3 tablespoons cornstarch
1 and 1/2 cups sugar (white or
  brown)
1/2 teaspoon cinnamon
1/2 teaspoon ginger

1/2 teaspoon nutmeg
1/2 teaspoon vanilla extract
1 and 1/2 tablespoons melted
  butter
1/4 cup molasses
1 and 1/2 cups milk
2 beaten eggs

Into a large bowl sift together the dry ingredients. Add the pumpkin and stir to blend. Add the molasses, beaten eggs, milk, and vanilla; again stir well. Lastly add the melted butter and beat with the egg beater. Then pour immediately into the pie shells, making sure that the pumpkin mixture coats all of the fruit. The apples will rise to the top, and the dates will remain on the bottom. Bake at 400° for about 45 minutes or until the filling is firm. Serve on Thanksgiving Day—"palm warm," with lightly whipped cream.

MINCEMEAT

Mrs. Samuel Barney
West Bend, Wis.

From a very old recipe. If this is made during the hunting season, the neck meat of the venison can be ground and used instead of beef.

2 pounds beef, ground
1 pound suet
5 pounds apples
3 pounds raisins
2 pounds currants
3/4 pound citron
2 and 1/2 pounds brown sugar

2 tablespoons cinnamon
2 tablespoons mace
1 tablespoon cloves
1 tablespoon salt
1 teaspoon nutmeg
1 quart sherry
1 pint brandy

Cook all together very slowly, uncovered, for about an hour and a half, or until the mincemeat reaches the right consistency. Can hot, or store in an earthenware crock in a cold place. The mincemeat will be protected by a coating of suet. This makes enough for 10 medium-sized pies and keeps forever improving with age. It is the best mincemeat you ever tasted.

ICE CREAM

A freezer of ice cream on Sunday all through the summer was as necessary to the American way of life a generation ago as firecrackers on the Fourth of July and Band Concerts on the warm Saturday evenings. Smooth ice cream and sherbet can be made in an old-fashioned ice cream freezer, in an electric one, or in the freezing compartment of a refrigerator. If the latter is used, it is convenient to freeze the mixture in a round plastic quart container saved from when you have bought commercial ice cream. Freeze until nearly solid, then remove from the freezer and beat vigorously for several minutes with a hand beater, an electric beater, or at top speed in a blender. The latter method will produce the lightest texture. The ice cream will increase in bulk by about one quarter. Return it to the freezer until solid.

VANILLA ICE CREAM

4 cups light cream	a pinch of salt
1 cup sugar	1 and 1/2 teaspoons vanilla

Heat 1 cup of cream very slowly (do not boil). Then stir in the sugar and salt until dissolved. Add vanilla. Chill. Add the rest of the cream and freeze.   1 and 1/2 quarts

PEACH ICE CREAM

Add 3/4 cup sugar to 1 and 1/2 cups of peach pulp; reduce the vanilla to 1 teaspoon and add 1/2 teaspoon of almond extract. Mix well; add to the ice cream mixture and freeze.

STRAWBERRY ICE CREAM

Add 3/4 cup sugar to 1 cup crushed strawberries and let stand 1 hour at room temperature. Add to ice cream mixture and freeze.

BANANA ICE CREAM

Mash 3 ripe bananas with a silver fork; beat until smooth; add to ice cream mixture and freeze.

MAPLE ICE CREAM

Substitute maple sugar for the ordinary kind. If you wish, stir a cup of broken nut meats into the ice cream just before it solidifies.

SHERBETS

Sherbets make a refreshing finish to many meals when a heavier dessert might seem too filling. Lemon, orange, and raspberry are fairly usual but there are other more surprising flavors that are easy to concoct from the frozen and bottled fruits and juices that are now available.

BLUEBERRY SHERBET

1/2 cup sugar
2 and 1/2 cups boiling water
1 cup puréed fresh or frozen
    blueberries

juice of 1 lemon
2 egg whites beaten stiff

Boil together the sugar and water. Add the lemon juice and the puréed berries. Freeze until nearly solid; beat the egg whites until stiff; beat together with the frozen sherbet and return to the freezer.

1 quart

LEMON OR LIME SHERBET

3 cups water
1 and 1/2 cups sugar

2/3 cup lemon or lime juice
2 egg whites, stiffly beaten

Boil the water and sugar until the sugar is dissolved. Add the fruit juice, cool and freeze until nearly solid. Beat the egg white until stiff; beat together with the frozen sherbet and return to the freezer until stiff.

1 quart

FRESH STRAWBERRY SHERBET

3/4 cup sugar
1 cup boiling water
2 cups fresh strawberry purée
juice of half an orange

juice of half a lemon
drop of red food coloring
2 egg whites, beaten until stiff

Combine according to the rules given for sherbet.

1 quart

BAKED ALASKA

And last, a tribute to our fiftieth state. Baked Alaska, easy to prepare, festive to serve, makes a light flattering end to a dinner that is a special occasion. Children love it, too, and a few candles make it into a birthday cake.

an 8-inch layer of angelfood or
  sponge cake
1 round quart container of ice
  cream, frozen very hard
jam, fruit, or marrons, liqueur if
  desired

6 egg whites
1/4 teaspoon cream of tartar
2/3 cup sugar
a wooden board approximately
  10 inches square

Beat the egg whites until stiff, then add the cream of tartar and, little by little, the sugar. Beat until very stiff. Place the layer of cake on the wooden board, unmold the ice-cream on the center of the cake, leaving a margin of an inch all round it. If you wish, make a hollow in the center of the ice-cream and fill it with jam, fruit, or marrons and splash it with liquor. Work quickly. With a spatula, cover the entire block of ice-cream with the meringue to a thickness of about an inch. Be sure that there are no holes in the meringue, for heat must not get through. Decorate the meringue, as you like, with a sprinkling of ground or chopped nuts, almonds, coconut, filberts, and return it to the freezing compartment of the ice box where it can wait for several hours until dinner. When ready to serve, slip the Baked Alaska on its board onto the middle shelf of an oven pre-heated to 500° and bake for about 5 minutes until the meringue is slightly browned. Serve immediately. Cut into wedges.

There are countless combinations for the flavors filling a Baked Alaska. Children love peppermint stick ice cream topped with fudge sauce, the meringue smothered in grated coconut. Peach ice cream topped with cherry jam and a jigger of kirsch pleases a more sophisticated palate and so does coffee ice cream covered with marrons and a tot of cognac or crème de cacao.

Serves 8-10

HARD SAUCE

Mrs. Robert Derby
Peterborough, N.H.

1/2 cup softened butter
pinch of salt
1 pound confectioners' sugar

1 teaspoon vanilla
grated nutmeg

Beat the butter, salt, and sugar up together, then add the vanilla and sprinkle with nutmeg, if desired. This sauce may be packed into small molds, refrigerated, and served unmolded, sliced thin.

FRENCH HARD SAUCE

1/2 cup butter at room temperature
1 and 1/2 cups confectioners'
   sugar

1 egg yolk
3 tablespoons brandy or rum

Beat the butter and sugar in the small bowl of the electric blender at high speed until light and fluffy. Stir in the rum and egg yolk. Chill before serving.

1 and 1/2 cups

BRANDIED APRICOT SAUCE

Good with various steamed puddings. For the Christmas pudding, it can be passed with the hard sauce.

1 jar apricot jam

2/3 cup brandy

Mix together over low heat. Serve hot.

SOFT SAUCE

Mrs. Robert Derby
Peterborough, N.H.

1/2 cup softened butter
pinch of salt
1 pound light brown sugar
1 egg

1 teaspoon vanilla
1/2 cup heavy cream,
   whipped

Beat together the butter, salt, and brown sugar until creamy (not *too* soft), then beat in the egg until the mixture is fluffy. Add the vanilla. Just before serving, fold in the whipped cream.

FLUFFY SAUCE
For Christmas Pudding.

1 egg
1/2 package confectioners'
   sugar
1 cup heavy cream, whipped

1 tablespoon rum
1/2 teaspoon vanilla extract
pinch of salt

Beat the egg until thick and lemon-colored. Add the sugar gradually and fold in the whipped cream and flavorings.

About 2 cups

HOT FUDGE SAUCE

2 cups sugar
2 squares chocolate
3/4 cup milk

2 tablespoons butter
dash of salt
1/2 teaspoon vanilla

Combine all of the ingredients except the vanilla and cook in the top of a double boiler over rapidly boiling water for about 15 minutes, or until a drop forms a very soft ball when dropped in cold water. Add the vanilla and serve.

2 cups

CHOCOLATE MINT SAUCE

Follow the directions for Hot Fudge Sauce; omit the vanilla and add 1/2 teaspoon peppermint extract or 1/4 cup crushed peppermint candy.

BUTTERSCOTCH SAUCE

3/4 cup brown sugar
1 cup corn syrup
1/4 cup butter

1 cup light cream
dash of salt

Boil the sugar, syrup, and butter, stirring constantly, for about 5 minutes. Add the cream and salt and bring back to the boiling point. Serve hot or cold.

3 cups

MAPLE SYRUP SAUCE

Good on puddings or an unfrosted cake.

1/3 cup butter
1 cup powdered sugar, sifted
1 egg, separated

1/2 cup maple syrup
1/2 teaspoon vanilla
1/3 cup heavy cream

Cream the butter, add the sugar gradually and beat until blended. Add the egg yolk, beat well, add the maple syrup and vanilla. Beat until creamy. Whip the egg white until stiff. Whip the cream until stiff. Fold them into the butter mixture.

About 2 and 1/2 cups

MAPLE SAUCE

1 cup maple syrup   1/2 cup marshmallow cream

Combine and beat with a hand beater until thoroughly mixed. Serve on ice cream, cake, or pudding, with or without nuts.

About 1 and 1/2 cups

MARSHMALLOW SAUCE

This sauce is very good served on chocolate or coffee ice cream or on chocolate cake or gingerbread.

2 and 1/2 cups sugar   about 3/4 jar of marshmallow fluff
4 tablespoons butter   3/4 teaspoon salt
1 small can (3/4 cup) evaporated   1 teaspoon vanilla
  milk

Combine all of the ingredients except the vanilla and stir over a low flame until blended. Remove from the flame and add the vanilla.

STRAWBERRY SAUCE
Mrs. Herbert M. Dickman
Newtown, Penna.

1/3 cup butter   1 pint strawberries, mashed
1 cup confectioners' sugar   1 beaten egg white (optional)

Cream together the butter and the sugar. Add the strawberries, and if desired the beaten egg white. Spoon over hot fluffy rice, over ice cream, cut up pears, or other fruit.

Serves 6

VANILLA SAUCE

1/2 cup sugar   1 cup boiling water
2 tablespoons butter   1 teaspoon vanilla
1 tablespoon cornstarch   dash of nutmeg
dash of salt

Mix together the sugar, butter, cornstarch, and salt and gradually stir in the boiling water. Boil while stirring until smooth and thick, about 5 minutes. Stir in the vanilla and nutmeg.

Serves 6

LEMON SAUCE

Follow directions for Vanilla Sauce, but omit the vanilla and add 2 tablespoons of lemon juice and 1 teaspoon grated lemon rind.

ENVOI

If you're doubtful about detergents and phosphates and their effect on the ecology, here is the old fashioned way to cleanliness which kept our forefathers in tune with their environment.

AUNT EM'S HARD SOAP

5 pounds lukewarm melted animal grease (beef suet produces the hardest soap; hog or bacon fat is somewhat softer.)
1 pound can lye
1 quart cold water

1/2 cup cold water
1/4 cup ammonia
3 tablespoons sugar
4 tablespoons borax
1 tablespoon salt

Dissolve the lye by putting it in a *enamel* (not aluminum) mixing kettle. Slowly pour 1 quart of cold water over it, stirring with a big *wooden* spoon or paddle. Stir occasionally until cool. Dissolve the borax, sugar, and salt in the ammonia and 1/2 cup of cold water.

When the lye is cool pour the grease in *slowly*, stirring constantly to mix well. Add the other ingredients. Stir until the mixture is very thick. Pour into pans (not aluminum) or heavy cartons lined with cloth. Cut in squares before the soap hardens.

If the grease has scraps in it, pour it through a strainer lined with two or three layers of cheesecloth.

The lye is apt to boil up when you pour the cold water on it. Be careful not to get spattered.

This is a dirty, time consuming job—but highly rewarding.

Stephen T. Whitney, of Peterborough, N.H., who gave us this recipe, says "I should call this *Tower Hill Soap* for that is where I knew it as a boy. The wonderful smells of the kitchen and well stocked pantry—the old iron range, the soapstone sink, and Aunt Em's soap. It did get a small boy's hands clean."

Mrs. Pierpont Blair
Wayland, Mass.

Index

A

Acorn squash, stuffed, 222
Alaska, baked, 286
Almond soup, 94
Anchovy: bread, 7; canapés, 79; mayonnaise, 243; puffs, 79; Roquefort salad dressing, 240
Angel pie, 261
Angels on horseback, 79
Anytime cake, 70
Appetizers (see Hors d'oeuvres): hot cheese, 83; sportsman's, 88
Apples: autumn delight, 259; and celery mold, 233; cornbread, 25; dumplings, 279; oatmeal crisp, 258; pancakes, 14; pandowdy, 258; pie, 279; pudding, crunchy, 258; rolls, old-fashioned, 259; soup, 94
Applesauce cookies, 58
Apricot streusel coffee cake, 23-24
Aroostook savory supper, 219
Artichokes, 201
Arundel rum pie, 282
Asparagus, 201-202: amandine, 202; au gratin, 201; tips with ham, 202; on toast, 201
Aspic: cucumber, 235; fish in, 236
Autumn delight, 259
Avocados: mix, 80; with hot sauce, 80; with red caviar and sour cream, 80; ring, 233; soup, 94

B

Bacon: biscuits, 12; and egg salad, 229; roll-ups, 80
Bag pudding, Christmas, 272
Baked Alaska, 286
Baked beans, 31; soup, 107
Baked seafood, 33
Baking powder biscuits and variations, 12
Banana: cream pie, 264; ice cream, 284

Barbecue sauce, 248
Basil beans, 81
Bass, poached striped, 128
Beacon Hill cookies, 58
Beans: baked, 31, soup, 107; basil, 81; black (soup), 108; cassoulet, 33; dill, 81; green, 202-203, lima, dried with cream, 204; salad, 227, serving suggestions, 203; white, 204
Béarnaise sauce, 247
Bedford cookies, 58
Bedspread for two, 35
Beef, 179-190: breaded, 180; chili, 185; corned beef and cabbage, 181; corned beef hash, 181; creamed dried, 45; eye roast, 180; frugal pie, 47; hamburgers, 189-190; Hungarian steak casserole, 51; marrow, 186; meat loaf, 187; New England boiled dinner, 184; pot roast, 182-183; roast, 179; Roquefort cheeseburgers, 190; steak, Cantonese, 187, and kidney pie, 48, tartare, 189; soup, vegetable beef, 92; stew, 186; stock, 92; Swedish meat balls, 188
Beets, 204-205: and beet greens in cream, 205; bright red soup, 97; in cream sauce, 205; Harvard, 204; jelly ring, 233; in orange sauce, 205
Bellevue broth, 95
Berkshire corn and tomato chowder, 107
Biscuits, 12-13, 86; baking powder, and variations, 12; pumpkin, 9; ragamuffins, 13; Roquefort, 86
Blackberry cobbler, 257
Blitz torte, 263
Blueapple pie, 280
Blueberry: cobbler, 257; muffins, 11; pancakes, 14; popovers, 10; sherbet, 285
Blue heaven cake, 70
Boiled dinner, New England, 184
Boola-boola topping, 108
Boston cream pie, 264

Bouillon: court, 126; cubes, 91
"Boys" (side dishes for curry), 146
Bran muffins, 11
Braumeister shrimp, 146
Breads, 3-8, 54-57: anchovy, 7; brown, 32; cheese, 7; cracked wheat, 5; date and apricot nut, 54; dill, 8; French, 7; garlic, 7; gingerbread, 55; herb, 7; hints, 3; homemade, 4; lemon, 56; oatmeal, 5; orange nut, 56; potato, 6; pumpkin walnut, 57; vanilla-flavored white, 4; wheat germ white, 6; Winchester nut, 56
Breaded beef, 180
Bright red soup, 97
Broccoli, 206
Broilers with oyster stuffing, 151
Brook trout, 127
Brown betty, 257
Brown bread, 32
Brown sugar cookies, 59
Brownies and bars, 68-69: butterscotch squares, 68; chocolate peppermint brownies, 68; date bars, 69; fudgy brownies, 68; Indians, 69; marble squares, 69
Brunswick stew, 155
Brussels sprouts and celery casserole, 207
Buckwheat cake, stump jumpers', 17
Buns: hot cross, 10, scone, 13
Butterball soup, 95
Butter cookies, 60
Butterfly leg of lamb, 193
Butterscotch: cookies, 60; squares, 68

C

Cakes, 70-76: anytime, 70; blue heaven, 70; cheese-filled chocolate, 71; cherry devil's food, 72; coconut, prize, 71; fruitcake, old English, 73; Grandmother Summers' 1-2-3-4, 74; jelly, Fasnacloich, 72; silver nut, 75; spice, 75, Roxbury, 75; sponge, Mother's, 76; Wellesley fudge, 74; white plum, 76
Caldeirada a pescadora, 129
Calves' liver, 198
Camembert balls, 82
Campfire smelt, 134
Canadian frosting, 77

Canapés (see Hors d'oeuvres): anchovy, 79; curried olive, 84
Cantaloupe dip, curried, 81
Cape Cod turkey, 129
Caper sauce, 246
Caraway cookies, 61
Carrots, 207-209: creamed in chicken stock, 208; and fresh mint, 207; glazed, 207; and parsnips, 209; purée of, 208; ring, 208; soup, cream of young, 98
Casseroles: Aroostook savory supper, 219; Brussels sprouts and celery, 207; clam, 138; corn-sausage, 45; Hungarian steak, 51; ratatouille, 221; shrimp and artichoke, 50; wild rice, 220; yodeling good Swiss, 52
Cassoulet, 33
Cauliflower, 209: salad, 227; soup, 98
Celery: braised, 210; casserole, Brussels sprouts and, 207; and chestnuts, creamed, 210; essence of, 99; hearts, creamed, 210
Charcoal-broiled chicken with garlic and herbs, 152
Cheese: appetizers, hot, 83; biscuits, 12; bites, 83; bread, 7; Camembert balls, 82; Chablis, 83; crock, 83; -filled chocolate cake, 71; Parmesan salad dressing, 228, 240; pear, 82; popovers, 10; pudding, Vermont Cheddar, 38; sauce, 245; Scotch woodcock, 39; soufflé, 40, ham and mushroom, 41, quick, 41; straws, 125; tray, 82; Welsh rabbit (rarebit), 39; woodchuck, 38
Cheeseburgers, Roquefort, 190
Cheesecake: no-bake, 266; with sour cream topping, 265
Cheesy Vermont maple apple Danish, 22
Cherry: devil's food cake, 72; muffins, 11; slump, 254; soup, 99
Chess pie, 282
Chestnut: cream, 260; croquettes, 43; stuffing, 164
Chick and oyster pie, New England, 47
Chicken: *breast of,* 149-151 — in bing cherry sauce, 149; with mushrooms and ham 149; in oyster and champagne sauce, 150; pâté, jellied, 159; with peaches, 149; pi-

NOTES

NOTES

NOTES

NOTES

SARA B. B. STAMM

Born and brought up in New England (Bellows Falls, Vt., and Milton, Mass.), Mrs. Stamm is now a resident of Walpole, N.H., where she and her husband, John Davies Stamm, like to work together in their roomy colonial kitchen inventing and perfecting the delectable foods for which their dinners are famous. A graduate of Vassar College, Mrs. Stamm has written articles on cookery for *Vogue* and *Look,* among other publications.